WHY
MEN LIE
&
WOMEN
CRY

Allan & Barbara Pease

MANJUL

Manjul Publishing House Pvt. Ltd.

First published in India by

Manjul Publishing House Pvt. Ltd.
10, Nishat Colony, 74 Bungalows, Bhopal, India 462 003
Ph. : +91 755 5240340 Fax : +91 755 2736919
E-mail : manjulindia@sancharnet.in
Website : www.manjulindia.com

First published - 2003
Fourth Impression - 2004

Distributed in India by
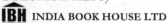 **INDIA BOOK HOUSE LTD**

This edition is authorized for sale in the following countries :
India, Pakistan, Bangladesh, Nepal, Bhutan, Burma & Sri Lanka

ISBN - 81 - 86775 - 32 - 3

Printed & bound in India by
Thomson Press India Ltd, New Delhi, INDIA & published by
Mr. Vikas Rakheja for Manjul Publishing House Pvt. Ltd., 10 Nishat
Colony, 74 Bungalows, Bhopal - 462 003 INDIA

Contents

Crying And Emotional Blackmail
How Blackmail Works
Case Study: Georgina's Story
Emotional Blackmail
Case Study: Rosemary's Story
Men and Emotional Blackmail
Case Study: Damian's Story
Common Emotional Blackmail Tactics
Case Study: Julia's Story
Case Study: Stephen's Story
Case Study: Irene's Story
How To Handle An Emotional Blackmailer
What You Can Say To A Blackmailer
When The Blackmailer Is Also In The Dark
When Blackmail Becomes A Life Sentence

4. Women's Top Secret Point-Scoring System   101
Men See Only The Big Picture
Our Experiment With Brian And Lorraine
How Brian Scored The Month
How Lorraine Scored Her Meek
Penalty Points
Lorraine and Brian's Reactions
Solution For Women
Solution For Men
Take The Test Now
Summary

5. Solving the Seven Biggest Mysteries About Men   117
1. Why Don't Men Know Much About Their Friend's Lives?
Solution
2. Why Do Men Avoid Commitment?
Case Study: Geoff and Sally
What Most Men Think
Solution
3. Why Do Men Feel The Need To Be Right About Everything?
Case Study: Jackie and Don

Acknowledgements

We wish to thank the following people who have contributed directly, indirectly and, sometimes, unknowingly to this book.

Our Team who have walked the steps with us on this journey: Ruth and Ray Pease, Dorie Simmonds, Sue Williams and Trevor Dolby.

Bill & Beat Suter, Adam Sellars, Melissa, Cameron & Jasmine Pease, Mike & Carol Pease, Len & Sue Smith, Fiona & Michael Hedger, Diana Ritchie, Dr Desmond Morris, Prof Alan Garner, Gary Skinner, Dr Dennis Waitley, Mark Victor Hansen, Dr Themi Garagounas, Bert Newton, Geoff & Sallie Burch, Tony & Patrica Earle, Debbie Mehrtens, Deb Hinckesman, Dorreen Carroll, Andy & Justine Clarke, Kerri-Anne Kennerley, Frank & Cavill Boggs, Graham & Tracey Dufty, John Allanson, Sandra & Loren Watts, John Hepworth, Esther Rantzen, Ray Martin, Kaz Lyons, Victoria Singer, Graham & Josephine Rote, Emma Noble, Yvonne & Barrie Hitchon, Richard Cranium, Ivor Ashfield and Helen Richardson.

Introduction

Why do men tell lies? Why do they feel they have to be right about everything? Why do they avoid commitment? On the other hand, why do women cry to get their own way? Why do they insist on talking a subject to death? Why don't they initiate sex more often?

The gulf between the sexes, the misunderstandings and the conflict, even in the twenty-first century, are still as present in all our lives as they were when Adam first fell foul of Eve. In three decades of research into the differences between men and women, conducting experiments, analysing miles of film footage, writing books, talking on television and sharing information at conferences, we've received tens of thousands of questions about why we men and women behave in certain ways. The letters, the phone calls and the emails all come from people baffled by the kind of things the opposite sex does, and who feel frustrated and helpless in knowing exactly how to deal with them. As a result, we wrote *Why Men Lie and Women Cry*. Here, we've catalogued 40 of the most frequently asked questions from readers and audiences around the world and have endeavoured to answer them using our experience, research, surveys, latest studies, the sciences and, lastly, common sense. We then developed workable solutions to get you on the right track to communicating with the opposite sex.

Why Men Lie and Women Cry tackles those big 'need-to-know' questions women ask themselves at 1am on Sunday morning. Questions like, "Why do men ogle other women?" and "Why do they always keeping telling me what to do and how to think?" Then there are those complexities men wrestle with at 10am on a Sunday morning, when they either wake up alone, or with their lover no longer talking to them. We go through all their questions too, like, "Why don't women ever get to the point?", "Why do they nag?" and "Why do I have to pick up my socks at 10am on a Sunday morning?"

*A woman worries about the
future until she gets a husband.
A man never worries about the
future until he gets a wife.*

Science can now explain why women talk so much, often 'beat around the bush', want to know the fine details about everyone around them and seldom initiate sex. We now know there are evolutionary and biological reasons why men can only do one thing at a time, hate shopping, won't ask directions, want the toilet roll to face out from the wall rather than in, and know hardly anything about their friends' personal lives, despite just having spent a whole weekend fishing with them.

In many ways, *Why Men Lie and Women Cry* points out the obvious things most people miss. You've probably noticed how many women seem to have a biological urge to examine and buy decorative cushions, or rearrange furniture for men to trip over when they creep in late at night. Or how few women understand the thrill of watching the same sports replay over and over, while it's rare that men will view the discovery of a designer dress on the clearance rack as one of life's major highlights.

Why It's So Tough For Men And Women

Being male today has become a tough call. Since the 1960s, when feminists became more vocal and successful, women's suicide rate has decreased by 34% but men's has risen 16%. Yet the focus is still on how hard a woman's lot is in life.

In the latter part of the twentieth century, when women

were discovering their freedoms and often regarding men as the enemy, relationships and families regularly came under enormous strain. Women were angry; men were dazed and confused. Over past generations, their roles were clearly defined. Man was head of the house. He was the principal breadwinner, his word was law and his areas of decision-making were clear-cut. He was the protector and provider. His wife was mother, housekeeper, social secretary and carer. He knew his responsibilities and his wife knew hers. Life was simple.

But suddenly everything began to change. Television sitcoms and commercials began to show men as stupid or incompetent in the face of more intelligent, superior women. More and more women embraced the call of equality. The trouble was that women seemed to know what they wanted and where they were going, while many men were feeling left behind.

> *If a woman slaps a man's face in public,*
> *everyone assumes he's in the wrong.*

Men often didn't seem to understand the rules. For instance, a woman speaking up about inequalities attracted sympathy; a man speaking up was often vilified as a woman-hater. Derogatory jokes about men now outnumber jokes about women by ten to one. This is a typical example of what you can get every day in your email:

"Have you ever noticed that all women's problems start with men?

Men-opause

Men-strual pain

Men-tal illness

Guy-naecologist

His-terectomy"

And the latest joke doing the rounds among women, a joke that most men find extremely demoralising and threatening:

The definition of a man?
A life support system for a penis.

In the face of what many men would see as open hostility, it can't be denied that this is one factor in the state of depression that seems to be sweeping through a whole generation of men. Men, both old and young, now have the highest suicide rate ever, with Japanese men at the top of the list. Men no longer know what their job specification is and there are no significant role models.

Women now have it tough too. Feminism began as a way of addressing the inequalities between men and women and it promised women freedom from the chains keeping them at the kitchen sink. Today, around 50% of women in the Western world work – whether or not they even want to. In Britain, one in five families is headed by a solo woman, as against one in 50 by a solo man. These women are now expected to be mother, father and provider. Women are now getting ulcers, having heart attacks and suffering stress-related illnesses, just as men always have done.

Bulimia is estimated to affect 4% to 5%
of college women, but only one in 300 men.

By the year 2020, it is estimated that 25% of all women in the Western world will be permanently single. This is an unnatural situation and is completely at odds with our basic human urges and biology. Women are now overworked, often angry and becoming increasingly lonely. Men feel women want them to think and behave like women. We have all become confused. This book provides the map that will help you through the relationship maze that has developed, and allow you to identify the false starts, tricky twists and dead ends.

Why Men And Women Have So Much Trouble

Women evolved as child-bearers and nest-defenders and, as a result, female brains became hardwired to nurture, nourish, love and care for the people in their lives. Men evolved with a completely different job description – they were hunters, chasers, protectors, providers and problem-solvers. It makes sense that male and female brains are hardwired for different functions and priorities. Scientific research, especially the new high-tech brain scans, confirms this.

Women write most of the books on human relations, and over 80% of the purchasers are female. Most of these books tend to focus on men, what they do wrong and how you can improve them. Most relationship counsellors and therapists are also women. To a neutral observer, this may give the impression that women care more about relationships than men.

In many ways, this is right. The concept of focusing on a relationship is not a natural part of the male psyche, thinking or scale of priorities. Consequently, men either don't try at all with relationships or they give up early, because they find the way women think and act too complex. It sometimes seems all too hard and it's easier to quit early than be seen as a failure. But the truth is that men want good, healthy, fulfilling relationships just as much as women. They simply assume that one day a perfect relationship will come along, without the need for prior study or preparation. Women regularly make the mistake of assuming that just because a man loves her, he must also understand her. But he usually doesn't. We call each other the 'opposite' sex for a good reason – we are opposite.

A woman needs to know but one man well to understand all men; whereas a man may know all women and not understand one of them.
HELEN ROWLAND

We are the only species that has continual trouble with the mating ritual, courtship and relationships – other species have it all worked out and get along fine. Even the Black Widow spider and the Praying Mantis, who kill their mates right after mating, know the rules of the mating game and stick faithfully to them. Take the octopus, for example. It's a simple animal with a tiny brain. But octopi never argue about male and female differences, sex or the lead up to it. The female comes on heat at a certain time and the male octopi all come around waving their tentacles; she picks the one with the tentacles she likes best and gives him the green light. She never accuses him of not paying her enough attention, and he never worries whether it was as good for her as it was for him. There are no interfering in-laws giving advice, and the female octopus doesn't worry whether she looks fat, and she never yearns for a mate with a 'slow' tentacle.

But humans are infinitely complicated. Women say they want sensitive men, but they never want them to be *too* sensitive. Men have little idea about the subtle distinction. Men don't realise they need to be sensitive to a woman's feelings, but tough and manly in other ways. Charting a way through this maze is one of the learnable skills men will discover in this book. Understanding what men want, and how to give it is one of the skills women will be taught.

Put the words 'relationships' and 'sex' into your Internet browser and you'll currently get 36,714 references in English alone to help you to improve things. For all other animals, relationships are a fairly straightforward procedure driven by each species' survival needs. They don't think about it – they just do it. We, however, have evolved to the point at which we now need to know how best to get on with the opposite sex to stand any chance of living happy lives, enjoying a fair share of the fun, excitement and enrichment that good relationships can bring.

Travelling The World

Why Men Lie and Women Cry is the next step on the relationship ladder from *Why Men Don't Listen and Women Can't Read Maps* and covers many of the areas of life most of us rarely think about, or simply don't notice. In order to write this book, we travelled to over 30 countries, and collected and collated information and research about relationships everywhere. In our work, we've tried to establish universal themes and define common problems, and then come up with what we believe are practical solutions. The behaviours and scenarios we describe in this book don't apply to all people all of the time. They are all true stories and the principles apply to most people, most of the time in their relationships with the opposite sex.

If you get it right with most people most of the time when it comes to living with, working for, managing and loving the opposite sex, your life will be so much happier. Unfortunately, we find most people still get it wrong a lot of the time.

In Britain, for example, the divorce rate is now over 50% within 4 years of marriage and, if you include couples who never get round to marrying, it's reasonable to assume the real split rate of all couples is probably more likely to be 60%–80%.

....
100% of divorces begin with marriage.
....

Why Men Lie and Women Cry offers a real chance to cut some of that misery, anguish and confusion out of your life. It will make everything easier. It's full of common sense and scientific facts that are immensely powerful, yet always presented in a humorous, easily digestible way. It explains the behaviour of the 'other side', whether it happens to be your partner, son, daughter, mother, father, in-laws, friends or neighbours.

Learning A Second Language

To succeed with the opposite sex you need to be able to speak two languages – 'Manspeak' and 'Womanspeak'. If you speak only English and you visit France, there's no point in speaking English and ordering fish and chips. French people don't understand either. If you are French and travel to an English-speaking country, there's no point in speaking French and asking for grilled snails. The locals just won't get it. But if you buy a simple translation book that shows you how to speak the basic words and phrases of another language, it will help you get around, the locals will love you for it and want to help you even if you're not particularly good at it. Others are impressed when they know you are attempting to understand and communicate with them.

"Do I Have To Change Sex?"

People often ask us, "Are you saying that I should think, talk and act like the opposite sex?" Absolutely not. When you buy a mobile phone, it comes with an instruction manual. When you learn how your phone works and program it to do what you want, it will give you lots of pleasure, profit and fun. You'd never accuse the phone company of trying to turn you into a telephone technician because they gave you an instruction manual. *Why Men Lie and Women Cry* is an instruction manual for understanding the opposite sex and knowing which buttons to press to get the best results.

When a woman realises how men evolved, it's suddenly easier to make allowances for the different way they behave and process thoughts. When a man understands that a woman is coming from a different direction, then he too can profit from her experiences and outlook on life.

First-hand Experience

We, the authors, are happily married, faithful lovers, and best friends. We are also the parents of four beautiful children. In *Why Men Lie and Women Cry*, we have also drawn on our personal experience and feel we have given you a balanced view of male and female relationships from many different points of view and, hopefully, without bias. Writing and researching this book has given us a greater understanding of each other, our parents, brothers, sisters, cousins, co-workers and neighbours. We don't always get it right, but feel we do most of the time with most people. As a result, we are rarely in an argument with anyone close to us and they all love us for it. It's not always perfect but regularly, it is.

How To Give This Book As A Gift

Following the worldwide success of our last book *Why Men Don't Listen and Women Can't Read Maps* (over six million books sold and translated into 33 languages to date) some men accused us of making their lives difficult. They felt their women were using our book to persecute them by saying, "Allan said this" or "Barbara said that…" *Why Men Don't Listen and Women Can't Read Maps* was a favourite of women everywhere and we are aware that some did give it to the males in their lives with the comment "You need this! Read it from cover to cover – in fact, I've highlighted the parts you need to read."

When a woman gives a personal development book to another woman, the woman who receives it is honoured and thankful for a gift that may help her improve. A man, however, may feel insulted and feel the woman is saying he's not good enough the way he is. "I don't need this!" he'll say dismissively as he hands it back to her, leaving her feeling hurt and upset.

So, if you're a man reading this, you're part of a minority

who want to get a handle on how women think and behave – Congratulations! If you're a woman, it could be safer to ask a man his opinion on the book's advice because men love to give opinions. Highlight the pages you want him to read and leave the book on the coffee table or in the toilet. Or buy him a ticket for one of our relationships seminars.

Finally...

They say it's great to be a man because motor mechanics tell you the truth, wrinkles add character, your underwear is only £4.95 for a six-pack and chocolate is just another snack. People never stare at your chest when you're talking to them and you don't have to leave the room to adjust yourself.

They say it's great to be a woman because you can talk to the opposite sex without having to picture them naked, taxis stop for you and you can scare male bosses with mysterious gynaecological disorders. You don't look like a frog in a blender when you dance and if you marry someone 20 years younger, you're aware that you look like a cradle snatcher.

Maybe one day, men and women *will* be like each other. Perhaps women will love watching racing cars drive in a circle, shopping will be considered an aerobic activity and men will have to spend one month a year in a PMT simulator. Maybe all toilet seats will be nailed down, women will only talk during the commercials and men will only read *Playboy* for its literary value.

We doubt it – at least, not for a few thousand years. Meanwhile, we'll continue to understand, manage and learn to love our differences. As a result, we'll be loved and cherished back.

Enjoy our book!

Barbara & Allan Pease

Chapter 1

NAGGING

When someone just won't let up

Nag: *verb* to annoy, badger, bend someone's ear, berate, breathe down someone's neck, worry, harass, hassle, henpeck, pester, plague, provoke, scold, torment; *noun* a person, especially a woman, who nags

Nagging is a term used almost exclusively by men to describe women.

Most women deny they nag. They see themselves as reminding the males in their lives to do the things that must be done: household chores, taking their medication, fixing broken things and picking up their mess. Some nagging is considered constructive. Where would many men be without a woman in their lives cajoling them not to drink too much beer and eat too much fast food and, if they can't stop, to make sure they exercise and take regular cholesterol tests? Nagging might even, at certain times, keep them alive.

If men nag, however, that's viewed very differently by society. Men are not naggers. They're assertive, they're leaders, and invariably they're passing on their wisdom – and gently reminding women of the path to take if they happen to forget along the way. Sure, they criticize, find fault, moan and complain, but it's always for the woman's benefit. The repetition of their advice, like "Read the map *before* you set off! How many times must I tell you?" and "Can't you make more of an effort with how you look when my friends come round?" shows admirable persistence and, above all, shows that they care.

Women, similarly, feel that nagging shows that they care, but men rarely see it in the same light. A woman will chide a man about throwing wet towels on the bed, peeling off his socks and leaving them all around the house, and not remembering to take out the garbage. She knows she's being irritating, but believes the way to get through to a man is by repeating, over and over, the same instructions until they one day, hopefully, sink in. She feels the things she's complaining about are based on truth so, while she knows she's being annoying, she feels justified in continuing. A woman's female friends won't see her as nagging either – they'll see the man as lazy or hard to handle and feel nothing but sympathy for his long-suffering partner.

'The Man Song', a comedy song penned by Sean Morley and reproduced thousands of times over the Internet, was an instant hit when released. Women love it because it says that nagging can sometimes yield results; that is, men understand who's boss. Men love it because it says something they've perhaps always, secretly, known too. One of the verses starts:

> *'The sooner you'll learn who's boss around here,*
> *the sooner you can give me my orders dear...*
> *Cause I'm head-honcho around here...*
> *but it's all in my head...'*

But usually, when a woman starts repeating her orders, the male brain hears only one thing: nagging. Like a dripping tap, nagging wears away at his soul and can gradually build a simmering resentment. Men everywhere put nagging at the top of the list of their pet hates. In the USA alone, there are more than 2,000 cases a year of men murdering their wives and claiming that their nagging drove them to it. In Hong Kong a husband who hit his wife on the head with a hammer, causing her brain damage, was given a reduced jail term by a judge who said he had been driven to violence by nagging.

Women's Nagging vs Men's Moaning

Women nag; men instruct.

After reading *Why Men Don't Listen and Women Can't Read Maps,* a man who called himself 'Henpecked Jeremy' sent us this email:

"I need your help. I'm married to the Queen of Naggers and I can't take another minute of her nitpicking, complaining and harassment. From the moment I arrive home until the moment I go to bed, she starts her nagging and never lets up.

It has come to the point where the only communication involved between the two of us is when she tells me all the things I didn't do during the course of the day, week, month, or since we've been married.

The situation has become so negative that I'm even asking the boss for overtime at work. Can you imagine that? I'd rather stay at work than go home. The stress of listening to her complaints is so strong that I get headaches while driving home from work. It shouldn't be like this – I should be excited about leaving work and getting home to see her.

My father used to tell me that all women complain and nag, and I never believed him until I got married. Even my buddies tell me their wives nag them all the time. Is it true that women are natural-born naggers? Please help me."

A group of women eating in a restaurant were overheard having a group discussion about their husbands.

Blonde woman: "You know, he's never satisfied. He's always complaining. If I don't want sex at the same time as him, he moans to me so much, sometimes I just give in to shut him up and then I don't enjoy it much. Maybe I don't feel in the mood. But he goes on and on and on until it's just much easier to go along with it than to listen to him moan."

Brunette: "Stephen's the same. He's always finding fault with what I do. If I dress up to go out to dinner with his friends, he complains that I make more effort for them than I ever do for him. He goes on about how maybe I find his friends more attractive than him. If I dress down, he whines that I don't care about him enough to take care with my appearance. Sometimes I feel I can't win."

Third woman: "So why is it that men always say women nag?"

Group laughter.

Nagging Through The Ages

Historically, it has always been women who have been described as naggers. The verb 'to nag' comes from the Scandinavian for 'to gnaw, nibble or pick at something'. In most dictionaries, a nag is a female noun with no male equivalent.

Until the nineteenth century, English, American and European laws allowed for a husband to complain to the magistrate about his wife's nagging or 'scolding'. If his case was found proved, his wife would be sentenced to the 'Ducking Stool'. The Ducking Stool was famously used in the USA and Britain to punish witches, prostitutes, minor offenders and scolds. The offending woman would be strapped into a seat, which hung from the end of a free-moving arm, and be dunked into the nearest river or lake for a pre-determined length of time. The number of times she was submerged depended on the severity of the offence and/or the number of previous misdemeanours.

A British court record from AD 1592 reads –

'... de wife of Walter Hycocks and the de wife of Peter Phillips are common scolds. Therefore it is ordered that they shall be told in church to stop their scolding. But, if their husbands or neighbours complain a second time, they shall be punished by the ducking stool.'

The following poem by Benjamin West, published in 1780, shows how seriously men took nagging in past centuries –

The Ducking Stool

There stands, my friend, in yonder pool
An engine called the ducking stool;
By legal power commanded down
The joy and terror of the town.

If jarring females kindle strife,
Give language foul, or lug the coif,
If noisy dames should once begin
To drive the house with horrid din,
Away, you cry, you'll grace the stool;
We'll teach you how your tongue to rule.
The fair offender fills the seat
In sullen pomp, profoundly great;
Down in the deep the stool descends,
But here, at first, we miss our ends;
She mounts again and rages more
Than ever vixen did before.
So, throwing water on the fire
Will make it but burn up the higher.
If so, my friend, pray let her take
A second turn into the lake,
And, rather than your patience lose,
Thrice and again repeat the dose.
No brawling wives, no furious wenches,
No fire so hot but water quenches.

If the ducking stool wasn't considered punishment enough, there was even worse in store. Some women ended up being paraded around town, as a warning to other women, with an iron mask, 'the branks', clamped onto their heads with a metal bar going into their mouths to hold the tongue down. The last woman to suffer the ducking stool after being convicted of being 'a common scold' was Jenny Pipes from Leominster, England, in 1809.

How the Nagger Feels

The nagger always hopes their victim will be motivated into some positive action by being made to feel guilty. They hope he'll be spurred into action, if not by realising he is in the wrong, then maybe simply to stop the tirade. Women know they nag, but that doesn't mean they enjoy it. Usually they're only doing it as a means to an end.

Some women have turned nagging into an art form. We have identified five basic nags –

The Single Subject Nag: "Kurt, how about taking out the rubbish?" A pause. "Kurt, you said you'd take out the rubbish." Another five minutes later. "What about that rubbish, Kurt? It's still sitting there."

The Multi-Nag: "The grass in front of the house looks a mess, Nigel, the doorknob is falling off the bedroom door, and the back window is still stuck. When are you going to tune the TV aeriel and…" etc., etc.

The Beneficial Nag: "Have you taken your pills today, Ray? And stop eating that pizza – it's bad for your cholesterol and weight…"

The Third Party Nag: "Well, Moira says Shane has already got their BBQ cleaned out and they're having people over tomorrow. Summer will be finished at the rate you're going."

The Advance Nag: "Well, I hope you're going to watch your drinking tonight, Dale. We don't want a repeat of last year's fiasco."

Usually, women laugh hardest at these descriptions. They recognise themselves and their words, but still they see no real alternative.

When nagging gets out of hand, the nagger's relationships with others can really suffer. Men may ignore her even more, which will only fuel her irritation and, sometimes, rage. She may end up feeling alone and may become resentful and miserable. When it gets out of hand, it's been known to destroy relationships completely.

How The Victim Feels

From a male standpoint, nagging is a continual, indirect, negative reminder about the things he hasn't done, or about his shortcomings. It happens mainly at the end of the day when a man needs fire-gazing time.

The more the nagger nags, the more the victim retreats behind the kind of defensive barriers that drive the nagger crazy. These barriers include newspapers, computers, homework, a gloomy face, amnesia, apparent deafness and TV remote controls. No one likes being on the receiving end of subdued rage, ambiguous messages, self-pity and blame or having guilt continually thrust at them. Everyone avoids the nagger, leaving her alone and feeling resentful. When she starts feeling even more trapped, unrecognised and isolated, the victim may suffer even more.

The more the nagger nags,
the more isolated she becomes.

The only real outcome from nagging is the destruction of the relationship between the nagger and the victim because the victim feels he has to continually defend himself.

Why Do Women Make Better Naggers?

Most women have the brain organisation to out-talk and out-nag any man on the planet. The illustrations overleaf are created from brain scans of 50 men and 50 women, showing the active areas of the brain (in black) that are used for speech and language. It's a graphic image of men and women talking and communicating with each other.

The shaded areas are used for speech and language function. You can clearly see women have far greater capacity for talking than men. This explains why, from a woman's stand-point, men don't say much and, from a man's standpoint, women never seem to shut up.

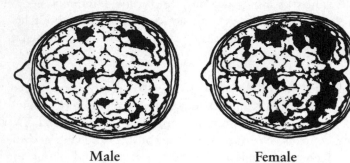

Male   **Female**

The areas of the brain used for speech and language,
Institute of Psychiatry, London, 2001.

A female brain is organised for multi-tracking – she can juggle four or five balls in the air at the same time. She can run a computer program while talking on the telephone plus listen to a second conversation behind her, all the time drinking a cup of coffee. She can talk about several unrelated topics in the one conversation and uses five vocal tones to change the subject or emphasise points. Men can identify only three of those tones. As a result, men often lose the plot when listening to women talk.

Multi-tracking can even occur in a single sentence –

Bill: "Is Sue coming over for Christmas?"
Debbie: "Sue said she'll come depending on how things go with carpet orders which have slowed down because of the economy and Fiona may not come because Andrew has to see a specialist and Nathan has lost his job too so he has to get a new one and Jodi can't get time off work – her boss is so tough! – so Sue said she could come down early and we could go dress shopping for Emma's wedding and I thought that if we put her and Len in the visitor's bedroom we could ask Ray to arrive early so…"

Bill: "Does that mean 'yes' or 'no'?"

Debbie: "Well, it also depends on whether Diana's boss Adrian will give her time off work because his car is off the road and she has to…"etc., etc…

Bill thought he had asked a simple question and he would have been happy with a simple answer like 'yes' or 'no'. Instead, he got a multi-tracked answer involving nine different subjects and eleven people. He feels frustrated and goes outside to water the garden.

Men have selective hearing.

Male brains are organised for mono-tracking. They can only concentrate on one thing at a time. When a man opens a map, he turns the radio off. If she talks with him when he's driving on a roundabout, he'll miss his exit and then blame her because she was talking. When a telephone rings he asks everyone to be quiet so he can answer it. For some men, often in the most powerful positions, it can even prove hard to walk and chew gum at the same time.

Men's brains are mono-tracked.
They can't make love and answer
questions on why they haven't taken
out the garbage at the same time.

One of the big problems for men is when multi-tracking happens during the nagging process. It's all too much for him so he simply shuts off. This goes on to begin a vicious cycle of the nagger increasing her volume and the strength of her accusations or claim to entitlement while the victim retreats further behind his barrier, often to the point of putting physical distance between himself and the nagger. Leaving the scene may not always be possible and the pressure will build up to a point where the victim will strike back resulting in a bitter argument. Sometimes that could even spill over into physical violence.

Why Nagging Never Works

The main reason nagging doesn't work is that it has the built-in expectations of failure. While naggers hope their words will push their victims into action, they often expect them to fail or they invite a negative response.

Their major mistake is the way they approach the problem. Instead of saying "I expect this as my right," they say, "...you never take the garbage out, you refuse to pick up your clothing..." They deal with their problem in small, trivial, niggling bits. They make feeble, indirect requests that are heavily laden with guilt. The 'requests' usually come in random groups that are framed in indirect speech which male brains have limited ability to decode. For a male, it's like being continually bitten by a plague of mosquitoes. He gets small, itchy bites all over and can't seem to swat them. "I don't ask you to do much around here you know... taking out the garbage is not a big deal you know... and you know the doctor said I can't lift heavy things... I spend my weekend working my fingers to the bone to make this place look nice while you just sit there all day watching the television... if you had a decent bone in your body you'd fix the heating because it's been freezing this week and..."

This kind of nagging is pointless, self-defeating and creates a lose/lose situation. With this approach, nagging becomes a corrosive habit that causes great stress, disharmony, resentment, anger and may easily end with a violent physical reaction.

Where Does The Worst Nagging Take Place?

Nagging rarely happens in the working environment unless the nagger and victim are intimately related. A clear sign that intimacy exists between the male boss and his secretary is when she begins to nag him about the things he hasn't done.

Nagging is all about the balance of power between two people. When a secretary notices her boss hasn't done certain things, she may gently remind him or simply do them for him. After all, that's a big part of her job. But when she feels more secure in her position, and feels more powerful and even indispensable, she may well start nagging the boss to do his job better. There may even come a point where she feels she could do the job much more efficiently than the boss. At that stage, nagging may reach a crescendo. She may be powerless to actually take his job from him, but, perhaps even unconsciously, she sees nagging as a way to wear him down, to 'bring him down to her level', and make him realise how lacking he is.

Career women who are happy and feel fulfilled in their work rarely nag at home. The Career Woman doesn't have the time or the energy. She is usually too concerned with the 'bigger picture' of her working life where she can receive compliments, accolades and proposals. If her male partner won't do his share of domestic chores, she either pays someone else to do it, ignores it or finds another partner who will. She's operating from a position of power.

Sex Sirens don't usually nag, either. They have power too, although of a different kind. They use their sexual power to get their own way with men. They could never be bothered nagging about dirty clothes on the floor – they drop their own clothes on the floor, and very sensually, too. When a relationship becomes permanent however, Sex Sirens can become the biggest naggers of all.

Sex Sirens don't worry about clothes on the floor – they drop their own there.

Women madly in love don't tend to nag. They're so tied up with romantic visions of their partner, or busy hatching plans to make mad, passionate love in every part of the house, they never notice clothes on the floor or breakfast plates left on the table. Their partners, also in the first flushes of a relationship, are eager to do everything they can to please them too. No one needs to nag.

Nagging occurs between people who are intimately connected – wives, husbands, mothers, sons, daughters and live-in partners. That's why the stereotypical nagger, the nagger of comic routines, is a wife or mother – those who are tied down with domestic responsibilities, who feel generally powerless in life, and who feel unable to change their lives in an upfront, direct way.

The Career Woman radiates material and mental power. The Sex Siren oozes sexual power. She is strong, independent and free. The woman who resorts regularly to nagging, however, is the one who feels powerless, frustrated and stuck. She can end up stomping around, more and more, in a confused, suppressed rage. She knows there is more to life than what she has, but she feels too guilty to admit she doesn't like her role. She is confused because she doesn't really know what to think.

Centuries of stereotyping, family attitudes, women's magazines, movies and television commercials have convinced her the role a truly womanly woman prefers is that of Perfect Wife and Mother. She secretly knows she deserves better but has become brainwashed into trying to live by a 'truth' she knows may no longer be appropriate. She doesn't want the epitaph on her grave to read, 'She always kept her kitchen clean,' but she doesn't know how to break free and build a better life for herself. She often doesn't even realise her feelings are widespread, normal and healthy.

Our research shows that women who are goal-oriented, work more than 30 hours per week or who happily accept the monotonous and repetitive ritual of housework and motherhood, rarely nag.

Nagging Can Be a Cry for Recognition

Nagging is a sign that a woman wants more: more recognition from her family for what she has given so far, and more opportunities to move on to something better.

"Every time my mother does something she just *has* to make a point about it," sighs Adam, a constantly nagged teenager. "Every time she washes the dishes or vacuums a carpet, she makes some loaded little comment to draw attention to herself. I'd rather she didn't do it in the end. Why does she have to go on about every little thing?"

She goes on about 'every little thing' because her life has become a collection of little things. It's hard to feel confident and powerful if all you've done from morning til night is trivial, predictable and commonplace. Anyone can vacuum a carpet. Unlike the soldier who is lauded for giving his life for the well-being of his country, no one will carve your name on a granite memorial for dedicating your life to your family's well-being. There are no Nobel Prizes for keeping peace in the home. It is because her tasks are so unappreciated that Adam's mother nags at him for recognition.

There are no Pulitzer prizes for
writing brilliant shopping lists.

The Perfect Wife and Mother has not been tortured (at least not in the sense normally understood by the word), blown up, or suffered in any grandiose way. Her daily tasks seem too mundane to justify powerful protests or claims to high public honour. Her suffering is of an invisible kind. It is the anguish of the downtrodden, of the silent, suffering majority.

If Adam gave her some of the recognition she craves – and deserves – the quality of his life would dramatically improve.

The women for whom nagging has got out of hand tend to be wives or mothers who are frustrated, lonely and disappointed, and who feel unloved and unappreciated. And therein lies one of the keys. Giving the nagger recognition for performing small, routine tasks eliminates most nagging.

The Mother Complex

Many women sometimes feel they are the only sensible adult in the family. They feel their husbands or boyfriends act like children. Of course, in a man's working environment he can communicate, problem-solve and produce positive outcomes and, indeed, gets paid significantly more than the women doing the same jobs. His female partner knows he has these skills, so thus gets enormously frustrated that he doesn't seem to use them at home.

> *Studies show that married men*
> *live longer than unmarried men.*
> *Some men say it just feels longer.*

The trouble is that the woman is then tempted to treat her partner more as a naughty little boy than as a capable man. His reaction, as a result, is to start behaving like one. This shift in attitude is a start along the precarious path of depreciating the relationship. The more the man rebels, the more the woman nags. The more he resists, the more she starts to act like his mother. Eventually, they both reach a point where they no longer see each other as partners, lovers and best friends. And there's no greater passion-killer for the man than starting to feel he's with his mother, nor for the woman than feeling she's with an immature, selfish and lazy little boy.

Solutions to Nagging: Saying What You Mean

A couple were having a massive row in a pizza restaurant. The whole restaurant became quiet as they raised their voices louder and louder. The argument had started off about which giant pizza they'd choose to share. He wanted pepperoni and capers; she wanted Hawaiian. She started off accusing him of never listening to what she wanted and she *hated* capers. It was nonsense to suggest that a perfectly good pizza could be ruined by pineapple. Besides, if he ever took the trouble to shop or cook, they wouldn't have to go out so often to eat at a pizza restaurant. Anyway, she didn't want to eat pizza regularly because she always preferred to eat more healthily. And all this pizza was giving her a weight problem. Was it really too much to ask that she be allowed to choose the pizza type just this once?

After this last sentence, there was silence. The whole restaurant listened in to see what the man's response would be. He took his time. He sipped his wine, looked at the floor, at the menu, then, finally, back at his wife. "This isn't about the pizza, is it?" he said at last. "This is about the last 15 years."

Nagging is so often a clear signal that a communication problem exists between two people. Instead of addressing that problem, however, it's usually far easier to pick on little trivial things and bait each other with those instead. This is particularly a tendency many women have. Many little girls are still brought up believing that they should be nice and sweet, and put their own needs and feelings last. They grow up into women who believe it's their role to keep the peace, to smooth over problems, to be liked and loved. Many women find it extremely difficult to just come out and say, "I'm not happy living like this. I feel stifled. I want to take a break from everything for two weeks to go off by myself and have some time out. How would you feel if I dropped the kids at my mother's for one week, you took the other week off from work to look after them, and I had some time to myself? I think I'd come back much happier, and be a much nicer person to live with." That's much harder to say and do than publicly picking on his pizza preference.

Women often expect men to intuitively pick up on what they're thinking, without actually saying it. They assume that if they yawn and say, "I'm so tired, I think I'll go to bed now" and wander off, men will brush their teeth, gargle with breath-freshener, put on some deodorant and slip into something more comfortable to join them there for a session of making love. Instead, many men grunt, go back to the fridge for another beer and settle down on the sofa to watch sport on the TV. It's never occurred to them that the woman in their life is talking in indirect code. The woman, sitting alone in bed, eventually falls to sleep alone, feeling unloved and unwanted.

Constant nagging merely masks a deeper communication problem. When women learn to say directly what they mean, men respond more readily. Women need to understand that male brain function is comparatively simple and men can rarely guess what their wives and partners *really* mean beyond the actual words they've uttered. Once both sexes have realised this, it makes communication much simpler, and removes the need for much of the nagging that takes place.

Solutions to Nagging: Saying How You Feel

A man won't tell you he feels emasculated when you correct his behaviour. He won't say that when you chastise or nag him it gives him the same aggravation he used to get from his mother when he was a teenager. And he won't tell you when he finds you as sexually unappealing as he finds his mother. When you let him know you don't think he'll make good decisions, he feels he is a failure and can never meet your standards. Instead, he shuts off.

You both may be doing a lot of talking, but that doesn't mean you're getting the message across. Almost all problems within a relationship such as infidelity, physical or verbal abuse, boredom, depression and nagging are the result of poor communication. Rarely do women ask, "I wonder why he no longer talks to me?" At the same time a man may think, "My wife is no longer attracted to me" but never discuss it with her.

If the woman in your life is nagging you, then she has something to tell you and you're not listening, so she's going to keep on telling you until you do. The reason you're not listening is because she's not approaching you the right way. Women habitually approach their men the wrong way with indirect talk.

One evening, Daniel arrives home late from work, to find his wife Sue waiting for him with a face that looks like thunder. Before he even has a chance to say anything, she pounces –

Sue: "You are so inconsiderate! Why are you home late again? I never know where you are! The dinner is cold – you have no consideration for anyone but yourself!"
Daniel: "Don't raise your voice at me. As usual, you're

complaining and exaggerating again! I work late so I can earn enough money to keep us comfortable... but that's never good enough for you!"

Sue: "Huh! You are so selfish! How about putting your family first for once! You never do anything around here – you expect me to do everything!"

Daniel: (Walking away) "Get off my back! I'm tired and I want to get some rest. All you ever do is nag me."

Sue: (Raging) "Sure, that's right! Just walk out of the room! You're acting like a child again. You know what your problem is? You're always running away from things and you never want to talk about it!"

Instead of Sue communicating what she really feels by using direct speech, she expressed hostility in an indirect way that led to Daniel's defensive behaviour.

Once Daniel goes into defensive mode, communication breaks down, preventing them from resolving the situation. But neither is listening or paying attention; Sue keeps repeating the same old message, and Daniel keeps walking away, thinking she is just a big nagger.

They're just not saying how they both truly feel. And their problems are only going to get worse.

Solutions to Nagging: The 'Me, I' Technique

In order to get Daniel's attention, Sue's first goal should be to avoid jumping down his throat and making him defensive. She can do this by using the 'Me, I' technique instead of using the word 'you' all the time.

Here are some of the 'you' phrases Sue used that got up Daniel's nose:

You are really inconsiderate!
You are so selfish!

You are acting like a child again.

You know what your problem is?

You're always running away.

Using 'you' language provokes defensiveness. Using a 'you' statement puts Sue in the position of judge and jury – a position that Daniel won't accept. The 'Me, I' technique lets Sue communicate her feelings about Daniel's behaviour without passing judgement. This technique will let you have a normal conversation with your partner, without ever having to fight again. And it stops arguing – forever.

The 'Me, I' technique has 4 parts. It describes your partner's behaviour, your interpretation of it, your feelings, and the consequences their behaviour has on you.

Here's how Sue could have handled Daniel:

Sue: "Daniel, you've been coming home late all week now without calling me once [behaviour]. Are you trying to avoid me, or are you seeing someone else? [interpretation] *Me, I'm* starting to feel unappreciated and unattractive. *Me, I'm* really hurting inside [feelings]. If this keeps up, *(me), I'm* going to go crazy worrying about you [consequence]".

Daniel: "Oh Sue, *me, I'm* so sorry. I never thought that you felt this way. *Me, I'm* not avoiding you. *Me, I* do appreciate you. And no, *me, I'm* not seeing anyone else, darling. *Me, I've* been so bogged down at work lately, that I've had to work longer hours and the stress is really getting to me. When I get home, *me, I'm* just so tired that I need a bit of time to myself. *Me, I* don't want you to feel this way, and *I* promise that *I'll* call you from now on every time that I have to stay at work late."

The 'Me, I' technique is powerful because it reduces defensiveness, increases honesty and clarifies everyone's feeling. It's virtually impossible to aggravate anyone with this technique.

In the above example, the message was clearly communicated by both Daniel and Sue and that resolved the problem. Good 'Me, I' statements work best when they're delivered in the right way, in the right tone of voice, and at the right time, so wait a few moments before speaking to make sure that the other person is listening.

Solutions to Nagging: Give a Man 30 Minutes of Fire-gazing Time

At the end of a long workday, a man needs about 30 minutes fire-gazing time to recoup energies before he's ready to talk. Most women, however, are ready to talk and want to talk immediately. Here's how to apply the technique:

Daniel: "Darling, *me, I* had a really long, hard day – can you give me about half an hour to wind down and relax? *Me, I* promise I'll talk with you afterwards."
Sue: "Sweetheart, *me, I* need to talk with you about the things that happened today. What time can we discuss it?"

If Daniel agrees to a time (and keeps it) and Sue gives him space to fire-gaze, there's no arguments, no tension and no one feels intimidated.

Solutions to Nagging: Getting Kids To Do What You Want

Part of responsible parenting is to remind, persuade and even demand that children behave in a certain way for their own safety, well-being and success in life. But when does our concern become nagging? And who's to blame for a constantly nagging parent in the home – the disobedient child or the nagging parent? The answer is – the parent.

The parent has conditioned the child to automatically respond the way they do. The child has been taught it's not necessary to respond after the first request and that your standard is for you to remind, persuade or demand several times before you expect them to comply. The child has trained you to keep repeating your demands and they think you don't really want them to act.

As a parent, this is a vicious circle. The more you repeat yourself and complain, the longer the child will resist. The more frustrated you become with the child's non-compliance, the angrier you get and the louder you become. The child now starts to resent your anger because, in their mind, they have not done anything wrong. Now the child becomes confused and frustrated. What started out as a simple request like, "Come and have your dinner!" has turned into war.

The nagging parent/disobedient child situation can be easily corrected and all you need is discipline and toughness – on yourself, not the child.

....
Be tough on yourself, not your children.
....

You must be prepared to tough out any particular problem for 30 days without wavering. Explain to your child that you know that he only needs to be asked once for his co-operation and if he does not respond, that is his choice. Then point out the consequences of not complying.

For example: "Jade, I want you to pick up your dirty clothes from your bedroom floor and put them in the washing basket. If you don't, I won't wash them."

This is where the self-discipline and resolve comes into play. Who's going to give in first? If you give in and pick up the clothes you're back to where you started. If you have self-discipline, let the soiled clothes build up and turn a deaf ear to any complaints about nothing to wear. This may seem tough, but you will teach responsible habits, not to mention a happier home. And your kids' future partners won't blame you for your kids' bad habits.

A child's behaviour is a direct result of the parent training, good or bad.

Don't Nag them – Train them

If you find you are continually nagging someone, it shows that person has trained *you* to do what they want *you* to do. In other words, they are making the rules and you are complying. For example, let's say you are constantly asking this person to stop throwing their wet towels on the bathroom floor. It seems no matter how much you protest, this individual just keeps doing it. Consequently, you end up picking up the used towels because you don't like an untidy bathroom and you think if you don't do it, no one else will and there won't be any dry towels for anyone to use. The reality here is that the other person knows that you will eventually pick up the towels anyway – all they have to do is put up with a little nagging from you, which is probably a small price to pay. So, you have been trained by them.

Here's how to reverse the situation: Allocate a clean towel to each child and/or adult in the house and tell them that this is their personal towel and they are to be fully responsible for it and its condition. Tell them if they leave their wet or dirty towel on the floor you will move it because you don't like an untidy bathroom and it infringes on your right to have a neat home. Tell them you'll put the offending towel in the back-yard, or over the side fence, in the dog kennel or even under their pillow. You don't mind where you put it – the choice is theirs. When you first implement this strategy it will create lots of laughter, confusion and protests from the offenders but you must carry through with action or you will remain the trained person.

Let's say, for example, the next time it happens you place the wet towel out of sight in the bottom of a broom cupboard. When the offender goes to have their next shower they will ask you where it is and you give them the towel's co-ordinates. They will then discover how uncomfortable it is to dry themselves with a damp, smelly towel. It only takes two or three times for them to become trained in picking up and hanging their towel. The same technique works well for dirty socks, underwear or any item that you don't want left around. With this technique, you become the trainer and not the trainee and nagging will no longer be necessary. If, however, you choose to continue to pick up after everyone, you will have chosen to remain the trained person and so lose the right to nag anyone about leaving mess on the floor.

Solutions to Nagging: A Case Study With Kids

Cameron, aged 13, was given the job of taking the garbage out every Wednesday night. He usually said he would do it after dinner or when his movie finished, or as soon as he'd had a shower, but he would continually forget to do it. Week after week the smell of rotting food would waft through the house as the garbage piled up. His mother had passed the point of asking and had slipped into nagging mode. The entire household was sick of hearing about the garbage and smelling it. But it didn't bother Cameron – he would simply forget about it and was prepared to put up with being nagged.

Eventually, Cameron's mother realised he had trained her to nag so she decide decided to take control. She told him it was his responsibility to take out the garbage but, because of his failing to do so, the family was suffering as a result of rotting food smells. He was then told of his consequences for non-compliance. If the trash was not put out, she said, it would be placed in his bedroom. If he didn't mind the smell of rotting food, then he shouldn't care that he'd be sleeping with it. This was outlined in a jocular, relaxed, non-aggressive but direct way.

The whole family couldn't wait for Wednesday night to come and, as usual, Cameron forgot to take the garbage out. The next night, when he went to bed, he peeled back the sheets and found it full of rotting garbage. His bedroom stank! The cost of this lesson was some dirty, smelly sheets (that Cameron was asked to wash – he knew the consequences). And he never failed to put the garbage out again.

How to Understand a Nagger

If a victim is honest with himself and admits the elements of truth in the nagging and recognizes that nagging is usually a cry for recognition, he could quickly turn the situation into a win/win. The greatest urge in human nature is to feel important. Research shows time and time again how people who work full time nag less than those who spend long periods isolated from other adults in the home. They see their contribution to the big scheme of things as important and feel their effort is recognised. Similarly, homemakers who really enjoy being at home and take pride in creating a clean, comfortable home, cooking good, healthy meals and caring for their family tend not to nag either – providing they get the same type of recognition and thanks.

So it's people in boring, repetitive work or those who resent being in the home, who tend to be naggers. Some women undoubtedly feel their lives are a non-event. Washing the clothes, vacuuming carpets, cleaning the kitchen, making the beds, and shopping for food can all be mind-numbing after a couple of years. When you add to this cocktail children who misbehave and who undo in ten minutes all the work that has been done during the day, and you end up with someone who'll resort to nagging for attention and to try and make everyone else feel as miserable as she does.

Because the basis of nagging is truth, the victim must accept equal responsibility for nagging. Nagging is the result of poor communication.

The Challenge for a Victim

To achieve a win/win situation both parties must want to change and share the responsibility. The victim needs to recognize and accept his contribution to the problem.

Victims develop patterns of avoidance, which compound matters. They may ignore the nagger, try to shout them down, leave the room or the house or make excuses for not complying with the nagger's request. Victims get it easy because they can always blame the nagger. But the only way out is for the victim to stop, take stock of themselves and consider their contribution. They should see nagging as a cry for help.

As a victim, you should ask yourself:

Are you listening to the other person?

Do you understand the other person's frustration?

Do you display a sense of superiority, making them feel worthless?

Do you recognize the other person's achievements?

Do you refuse to share the household activities because you consider yourself the breadwinner and therefore deserve to get it easy in the home?

Are you just plain lazy and uncaring?

Is there some other deep-seated anger, which motivates your unwillingness to understand the other person's problems?

Do you want to be happy?

If you do want to be happy, are you prepared to sit down with the other person and talk it out?

The Challenge for a Nagger

If you are a nagger, have you thought that the other person may be unable to meet your request? Are you behaving like a parent towards them? Do you insist on instant action, regardless of the needs of the other person at the time? Do you continually repeat your demands?

If your answer to any of these questions is yes, sit down with the other person and be prepared to communicate using the 'Me, I' language:

Tell him what is frustrating you.

Agree to a time frame for your requests.

Stop repeating yourself.

State your needs, then stop and listen to the response of your spouse.

Seek input from your partner. He may have a better idea.

Avoid 'you' statements, which cause resistance from the other person.

What will be the solution or the consequence if he does not reconsider his thoughtless action?

What are you doing to improve your own self-image?

Do you reward yourself for achieving your own goals on a day-to-day basis?

Do you want to be happy?

Nagging can be a way of life for many people, the means by which they always end up communicating, which makes them angry, resentful and miserable towards the one person in their lives who should really be an everyday source of great joy, warmth and support. But it doesn't have to be so. Follow our simple strategies to build a much happier, loving future for you both.

Chapter 2

SEVEN THINGS MEN DO THAT DRIVE WOMEN INSANE

Three Wise Men followed the Star in the East to Bethlehem to find baby Jesus. They brought gifts of gold, frankincense and myrrh. But what if they'd been Three Wise Women?

The story of the Three Wise Men and the birth of Christ is one of the world's most told tales. It's also one, which, for women, illustrates all of the male species' traits that frustrate them. First of all, they simply assumed the heavens revolved around them – the star shining in the East had been put there expressly for them to follow. Secondly, they didn't arrive at the stable where Jesus was born until more than two months after the event, most probably because they refused to stop on the way and ask for directions. Thirdly, what possible use would a newborn baby and his exhausted new mother want with gifts of gold, frankincense (a resin used for fumigation) and myrrh (a strong-smelling plant oil used for embalming the dead)? And, finally, *Three* Wise Men? Who's ever seen such an unlikely sight?

Imagine if the story had starred Three Wise Women. They would have asked directions, arrived in time to help deliver the baby and brought practical gifts, like nappies, bottles, toys and a bouquet of flowers. They would then have put the animals outside, cleaned the stables, made a casserole, stayed in touch by mail, and there would be peace on Earth for ever more.

....

Moses wandered in the desert for 40 years.
He wouldn't ask for directions either.

....

It's hard to whittle down to a manageable figure the number of annoying traits women find in men but, from letters we've received from over 5,000 of our female readers, we've come up with the seven questions women most frequently ask about men.

1. Why do men continually offer solutions and give advice?
2. Why do men keep flicking through the channels with the remote control?
3. Why won't men stop and ask for directions?
4. Why do men insist on leaving the toilet seat up?
5. Why do men make such a fuss about going shopping?
6. Why do men have such disgusting personal habits?
7. Why do men love gross jokes?

What women see as male 'bad habits' fall into two categories: those he has learned from his upbringing, and those that are linked to the wiring of the male brain. But none are insoluble. Anyone can be retrained, if you know how.

1. Why Do Men Continually Offer Solutions and Give Advice?

"The man in my life is becoming too much for me with his constant problem-solving approach to everything. He gives me advice on how to handle everything in my life – whether I want it or not! When I just want to talk about my day or my feelings, he keeps cutting me off or interrupting me by telling me what I should do, think or say. He's great at solving problems involving 'things' – leaking taps, faulty lights, car and computer problems and so on – but when it comes to listening, he just won't do it. And if I don't take his 'advice' he gets upset.
'Going-crazy' Karen"

To appreciate why a man insists on giving solutions to every little thing, there are several things that need to be understood about the way the male brain works.

Men evolved as hunters, and their main contribution to the survival of the human race was the ability to hit a moving target so everyone could eat. They needed to be able to aim accurately at either edible targets or enemies who either wanted to steal that food, or who threatened their families. As a result, their brains evolved with a target-hitting area called the 'visual-spatial' area that allows them successfully to carry out their whole reason for being: hitting targets and solving problems. They turned into results-oriented people who measure their own success by results, accomplishments and their ability to come up with solutions to problems. As a consequence, a man still defines who he is and his self-worth by his problem-solving abilities and achievements.

> *A man's self-worth is defined by*
> *the results he can achieve or by how*
> *accurately he can hit a moving zebra.*

This is why men love to wear uniforms and hats with badges and insignia that display their competence or reflect their problem-solving abilities. A man feels that he is the one person most capable of solving his own problems and does not see the need to discuss them with anybody else. He will only ask another person's opinion about a problem if he feels he needs expert opinion and he considers this to be an intelligent, strategic move. In return, the man who is asked for his opinion feels honoured by the request.

> *If one man asks another man for advice, the man*
> *who is asked sees the request as a compliment.*

Consequently, for a woman to offer a man advice when he didn't ask for it is seen by him as a statement that she feels he is incompetent because he can't solve his own problems. A man sees asking for advice as a weakness because he feels he should be solving his problems himself and this is why he will rarely talk about what is bothering him. He loves to offer advice and solutions to others, but unsolicited advice, especially from a woman, is not welcome.

Why Women Become Upset By Men's Solutions

A woman's brain is organised for communication through talking and the main purpose of the talk is to talk. For the most part, she is not looking for answers, and solutions are not required. Herein lies the problem for most couples – at the end of the day she usually wants to talk about the events in her day and to share her feelings, but he thinks she is giving him her problems to fix and starts to offer solutions. She gets upset because he won't listen to her talking, and he becomes angry because she won't accept his solutions. "Why don't you just keep quiet and listen?" she'll yell as she heads for the door. "If you don't want my opinion," he'll shout back as the door slams behind her, "don't ask for it!" Each feels the other does not value what they say.

> *When she wants him to show empathy,*
> *he thinks she's asking him for a solution.*

He thinks he is being caring and loving by solving her problems – she thinks he is indifferent or is trivializing her feelings by not listening.

Case Study: Sarah and Andy

Sarah has had a tough day at work: the boss has been on her back, she was blamed for an administration bungle, she lost her purse and broke a nail. She feels like her world is falling apart and wants to talk to Andy about it when he gets home.

She phones Andy to find out what time he'll be back, and prepares a good dinner in the expectation that they'll have a long heart-to-heart as they eat. He'll be loving and sympathetic. She'll be able to pour out her heart to someone who cares and she knows she'll feel so much better as a result. She wants him to listen, make her feel loved and understood, and reassure her that she'll be able to solve her problems.

But Andy has also had a tough day. He left work with several major problems still outstanding that he'll need to solve before he returns to work next day. As he drives home, his mind is working overtime on the solutions. He knows from Sarah's phone call that she had a bad day, but he really needs time out to sort out his own problems.

He arrives home, says a quick 'Hi' to Sarah and then sits down in the lounge to watch the news on television. She checks the meal and tells him dinner will be ready in fifteen minutes. He thinks, 'Good! Fifteen minutes of quiet time before we eat.' Sarah thinks, 'Great! Fifteen minutes to start chatting before we eat.'

Sarah: "How was your day, darling?"

Andy: "Fine."

Sarah: "I've had the worst day of my life and I just can't take any more!"

Andy: (still with half an eye on the news) "You can't take any more of what?"

Sarah: "My boss is giving me a really hard time. When I got into work this morning he had a go at me about the quality of my work and demanded to know why I hadn't finished the new advertising campaign. Then he told me he wanted it by the end of the week and that he was scheduling for the client to come in Monday and see what we had done. When I tried to explain it wasn't done because I'm still working on the Seinfeld project that he'd told me was urgent, and that I wouldn't have time to finish both projects so quickly, he just cut me off and said he didn't want to hear any more excuses and just to have the campaign on his desk before I finish work Friday. Can you believe it? He just wouldn't listen to me... (becoming upset)... then he changed the subject and said he'd see me at 6 o'clock on Friday night to go over any last minute changes. I just feel like quitting. I don't think I can take this any more..."

Andy: "Look, it's simple, Sarah... what you should do is stand up for yourself and tell him you can't finish both projects and ask which does he want completed first? Go in tomorrow and tell him that his deadline is impossible and he needs to adjust it or get someone to help you with both projects."

Sarah: (becoming emotional) "I can't believe you! I'm telling you about this boss who just orders me around and never listens, and then you start telling me what to do. Why can't you just listen to me? I'm sick of men always knowing better."

Andy: "Come on, Sarah. If you don't want my opinion, stop telling me your problems. Sort it out yourself and stop complaining to me about it! I have enough of my own problems which, by the way, I always sort out myself!"

Sarah: (close to tears) "Well, you can go jump! I'll find someone else who'll listen to me and won't tell me what I did wrong! You can get your own dinner! I'm going out and I don't know when I'll be back!"

For men and women around the world, it's an all-too-common scenario. At the end of it, Sarah feels let down, unloved and hurt. Andy feels unappreciated and confused because Sarah has just criticized his number one skill: problem-solving.

How could Andy have handled it better?

Let's rewind this scene and see how Andy could have avoided having such a bad night.

Sarah: "How was your day, darling?"

Andy: "It was fine. I've got a few work problems to sort out by the morning; things will be much better after I've slept on it."

Sarah: "I've had the worst day of my life and I just can't take any more!"

Andy: "Oh no. You poor darling! I want you to tell me all about it, but can I have fifteen minutes by myself to sort out the problems I have at work, then I'll be able to give you my full attention over dinner."

Sarah: "OK... I'll check the dinner and call you when it's ready. Would you like a glass of wine now?"

Andy: "Thanks darling... I'd love one."

By Andy asking for time out and Sarah granting it, he now has the time and space to sit on his rock and think about his own problems. Sarah feels reassured and happy that he'll be there for her over dinner when she'll be able to get her problems off her chest and feel better about life.

Here's how the dinner went:

Sarah: "My boss is giving me a really hard time. When I got into work this morning he had a go at me about the quality of my work and demanded to know why I hadn't finished the new advertising campaign. Then he told me he wanted it by the end of the week and that he was scheduling for the client to come in Monday and see what we had done. When I tried to explain it wasn't done because I'm still working on the Seinfeld project that he'd told me was urgent..."

Andy: (showing interest with his face) "Darling... that's terrible. Doesn't he know how hard you've been working? You look so stressed..."

Sarah: "You can't begin to imagine how stressed I am! Anyway, I started to explain it wasn't completed because the Seinfeld project is so time consuming. But in the middle of my explanation he just cuts me off and says he doesn't want to hear any excuses and to have the campaign on his desk before I finish work Friday! Can you believe it?"

Andy: (looking concerned and resisting giving advice) "Sounds like he's really giving you a tough time..."

Sarah: "He just wouldn't listen to me... he changed the subject and said he would see me at 6 o'clock on Friday

night to go over any last minute changes. I am so stressed I
feel like quitting…"

Andy: (putting his arm around her) "You've had a really hard
day honey. What would you like to do?"

Sarah: "I'm going to sleep on it tonight and get up early
tomorrow and if I don't feel any better about it, I'd really
like you to help me work out how to handle it. I'm just too
tired and stressed out to discuss it tonight. Thanks for
listening to me, darling. I feel so much better…"

By not offering immediate solutions, Andy avoided an argument, got a glass of wine and didn't end up sleeping alone on
the couch. By giving Andy time to himself, Sarah avoided the
usual arguments, and felt happy about herself and her life.

When You Want to do Business with
the Opposite Sex

Men and women do business very differently, and if either side
doesn't fully understand the implications of that, then their
business relationship could prove financially disastrous.
Women want first to establish a personal relationship with a
man before they proceed to business, by chatting on a variety
of topics, often on quite a personal level, as a way of seeing
what kind of person he is and whether he seems trustworthy.
Men often completely misunderstand this approach. At worst,
some think she might be coming on to him for sex; at best
nearly all assume she is asking for advice for her problems.
They then feel justified in offering solutions, and telling her
what she should do, think or say.

The woman resents this very much. She's likely to write off
the man as someone who won't listen and who is unlikely to
take much notice of her if they do business together. She
becomes more hesitant about dealing with him, leaving the
man confused and bewildered that their business relationship
isn't working out. A man needs to understand that, even in

business, a woman is easier to deal with if she forges a personal connection first. A woman needs to understand that a man is uneasy discussing personal information, and prefers to get right down to business. When each side understands this, both are much more willing to compromise – which leads to a far stronger business relationship in the long run.

How to Avoid an Argument with the Opposite Sex

If a woman is upset or stressed and needs to talk, a simple technique is to say to a man, "I need to talk with you about several things. I don't need any solutions, I just want you to listen." A man will be happy with this approach because he knows exactly what he is supposed to do.

Solution
If a woman is talking, and a man does not know whether she is asking for solutions or just talking, he can find out by simply asking, "Would you like me to listen as a boy or a girl?" If she wants him to listen as a girl, he only has to listen. If she wants him to listen as a boy, he can offer solutions. Either way both will be happy because each understands what is expected.

> *A woman usually wants to be heard, not fixed.*

To sum up, advice-giving is perceived differently by men and women. A man sees giving advice as being caring and showing love, but a woman can interpret it as showing he's unwilling to listen. The lesson here is simple but powerful. For a man, listen with empathy, particularly if a woman is upset and, if he's not sure what she wants him to do, ask. For a woman, make it clear what you expect from the man to whom you're unburdening yourself.

2. Why Do Men Keep Flicking Through the Channels with the Remote Control?

> **Remote control:** *noun, female*: A device for changing one TV channel to another; *noun, male*: A device for scanning through 55 channels every 2.5 minutes

For thousands of years, men would return from the hunt at the end of the day and spend the evening just gazing into the fire. A man would sit in this trance-like state among his friends for long periods without communicating, and the other men made no demands on him to speak or participate. For men, this was a valuable form of stress relief and a way to recharge their batteries for the next day's activities.

For modern men, fire-gazing still occurs at the end of the day, but now involves tools like newspapers, books and remote controls. Once, we were at the remote Okavango Delta, north of Botswana's Kalahari Desert in Southern Africa. Noticing a satellite dish powered by a solar cell on a pole above a village hut, we went inside, and found a group of Kalahari bushmen dressed in loincloths in front of a television set with a remote control, all taking turns to flick through all the channels.

....

*In Heaven, every man has three remote
controls and all toilet seats are left up.*

....

Male channel-changing is a pet hate of women everywhere. It's a common joke that many would like to bury their husbands with the remote control firmly clasped in their hand.

At the end of a long day, women like to relax by becoming involved in a television show, especially any series involving human interaction and emotional scenes. Her brain is organised to read the words and body language of the actors and she likes to predict outcomes of relationship scenarios. She also enjoys watching the commercials. For men, however, watching television is a completely different process, done to satisfy two main impulses. Firstly, having a solution-oriented, problem-solving brain, he is interested in getting to the bottom line as quickly as possible. By flicking through the channels, he can analyze the problems in each programme and consider the solutions needed. Secondly, men like to forget about their own problems by looking at someone else's, which explains why six times as many men watch the TV evening news bulletins as women. Since his mind can only do one thing at a time, by looking at other people's problems and not feeling responsible for them, he can forget about his own worries. It therefore becomes a form of stress relief, just like surfing the Internet, working on his car, watering the garden, working out in the gym or, often his favourite, having sex. As long as a man concentrates on one thing, he's always able to forget his own troubles, and feel good about himself.

Men don't want to know what's on television, they want to know what else is on television.

If a woman is worried about a problem, it makes no difference if she does any of these things – the problem still preoccupies her multi-tracking mind and she needs to talk about it to get any relief.

This basic difference between the sexes frequently leads to trouble. A woman will often try to talk to a man while he's reading a newspaper or channel-surfing and, because he doesn't react to what she's saying, will frequently challenge him. "What's the last thing I said?" she'll demand. To her frustration, he'll usually be able to tell her. That's because he has heard her talking but, because his brain was mostly taken up with the single task of reading the newspaper, he wasn't really listening, or analysing what she was saying, he only recorded her words.

Women will often accuse men of being miles away when they're trying to talk to them. That confuses men; they feel their physical presence is often enough. Women, however, want them to be emotionally present too. Women will resent a man's apparent inattention and interpret it as being ignored. Men will resent not being allowed to have downtime, even after they've tried to offer solutions and been rebutted. The more a woman pushes, the more the man will resist. The more he resists, the more resentful she becomes.

A woman needs to understand that a man's fire-gazing is his way of relieving stress, and that she should not take it personally. When he talks, he talks about one thing at a time. Her multi-tracking brain allows her to talk about a range of things, past, present and future, all simultaneously.

> *Silence from a man doesn't*
> *mean he doesn't love her.*
> *It means he wants quiet time.*

A man needs to understand that a woman needs to talk about things without reaching solutions in order to relieve the stress she's feeling.

Solution

To solve the remote control problem, she needs to calmly discuss with him how much it drives her crazy, and could he please not do it when she is watching her programme. Alternatively, she can try hiding the remote somewhere he'd never think of looking. And if neither of those work, she should consider buying her own television set – or another remote control.

3. Why Won't Men Stop and Ask for Directions?

For over 100,000 years men have used the spatial part of their brain to track prey and hit targets. During this time men learned the art of a good sense of direction and how to retrace their steps by feel, so that they could hunt over long distances and then find their way home again. This is why, when entering a windowless room for the first time, more than one in three men can sense North within a range of 90 degrees and point towards it, something only one in five women is capable of. The unfortunate fact is that you can never learn to sense North; you can either do it or not. The most plausible explanation for direction-sensing is that men have a higher concentration of iron in the right hemisphere which allows them to feel magnetic North. This is the same skill a man uses to find his way back to his seat at a sports match, relocate his car in a multi-storey car park and return to a location he's only been to once before.

Nest-defending females did not venture alone past the horizon so they learned to navigate by landmarks – sensing direction was never a necessity and was not part of her job description. If she could see a tree, or a lake or a hill, she could find her way around it and find her way home again. This is also the key to how a man should give a woman directions. If he tells her to go to the road with the giant oak tree, then head to the pink building beside the National Bank opposite the lake she is likely to reach her destination. If he tells her to take the third exit at the West turnoff on Highway 23 and drive five kilometres North, she will possibly never be seen again.

Men don't get lost – they simply discover alternative destinations.

For a man to admit he is lost is to admit he has failed at his number one skill – finding his way. And he would often rather be burnt at the stake than admit it to a woman. If you are a woman in the passenger seat and you've just passed the same garage for the third time, it's important not to criticise him or offer advice, especially if you don't want to end up walking.

Solution

Buy a map or directory and leave it in the car for him. If he likes computers, there are now CD-ROMs available for most major cities that plot the perfect route, which you can print out and take on the journey. For a relatively small amount of money, an excellent solution is to buy him a hand-held Satellite Navigation System for his birthday/Christmas which is an excellent spatial boy's toy that will allow him always to be right, never be lost, and to love you forever.

> *Why does it take 4 million male sperm*
> *to find and fertilize an egg?*
> *Not one wants to ask for directions.*

A quick, safe emergency strategy is to tell him you urgently need to go to the toilet, which will force him to stop, and preferably at a service station. While you're in the toilet, he'll have time to pretend he's buying something and to ask for directions.

4. Why Do Men Insist on Leaving the Toilet Seat Up?

Until the end of the late 1900s, toilets were small boxes out the back of a home. Whenever a woman was going to use the toilet, she would take other women with her for security. Men, however, were expected to go alone and defend themselves if necessary. Men never peed in the toilet – they did it in a bush or up against something, a habit that modern men have inherited from their forefathers. This is why you rarely see a man peeing in an open field, it's always up against something like a wall or a tree and, just like other animals, there's an intrinsic element of marking one's territory. When the flushing toilet was invented in the late nineteenth century (purportedly by Thomas Crapper), the humble loo moved to its own room inside houses and public establishments. Yet the practice of going to the toilet in groups still persists for women. A man will never be heard to say, "Hey Fred, I'm going to the toilet... would you like to come?"

When men go to the bathroom,
they never take a support group.

Today, public toilets everywhere have separate sex toilet facilities, with seats for women and wall-mounted urinals for men. Women always sit down, but men only sit 10 to 20% of the time. Modern homes are supposedly designed and built to accommodate both men and women equally, but men are disadvantaged in that home toilets only accommodate women's needs. In the home, a man will lift the seat so as not to wet it for a woman who will sit on it. But when he fails to put it down afterwards, he's roundly criticised. Many men resent that a great deal. Why shouldn't women take a turn in putting the seat up for men? In some parts of the world like Sweden, it's even become law for a man to sit when peeing in a public toilet because it is politically correct.

When God had finished creating the Universe he realised he had two things left over to divide between Adam and Eve. One, he explained, was an implement that would allow its owner to pee standing up. Adam was thrilled, and begged and begged that he be allowed to have it.

Eve smiled graciously and told God that if Adam really wanted it so badly, he should have it. So God gave it to

Adam, who immediately went off and excitedly peed up against a tree, and drew a pattern in the sand. And God saw that it was good.

God then turned to Eve. "Well, here's the other thing," He said, "I guess you can have it."

"Thanks," replied Eve. "What's it called?" God smiled back as he answered, "Multiple orgasms."

In Sweden a few years ago, a feminist group called for men's urinals to be banned on the grounds that men standing up to pee were 'triumphing in their masculinity' and thus degrading women. They didn't win too much support. In some places, usually trendy advertising offices in the USA, urinals are increasingly being phased out, however, in preference for unisex toilets, all with their individual cubicles, although more on the grounds of saving money and optimising space than any arguments about the equality of the sexes. A Dutch company in the year 2000 announced the launch on to the market of the world's first 'female urinal'. So far, they haven't made a huge impact on global toilet habits.

One of our male readers wrote to us about how he and his wife tackled the ongoing toilet seat argument:

"Women should understand that sometimes a man's penis has a mind of its own. A man can go into a toilet cubicle (because all the urinals are being used), take perfect aim at the toilet, and his penis will still manage to pee all over the roll of toilet paper, down his left pant leg, and on to his shoe. I'm telling you, John Thomas can't be trusted.

After being married 28 years, my wife has now trained me. I'm no longer allowed to pee like a man – standing up. I'm required to sit down and pee. She has convinced me that this is a small price to pay. Otherwise, if she goes to the toilet one more time at night and either sits on a pee-soaked toilet seat, or falls into the toilet because I didn't put the seat down, she's going to murder me in my sleep."

There's also the problem of the morning erection, which makes it doubly difficult for a man to have a true aim, and explains how the wallpaper gets wet. Even sitting down, he reported, there are major mechanical problems that only men understand. He's now perfected the art of lying face down over the toilet bowl in a 'Flying Superman' position in order to make sure that nothing escapes.

> "Women need to understand that men are not totally to blame. We are sensitive to their concerns about hygiene and bathroom cleanliness, but there are times when things just get beyond our control. It's not our fault, it's Mother Nature. If it was Father Nature... there wouldn't have been a problem..."

In truth, men don't really care about whether the seat is up or down, but can get annoyed with a woman who demands it is lowered, rather than asking him politely – or doing it herself.

Solution

Asking a man to sit down when he pees will usually mean no more problems. If the man refuses, it should be quietly, but firmly, pointed out that many hundreds of thousands of men in the Muslim world sit down to pee every day – without feeling their masculinity is in the slightest bit compromised. The Prophet was said to only have urinated once standing, and that was when he was in a garden where it was impossible to sit down. If that fails to persuade a man, simply set new house rules. From now on, it's his job to clean the toilet, and that means mopping the floor every day to clear up all the stray droplets. That might very soon put a whole new positive light on the seated position...

If you can afford it, the ideal solution is always to buy a home with two toilets – one for him and one for her – or renovating a current home to include an extra bathroom. That way, you can both enjoy the standards of cleanliness and hygiene you choose, without having to feel stressed about the other's.

5. Why Do Men Make Such a Fuss About Going Shopping?

The great thing about being a man is you can buy two suits, three shirts, a belt, three ties and two pairs of shoes in under eight minutes. And that's enough clothing to last a man for up to nine years. He can buy Christmas presents for the entire family in less than 40 minutes at 4.30pm on 24 December and he can do it completely alone.

For a man, one pair of shoes, one suit and a couple of shirts will last for many seasons. The same hairstyle endures for years, perhaps decades. And, even better, his wallet, as a consequence, will last far longer too.

Most men rate shopping on a par with having a prostate examination by a doctor with cold hands. British psychologist Dr David Lewis found the stress men experience while Christmas shopping ranks with the kind of stress experienced by a police officer dealing with an angry mob in a riot. For most women, on the other hand, shopping is a much-loved form of stress relief.

The reasons are obvious for anyone who has studied the different ways men and women evolved, and who understands how their brains are wired. Men's earlier lives as hunters have given them a form of tunnel vision, which enables them to move directly from point A to point B in a straight path. The amount of zig-zagging through shoppers and stores needed for a successful shopping expedition makes him feel extremely uneasy, as a change of direction requires a more conscious decision. Women with their wider peripheral vision, however, navigate a crowded shopping mall and zig-zag with ease.

Men's shopping tip #62: you can get new shoes for £4 at bowling alleys.

Men evolved into creatures that made a quick kill and then went home again. Today, that's exactly how men like to shop. Women shop the same way as their ancient ancestors would gather food: heading off for the day with a group of other women to a place where someone remembered some tasty things were seen growing. There does not have to be a specific goal or directive and time limits are not important. They spend the day wandering from place to place in an unstructured way, squeezing, smelling, feeling and tasting all the interesting things they can find, while at the same time talking with each other on a range of unrelated topics. If nothing was available or ready for picking and they returned home at the end of the day with little to show for their efforts, they still felt excited that they had had a great day. For men, this is an inconceivable concept. For a man to go out for the day with a group of other men with no clear destination, no clear goals, objectives or time limits, and to return home empty-handed, would class him as a failure. This is why, when a man is asked to buy milk, bread and eggs on the way home from work, he may come home with sardines and marshmallows. He forgot what she asked him to get and came home with a couple of 'bargains' instead – his very own quick kill.

A woman will dress carefully according to the weather, the season, fashion, her own colouring, where she's going, how she feels about herself that day, who she's seeing, what she'll be doing. A man merely performs the sniff test on a piece of clothing he's left lying over the arm of a chair.

Research shows that not only do men dislike food and clothes shopping, it's detrimental to their health because of the stress it causes them. But there are ways to help a man feel positive about the shopping experience.

How to Shop for Food

Always let a male push the shopping trolley. Men like to be in control and they like to 'drive' it and to use their spatial ability – cornering, angles, speeds and so on. Men even like the trolley with the dummy wheel because that represents an even bigger challenge to their spatial and directional skills. Many men quietly make a *Brrrrrmmmmmm* sound in their heads just like when they were boys. Ask him how he thinks the food will best fit in the trolley – this lets him use his spatial skills again to get the right answer. Women prefer to zig-zag when they supermarket shop and work from a list but men prefer to take a straight line, shop by memory and examine every item that looks good. As a result he always brings home the same items – for example, a single man's kitchen cupboard has 26 cans of baked beans and 9 bottles of tomato sauce but not much else. While you zig-zag the aisles, give him clear goals – brands, flavours and sizes and challenge him to find the best prices and congratulate him when he gets a result. Always ask him what he likes to eat, give him lots of positive strokes and buy him a special treat such as chocolate. A woman may be sticking her fingers down her throat at this point and saying "All this just to go food shopping?!" But remember, shopping is not hardwired into the male brain so incentives are needed.

Clothes Shopping

To many women, it seems as if men are hardwired to buy ugly clothes for themselves and this is not far from the truth. For at least a hundred thousand years, women dressed to attract while men have dressed to frighten away their enemies. Men would paint their faces and bodies, put bones through their noses, wear a dead buffalo on their head and have a rock connected to the end of their penis. We should not be surprised if scientists discover men, particularly heterosexual men, have a 'bad taste' clothes gene.

We always hold hands.
If I let go, she shops.
ALLAN PEASE

The same motivational principles apply to clothes shopping as for food shopping – give a man sizes, colours, fabrics and price ranges, and send him on the hunt. The male brain is organised to concentrate on a singular task.

What can you tell from a well-dressed man?
His wife is good at picking out his clothes.

A key to how men shop was revealed in a study with chickens. When chickens were fed male hormones, they pecked at their coloured food in different ways. They ate all the red seed first until it was gone, then all the yellow. The other chickens (with no male hormones) ate all the different coloured food in no order.

Solution

Only give a man one thing at a time to do and don't try to convince him you are saving lots of money by buying more. Never ask him, "Do I look better in the blue dress or the gold?" A man will become anxious because he knows he can never get the right answer and will therefore fail. Most men own two pairs of shoes, male brains have limited skill to match patterns and designs, and one in eight men is colour blind to either red, blue or green. If a woman asks a man to shop for her or get her an item from the clothes rack, she must give him the exact size of the garment she wants. If he gets one size too big she accuses him of saying she's fat. If it's one size too small she thinks she's putting on weight. If she is modelling outfits for a man she only needs to instruct him to rate each outfit from one to ten and never ask comparison questions like "Is the green better than the yellow?" If a woman leaves a man waiting outside the changing room in the 'Bored-Husband-Seat', she must always get him something to eat.

Even with these strategies, most men still only have a shopping attention span of about 30 minutes. If you insist on taking him shopping however, do it near a large hardware store so that, at worst, he can return home having road-tested the latest Black & Decker double electric reverse router saw which would let him drill perfectly round tiny holes upside down in a plaster ceiling without a ladder, should the need ever arise.

6. Why Do Men Have Such Disgusting Personal Habits?

Women everywhere complain that men have far more unacceptable personal habits than women, but research does not back this up. Men are more accepting of what they consider are female bad habits and men pay less attention to detail than women. They are therefore less likely to even notice an offending woman's indiscretion.

------

*It's good to be a man because
you don't have to leave the room
to adjust your private parts.*

At the top of the list of men's habits women won't tolerate are nose-picking, burping, body odour, wearing ancient underwear and crotch scratching. But number one on her list is farting.

Flatulence: *noun, female*: An embarrassing by-product of digestion; *noun, male*: An endless source of entertainment, self-expression and male bonding

Farting is universally unacceptable by women even though it is a sign of a healthy body and diet. For males, the appreciation of farting as a pastime begins at about age 10 when a boy's level of achievement is related to his ability to drop a range of farts under a variety of circumstances such as imitating voices or using a cigarette lighter to send a blue flame of fire shooting across the room. These acts are seen as a greater achievement than the discovery of the cure for polio. Burping routines rate as a close second.

The world's most famous farter was Joseph Pojul who, in 1892, had a famous act at the Moulin Rouge in Paris under the name 'Le Petomane'. His act opened by telling a story using a remarkable range of farts for the voices of the characters. He could smoke a cigarette through a tube placed up his bum and also play the National Anthem with a flute connected to the end of the tube. Women were reported to laugh much more than men to the extent that some would pass out and be taken to hospital to recover.

Flatulence Facts

While 96.3% of men admit to farting, only 2.1% of women will ever acknowledge they fart. Men let loose an average of 1.5–2.5 litres of gas a day delivering an average of 12 farts a day which is enough to fill a small balloon. Women fart an average of seven times a day and emit 1–1.5 litres of gas. The main cause of excessive farting is talking too much and talking while eating. Wind becomes trapped in the system and although much of it is belched out, the rest passes through into the small intestine where it mixes with other gases and prepares to burst out on an unsuspecting world. In 1956, Bernard Clemmens of London managed to sustain a fart for an officially recorded time of 2 minutes 42 seconds.

Why do men fart more than women? Women don't stop talking long enough to build up pressure.

Fart gas is 50–60% nitrogen and 30–40% carbon dioxide. The other 5–10% is methane, which causes underground mines to explode and hydrogen gas, which, in a bomb, can destroy cities. One of the biggest sources of these gases is eggs, giving rise to what is known as the 'rotten egg fart'.

Offending foods

The biggest fart-producing foods include cauliflower, onions, garlic, cabbage, broccoli, bran, bread, beans, beer, cask white wine, and fruit and vegetables generally. As a result, vegetarians fart much more but smell a lot less.

Products that reduce the amount of gas produced include charcoal tablets, 'de-gas' preparations and both peppermint and ginger products. There is also a charcoal-based cushion available. You sit on it and it guarantees a 90% reduction of fart smell.

Cattle and sheep fart around 35% of the methane gas in the world's atmosphere causing increased global warming and enlarging the hole in the ozone layer. Terrorism is not the world's biggest threat – it's farting cows!

Solution

An obvious remedy is to serve up healthy meals with fewer of the fart-producing foods, and give a man a cup of peppermint tea afterwards, rather than coffee. Food-combining diets are also shown to help too, where meals never involve both carbohydrates and protein in the same sitting.

Men should not be allowed to eat gas-producing foods within two hours of bedtime.

Also, encourage a man not to drink water during the meal. Beforehand is fine, but to drink while eating dilutes the digestive juices so makes him more likely to fart afterwards. Lead by example. Chew food very well, eat slowly, and don't watch TV at the same time. If he still insists on eating quickly and farting often, however, you may need some more dramatic tactics. Take one of our reader's examples:

Nigel always got a big kick out of farting in a public place like a department store whenever he was out with Sharon. After he'd let one fly, he'd keep a straight face so no one would see who did it. When bystanders turned to look at the couple, Sharon appeared to be the obvious culprit because she usually went bright red, and looked embarrassed. Nigel thought the whole thing was hilarious – until the huge fight that followed. At home, he would fart in bed and call it a 'test of true love'.

Sharon decided to establish 'fart-free zones' in the bedroom and kitchen. When they were out in public she told him to give at least two minutes' warning if he felt he had to let fly. If he didn't comply with this request she would produce a toilet roll from her handbag and loudly say "Perhaps this might help?"

Pets can often help too. At the sound, or smell of a fart, it's often easy to turn to your dog or cat and reprimand him loudly.

Often the most useful persuasive device with any man is the promise of sex if he behaves well. A woman can make it clear how much she's turned off sex by farting in the bedroom. If he works at his diet to make sure he farts less, he may, in return, enjoy a far more active sex life.

7. Why Do Men Love Gross Jokes?

The main purpose of humour for men is threefold: first, to gain status with other men by having a good repertoire; second, to allow him to deal with tragic events or consequences; and third, to acknowledge the truth about a topical issue. This is why almost all jokes have a punchline, which is usually a disastrous ending. Laughter is rooted in our ancient past where it was used as a warning signal to tell other humans that there was imminent danger, just like it's used in the ape family. If, for example, a chimpanzee narrowly escapes being attacked by a lion, it will scamper up a tree, throw its head back and make a series of HOO-HOO-HOO-HAR-HAR-HAR sounds that resemble human laughter. This warns other chimps about the danger. Laughing is an extension of crying and crying is a startled fear reaction, which is evident in infants from birth. If you intentionally frighten a child by playing peekaboo, its first response is to cry out of fear. When the child realises the situation is not life-threatening it will laugh, signifying that, while it experienced a fear reaction, the laughter signals it now knows it was only a trick.

Brain scans show that men laugh more at things that stimulate the right brain than the left, but for women it's the opposite. In America, Rochester University claims to have found where the male sense of humour comes from – it's located in the right frontal lobe of the brain above the right eye. Men love humour or any joke that has a logical, step-by-step approach with a conclusion that is hard to predict. Here are some relatively tame jokes that stimulate male brains:

1. What's the difference between a tart and a bitch?
   A tart will sleep with anyone.
   A bitch will sleep with anyone except you.

2. What's the difference between a woman with PMT and a terrorist?
   You can negotiate with a terrorist.

3. Why do men give their penis a name?
   Because they don't want a complete stranger making their major decisions.

A major difference between the sexes is men's obsession with telling jokes about tragedies, horrific events and male genitalia.

Women's sex organs can perform astounding feats of human reproduction, are securely hidden away and if unravelled, would stretch over four kilometres. But women never make jokes about them, give them pet names or treat them as a source of laughter.

Men's sex organs hang out the front in a vulnerable and precarious position (further proof that God is female) and are a constant source of male amusement and hilarity. Women's humour involves people, relationships and men. For example:

1. What can you say to a man who's just had sex?
   Anything you like – he's asleep.

2. What's the definition of the perfect male lover?
   He makes love until 2am then turns into chocolate.

3. Why don't men fake orgasm?
   Because no man would pull those faces on purpose.

Male brains have an amazing capacity for remembering and storing jokes. Some men can tell jokes they heard in fourth grade but don't know the names of their children's best friends. Males think it is hilarious to moon (give a 'brown eye') from a moving car to an unsuspecting group of elderly ladies, especially nuns, put superglue or cling wrap on a toilet seat, hold a farting competition or chain a drunken, naked groom-to-be to a lamp-post. To most women, none of these things is remotely funny.

Jokes are so important as a communication medium to men that whenever there is a global tragedy, the world's email networks and faxes are literally swamped with men sending tragedy-related jokes. Whether it's the death of Princess Diana, September 11 or the hunt for Osama bin Laden, the male brain instantly swings into action.

Osama bin Laden has 53 brothers and sisters, 13 wives, 28 children and is worth over $300 million. But he hates Americans because of their excessive lifestyles.

Herein lies the difference between men and women in handling serious emotional issues. Women deal with calamity or tragedy by openly expressing their emotions to others, but men withhold their emotions. Men use joke-telling as their way of 'talking' about the event without showing any strong emotions which could be seen as a weakness.

How Jokes and Humour Ease Pain

Laughing and crying instruct the brain to release endorphins into the blood stream. An endorphin is a chemical that has a similar composition to morphine and heroin, and has a tranquillizing effect on the body while, at the same time, building the immune system. This explains why happy people rarely get sick and miserable people who complain a lot often seem to fall ill.

Laughter and crying are closely linked from a psychological and physiological standpoint. Think of the last time someone told you a joke that made you buckle up with uncontrollable laughter. How did you feel afterwards? That tingling sensation came from your brain releasing endorphins into your blood system, giving a natural 'high'. In effect, you were 'stoned'. Those who have trouble with laughing at life often turn to drugs, alcohol or sex to achieve that same feeling. Alcohol loosens inhibitions and lets people laugh, releasing endorphins, which is why most well-adjusted people laugh more when they drink alcohol and unhappy people become even more miserable or even violent.

At the end of a big laughing session, you will often cry. "I just laughed until I cried!" Tears contain encephalin, which is another of the body's natural tranquillizers to relieve pain. We cry when we experience a painful event, and endorphins and encephalin aid in self-anaesthesia.

*John sat still as the fortune-teller gazed into
her crystal ball. Suddenly, she started to laugh loudly
so he leaned across and punched her on the nose.
It was the first time he'd struck a happy medium.*

The basis of many jokes is that something disastrous or painful happens to a person. But because we know that it is not a *real* event happening, we laugh and release endorphins for self-anaesthesia. If it *were* a real event, we would go immediately into crying mode and the body would also release encephalin. This is why crying is often the extension of a laughing bout and why, when faced with a serious emotional crisis such as a death, many people cry, but a person who cannot mentally accept the death may begin laughing. When reality hits, the laughter turns to tears.

Laughter anaesthetises the body, builds the immune system, defends against illness and disease, aids memory, teaches more efficiently and extends life. Humour heals. Research around the world has now shown how the positive effects of laughing, with the release of the body's own painkillers, strengthen the immune system. After laughter, the pulse rate steadies, breathing deepens, arteries dilate and the muscles relax.

This is a predominantly male way of dealing with emotional pain. The harder it is for a man to talk about an emotional event, the harder he will laugh when told a joke about it, however heartless and insensitive it may seem to women. Men rarely talk about their sex lives to other men so they tell jokes about it as a way of discussing it. Women however, will discuss their sex lives with their girlfriends in graphic detail without the aid of any jokes.

Don't Feel Offended

As long as there are Irish men, there will be Irish jokes. Or Asian or Aussie or feminist jokes. And every time there's a tragedy, it will invariably spawn its own set of jokes.

Being offended is a choice. Others can't offend you – you *choose* to be offended. And choosing offence tells the world that you are unable to come to terms with the problem addressed by the joke. We are Australian authors living in England, and the English are always telling Australian jokes about us: "What's the difference between Australia and yoghurt? At least yoghurt has some culture!" "Why are Aussies so well-balanced?" "They have a chip on both shoulders." And "How can you tell a level-headed Australian?" "They dribble out of both sides of their mouth."

With all these jokes, we don't choose to be offended. If it's a good joke, we'll laugh just as hard as the English. And later, we might even adapt it to make it about Kiwis or Americans. Choosing offence is a negative choice, like shame, embarrassment or hurt. These choices may show others that you have low self-esteem, aren't in control of your own emotions or are not prepared to face a situation.

You can choose to feel *offended* because someone tells a joke that says anyone from your country is stupid. That doesn't mean they *are* stupid and even if you agree that they are, abusing the joke-teller won't make them any smarter. You can choose *anger* because the traffic is backed-up, but it won't clear the traffic. If you take a calm, analytical approach about why the traffic is backed-up you may come up with a solution that can help solve the problem. There's no point in choosing anger.

If a man insists on telling inappropriate jokes at the wrong time or place, tell him you don't like it and you want him to stop. If he continues to do it simply walk away and do something else.

At a dinner party, that can be more difficult, particularly if you happen to be the host. The man you're asking to stop telling inappropriate jokes may feel publicly humiliated, which may simply encourage him to tell even more outrageous jokes. It might be better to use the tactic of striking up a conversation about his jokes with the line, "Do you know any jokes that *aren't* nasty, or maybe all jokes are nasty?" That can then turn the dinner table conversation to a general discussion about the nature of humour. You can always then dazzle your guests with your extensive knowledge of why men and women laugh at very different kinds of jokes!

Learned Behaviour – Blame His Mother

Some women view men as naughty little boys who never grew up. They claim men throw their clothes on the floor, won't help around the home, can't find things, won't ask directions, expect to be continually waited on and will never admit to making a mistake. Women's brains are hardwired to nurture and mother others, particularly their sons. They pick up after their son, cook him his favourite meals, iron his clothes, give him money and protect him from the trials of life. As a consequence, many boys reach manhood with few domestic skills and abilities, and little understanding of how to make relationships work with women. Their sons become attracted to women who, like their mothers, will nurture and mother them. At the start of a new relationship, most women respond to the role of mothering a new man, but when they realise it could be a permanent role, things can turn sour. It is important for a woman to understand that, if she continually mothers a man, he will see her as a mother figure and respond by yelling, throwing tantrums and running away. And no man finds his mother sexually attractive.

Retraining a Man

Training someone to do what you want is the same whether they are a child or adult. You reward the behaviour you want and ignore the behaviour you don't want. For example, if a man leaves his clothes or wet towels on the floor instead of in the laundry basket, explain gently that you'd like these items put in the basket so they can be washed. If he continues to offend, do not pick up these items. If they interfere with your right to a tidy house, calmly explain that you will put them in a plastic bag in a cupboard, or under the bed or in his workshop. This way, if he needs them at least he knows where they are. The key is to give advance notice of your intentions and to avoid being sarcastic, judgmental or aggressive, as this usually has an opposite effect on males. When he eventually needs clean underwear, shirts or towels, it becomes his problem not yours. Similarly, if he leaves tools or uncompleted projects around the house, tell him you will also put them in a cupboard or drawer. Do not put them in his workshop or any place that is convenient for him, as that will simply reinforce the behaviour you don't want. If you want to retrain your man, you must resist the urge to pick up after him. When he puts his own things away, reward him for his contribution with a smile or thanks. Some women are appalled by the thought of thanking a man for doing something as basic as picking up his own clothes, but it's important to understand that men did not evolve as nest-defenders and general tidiness is not something which comes naturally to them. If a man's mother didn't train him to do these things, it will be up to you to train him. On the other hand, if you continue to pick up after a man (or boy), you have to accept that you've chosen to replace his mother, and you may as well feel happy in the role.

When you understand how the male brain works, you will find men can be great fun to have around. Men are the same everywhere – they may have different coloured skin, different cultures or belief systems, but their brains operate the same way regardless of whether they live in Trieste or Timbuktu.

The key is always to manage the males in your life, rather than arguing, becoming angry, or feeling frustrated with them. That way, both sexes will be able to live happily ever after. And, you never know, the next time we ask women for the seven things men do that drive them insane, maybe they won't even be able to get past three. Maybe.

Chapter 3

WHY WOMEN CRY

The dangers of emotional blackmail

To this point, we've taken a serious but humorous look at the differences between the sexes and what you can do about it. Now, we'll look at the serious side of how emotions are used to manipulate others to gain compliance. The stories here are all true – only the names have been changed to protect the guilty.

There are times when people cry as a direct response from the heart, but many times they cry as a way of manipulating others' emotions. While men will occasionally do this, women are more likely to use tears as a way of emotionally black-mailing others. Sometimes, they don't realize what they are doing. They cry in response to a situation, knowing that it will make the other person feel bad about themselves and, hope-fully, as a result, they will be able to manipulate them. It's a controlling mechanism that is either deliberate or subcon-scious. The goal is to force another person – a husband, lover, child, parent or friend – into a course of action they may not otherwise have taken. Women may also cry in an attempt to appear regretful and thus receive lesser punishment for misconduct such as having an affair or shoplifting. This chap-ter will help you identify people in your life who use these tactics to manipulate or bluff you into doing what they want.

Why We Cry

Cry: *verb* to bawl, blubber, boohoo, howl, shed tears, lament, sob, wail, weep, whimper, whine

Crying is something we share with other animals and that begins at birth, but humans are the only land-dwellers that weep with emotion. Tears serve three purposes for humans: to help clean the eye surface; to excrete stress chemicals from the body; and as a visual distress signal in a highly emotionally charged situation.

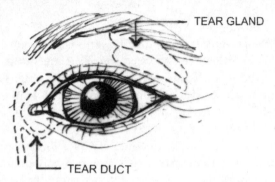

The tear gland is the tap, the tear ducts are the drain.

Tears are formed by a gland above the eye and are removed by two ducts in the inner corner of the eye that empty into the nasal cavity. In emotional or distressing circumstances, the excess tears that can't be drained quickly enough by the tear ducts will roll down the cheeks.

Why Women Cry More Than Men

Crying begins at birth and its prime purpose is to stimulate loving and protective feelings in adults. Crying is a way for the baby to get what it wants and, as adults, this behaviour is perpetuated by some women. Most women can identify seven different meanings behind a baby's cry to evaluate its needs. Women's tear glands are more active than men's, which is consistent with the greater emotional responses of the female brain. Men are rarely seen crying in public because, from an evolutionary perspective, a man showing emotion, especially around other men, would be put at risk. He'd look weak and this would encourage others to attack him. For women to show emotions to others, however, particularly other women, is seen as a sign of trust because the cryer becomes the baby and is putting her friend into the role of protective parent.

Crying has three known purposes:

1. As an eyewash

Many zoologists believe this function is a relic from an aquatic era when we lived mainly in the water and evolved webbed fingers, webbed toes and down-facing nostrils to allow effective swimming. The tear gland secretes liquid into the eye and the tear ducts act as a drain to remove it via the nasal cavity. Crying serves to remove salt and other impurities from the eye – a specialty not seen in other primates. Tears also contain an enzyme called lysozyme that kills bacteria and prevents eye infections.

2. As a stress reducer

Chemical analysis of tears reveals that stress tears, those that roll down the cheek, contain different proteins from those used for eye cleansing. The body appears to use this function to clear stress toxins from the body. This could explain why women say they feel better after 'a good cry', even when there appears to be no real reason for crying. Tears also contain endorphins, one of the body's natural painkillers, which act as a damper to emotional pain.

3. As an emotional signal

Seals and sea otters cry when emotionally distressed because they have lost their young. Humans are the only land animal that cries both from emotion and to manipulate emotionally. Tears act as a visual signal asking others to hug and comfort the weeper and they encourage production of the hormone oxytocin, the hormone that makes a person desire to be touched and cuddled by another person.

Seals and otters don't manipulate each other with tears. Only humans do.

Glistening or sparkling eyes occur when a person's emotions are intense but tears are not overwhelming to the point where they overflow onto the cheek. Glistening or sparkling eyes can be seen in a proud parent or a lover's eyes that sparkle or twinkle as light reflects off the tears produced.

Crying And Emotional Blackmail

How Blackmail Works
Now that you understand the purposes of crying, we'll examine the mechanics of how one person can set out to manipulate another.

Case Study: Georgina's Story

Georgina was an attractive, intelligent woman. She attended secretarial college before taking a position as an executive personal assistant. She loved the fast life: parties, an expensive apartment, designer clothes and a sports car. She earned enough money to meet her living expenses, but her extravagant social life was usually paid for by her male companions.

Georgina, however, hated working for a living. Getting out of bed and being at the office by 9am after a big night out was becoming too hard. Her social life and job commitment were not compatible.

At a party one night, she told her troubles to a man she met there. He was an older man who appeared to be wealthy, owned a Porsche and a yacht, travelled a lot and didn't seem to work. He suggested to Georgina that she might like to become a high class escort and, for a percentage of her fees, he could introduce her to a large clientele.

After a few days of deep thought, Georgina accepted his offer and was soon enjoying life the way she wanted. But not for long. Guilt, conscience and a violent incident soon made her realize that her previous life was not so bad after all. She moved away, changed her name to Pamela and got a position with a big accounting firm. Soon Georgina, now known as Pamela, was dating one of the business partners – her boss, Graeme. They eventually married and after three happy years had a child. Life was good for Georgina – a.k.a. Pamela. She had a wonderful husband who loved her, a beautiful baby, a new home, financial security and plenty of friends.

One morning she received a telephone call from Frank. Frank had been a regular client when she was an escort. He wanted to meet her again and suggested lunch. Pamela refused. That was in the past and it was over. Frank insisted that it was in Pamela's interests to meet him and said he was sure she would not want her previous life disclosed to her husband and friends.

Pamela was devastated. She could lose everything – her husband, her home, her child, her whole security in life.

Pamela met Frank, who demanded $10,000 to keep quiet. Pamela had some money saved and felt that she had no option but to pay up. Three months later, Frank was back with further demands but now he wanted sex as well as cash. Pamela went to the police. Frank was convicted of extortion and given twelve months in jail. Even though her husband Graeme handled the situation well, Pamela knew her life would never be the same again.

This was a classic case of how criminal blackmail works. This case has the strategies that apply to any situation where one person attempts to manipulate another for personal gain. Here are the main ingredients and the players:

The victim: someone who has a sense of guilt or obligation

The blackmailer: the person who knows the weakness of the victim

The demand: payment for silence or co-operation

The threat: threat of exposure, punishment, and the threat of loss of something highly valued or guilt

The resistance: the initial refusal by the victim to co-operate

The compliance: meeting the blackmailer's demands

The continuity: the inevitable ongoing demands

Most people never consider that those close to them could use this type of manipulative strategy; they just think these people are 'badly-behaved' or 'pushy'. This chapter will help you identify who these people are in your life and will show you what to do about it.

Emotional Blackmail

Emotional blackmail is where a person who is emotionally close to you subtly threatens to punish you or threatens or implies that you will suffer if you don't comply with what they want. They know your deepest secrets and vulnerabilities and use this intimate knowledge to get you to obey. Whatever strengths or weaknesses you have, the blackmailer will use them against you.

Case Study: Rosemary's Story

Rosemary's husband Greg and her mother had never liked each other. Her mother believed Greg was not good enough for her daughter and was always trying to create trouble between the couple.

One day, she'd told Rosemary one of her friends had seen Greg with another woman at a local bar. "It was probably just a work friend," Rosemary suggested. "We don't *own* each other."

Rosemary brought it up with Greg. He was furious, and accused her of spying on him. "Maybe if you don't trust me, we should look again at our relationship," he said. Rosemary persevered, and eventually Greg was forced to admit that the woman was the owner of the bar and he'd been drawing up plans for a surprise party for Rosemary's upcoming birthday. He then insisted on dragging Rosemary to the bar and introducing them to each other.

Two years later, Rosemary's mother had a bad fall. She spent four months in hospital and, when she came out, she was weak and had lost her confidence. Rosemary knew, with a sinking heart, that she'd have to ask her mother to live with them, but she could imagine what Greg's reaction to this idea. She carefully chose the time to broach the subject.

That evening, she took extra care over her appearance, and cooked Greg's favourite meal. When he came home she gave him a glass of wine, and asked him about his day. By the time they both sat down at the dinner table, she knew he was feeling calm and relaxed.

After dessert, she put her head in her hands. Greg was concerned and asked what was wrong. "I don't know how to tell you," she replied. "I just feel terrible." Greg put his hand on hers. "Rosie, what is it?" he asked. "Is it something I've done?" Rosemary shook her head sadly. "No, Greg, you haven't done anything. I just..." She then broke down into tears.

Greg put his arms around her and begged her to tell him what was the problem. Through her tears, she shook her head. "No, it's OK, Greg. I'll get over it. Sorry about this. Don't worry." "But Rosie," he pleaded, "Tell me what's happened. Surely it can't be this bad?" Through her tears, Rosemary looked up appealingly at him. "No, Greg, I'm afraid you'll be angry at me, and I couldn't bear that," she said in a soft, broken voice. "You won't understand." Greg was beginning to feel upset too. "Please tell me," he said. "Honestly – I'll try to understand." Greg started thinking the worst. Rosemary must be having an affair.

Rosemary shuddered, dabbed at her eyes and then took a deep breath. "It's mother," she said. "She's so frail now and I'm worried about her. I want to look after her, but I know how you'd feel about her living here with us. I've tried to put it to the back of my mind, but it's killing me – the thought of her in that house on her own with no one to help her if she falls over again. Oh Greg, I don't know what to do... if it was your mother I'd cope but..." She drifted off into long, shuddering sobs.

At first, Greg flatly refused to even entertain the thought of his mother-in-law moving in. But after two days of Rosemary's tears, he started to feel guilty. If he really loved Rosemary, shouldn't he be prepared to make sacrifices for her? Isn't that what true love was all about? Isn't marriage about compromises? He began to feel selfish and mean – just as Rosemary knew he would. Eventually, Greg agreed to a one-month trial period. Both Rosemary and her mother knew that once she was in the door, it would be virtually impossible to get her out again. And Greg knew that every time he protested, there'd be tears and accusations and he'd end up feeling bad. The pattern had been set.

Rosemary and Greg's story had all the typical blackmail ingredients where one person attempts to emotionally manipulate another for their own personal gain:

The victim: Greg – he had a weakness and a sense of guilt when the woman in his life appeared emotionally distressed

The blackmailer: Rosemary – she knew Greg's weakness

The demand: Rosemary's mother moving in

The threat: the implied withdrawal of love if Rosemary didn't get her way

The resistance: the initial refusal by Greg to co-operate

The compliance: Greg giving in to Rosemary's demand

The continuity: the inevitable ongoing arguments and tears

Everyone knows at least one person who has used emotional blackmail tactics to force them to do something they initially refused to do. It might have been a situation similar to Greg's, or it might happen regularly with a passive-aggressive person who never seems to say exactly what they want – they just end up playing games to get the end result. It's important that you identify any person in your life who uses these tactics to manipulate or bluff you into getting their way. Most people never realize their friends or family could use this type of conscious, well-thought-out strategy; they just think of these people as being assertive or aggressive. The results of being emotionally blackmailed are always destructive.

> *The most common emotional blackmailers*
> *are family members and close friends.*

You end up agreeing to something you never wanted to do or believe is wise in the circumstances. In the process of complying, the blackmailer has made you feel bad about yourself, and guilty for resisting. Inevitably, you'll resent being put in that situation. Whether or not you realize it, long term, your relationship with the blackmailer will never be the same.

Men And Emotional Blackmail

Men are far more often the victims of emotional blackmail than the villains. Men prefer to ask directly for what they want. Women, in their evolved role as the peacekeeper, tend to shy away from saying exactly what they want, when they want it. Many women lack the self-esteem to realize they deserve what they're asking for. As nest-defenders, their overwhelming urge is to be *liked* by others. They've always been the nurturers of relationships – with partners, children and other family or social groups. Their brains are organized to succeed in making relationships work. Therefore, they'll often resort to emotional blackmail to get their way, rather than asking for what they want directly and risk being rejected.

---

*Blackmail seems the easy route because
it lets the person avoid confrontation.*

Men will use emotional blackmail, but always to a much lesser extent. Men's brain functions are much simpler when it comes to emotions. When men were hunters, they preferred the direct, full-on approach and their brains have continued to evolve that way.

If a man wanted his mother to move in, he'd probably buy his partner a bunch of flowers before he asked, but that would be the extent of his manipulation. He'd then move on to broach the subject and discuss it plainly, without emotion, looking at the pros and cons. He may present a plan for building a home extension, having a home-carer visit his mother, weekends away without the mother, and so on. Men often demand or subtly insist that everyone else go along with what they want, and many women comply.

---

*Men will use a well-planned, direct
approach to get what they want.
Women prefer emotional blackmail.*

Historically, men were in more powerful positions than women, and could call the shots far more openly. Women were rarely dominant enough to have the upper hand, so for centuries had to rely on their wiles and cunning to get what they wanted.

In some situations, however, men do resort to emotional blackmail. Young men, for instance, in trying to persuade their girlfriends to have sex, use emotional blackmail as a contrivance to have their way.

Case Study: Damian's Story

Damian has been out twice with Erika, and their dates have ended, both times, with a long, deep kiss before she broke off the embrace and scrambled out of his car and up the pathway of her parents' house. Damian was growing impatient. He liked Erika and wanted to have sex with her, but she seemed to be resisting. He couldn't understand why. She said she liked him, and he felt it natural that she'd want to make love as much as he did.

On their third date, after they'd gone to the movies and he'd paid for a meal far more expensive than he'd intended, Damian pulled up in a dimly lit park and switched off the engine. He then turned to Erika and started kissing her, and fumbling with her top. She helped him undo her buttons, and they began caressing each other. After five minutes, he tried to pull up her skirt but she pushed his hand away. That happened a second time. And a third. Finally, he broke away and asked her what was wrong.

"Look I really like you," he told her. "I just want to make love with you. I feel like we're getting on so well, I want to show you how much I care." Erika looked unconvinced. "Sorry, Damian, I really like you too," she said. "But it's too soon. I don't feel ready. We've only been out three times. I'll know when the time is right. Please be patient with me."

Damian nuzzled her ear. "Come on baby," he said. "You know you want to. I really like you. For me, the time feels right now. I just want to know you even better. I've never felt like this about someone before."

Erika, however, moved away. "No, Damian... I'm sorry... but I don't want to," she said. "I *do* like you too, but I'm not ready."

Damian looked crestfallen. "But... I thought you felt the same about me as I feel about you," he said. "Erika, I'm so sorry... I completely got all the signals wrong from you..." He looked so upset, Erika couldn't help but feel for him. "No

Damian, I *do* like you," she insisted. "I just need a bit more time…"

Damian shook his head sadly. "No, you obviously don't feel the same way about me. I'm sorry, Erika, I really thought we had something good going here. I've made a complete fool of myself. I'm sorry. Let's just forget this ever happened." He reached for the car keys to start up the engine. Erika could feel herself getting more and more upset. "No, Damian," she said. "Look, I think you're a lovely guy and I want to spend more time with you."

"But, Erika," replied Damian, "I *really* like you, so for a man it's natural to want to express it physically. But if you don't feel the same, then I think it's better we call a halt now before I get *too* involved… Sorry, but that's the way I feel. I've been hurt before…"

Erika ended up having sex with Damian that night. Their relationship lasted another two weeks.

Damian was the blackmailer here, Erika was the victim, sex was the demand. He knew exactly where Erika's weak spots lay and played on them mercilessly. Women hate to see men emotionally upset; it brings out their maternal instincts and the desire to help get rid of the pain. They're used to seeing men as strong, infallible creatures, so when a man appears to crumble, women are deeply affected. When Damian subtly accused Erika of not caring about him, after she'd already made it quite clear that she did, she allowed herself to start feeling maybe the only way he'd understand she did like him was to agree to sex.

Finally, there was Damian's implied threat that he was prepared to call off the relationship if he didn't get his own way. If he'd said that straight out, she wouldn't have reacted the way she did. But because he couched it in terms of not being able to bear to be hurt any more, she ceased resistance and allowed herself to be emotionally blackmailed into a position she had not wanted to be in. This opened the way for Damian to expect sex every time her saw her.

A relationship that starts on such a manipulative basis is usually doomed. How can two people reasonably be expected to trust and respect each other, if their beginning together was built on manipulation? Emotional blackmail is destructive unless tackled immediately.

Common Emotional Blackmail Tactics

Emotional blackmailers may be lovers, husbands or wives, children, mothers-in-law, parents or friends. Sometimes they can be employers. Blackmailing runs in families and is a tactic passed on from one generation to the next.

Here are some of the typical threats or punishments emotional blackmailers use. Some may sound familiar to you.

Parents: "After all I've done for you."
"I will cut you out of my will."
"Why are you doing this? You're my flesh and blood!"

Husbands/Wives: "I can't believe you're behaving so selfishly."
"You don't really care about me."
"If you loved me, you'd do it."

Ex-partners: "I'll drag you through the courts. You'll never see the children again."
"I'll take you for every cent you've got."
"When we had sex, I always hated it."

Lovers: "Everyone else is doing it. What's wrong with you?"
"This is what lovers are supposed to do for each other."
"It's obvious that you don't love me. It might be better if we split up."

Children: "All the other parents do it for their children. Obviously they love their kids more than you love me."
"I'll run away – I must be adopted."
"You love my sister more than me."

Parents-in-law: "I'll leave everything to charity."
"If you don't look after me, I'll get sick and end up in hospital."
"Don't worry about me – I'm old and will be dead soon."

Friends: "If things had been the other way around, I'd do it
for you."
"You say I'm your best friend. Well maybe you had better
find another one."
"I've always been there for you. Look how you treat me
when I need you."

Employers: "You'll only make things more difficult for your
workmates. They'll have to carry the load."
"I'll make sure that you're never considered for promotion
ever again."
"Surely you owe me and the company some loyalty?"

Employees: "If you fire me, you'll need a great lawyer."
"I bet the media would like to hear about this."
"Haven't you heard of harassment?"

What the blackmailer is saying is, "If you don't behave the way
I want, you will suffer."

Children learn early that emotional blackmail is a way of
getting what they want – particularly when they know their
parents use it too. Children feel relatively powerless because of
their age and size, so blackmail looks the easiest and most
effective route to getting what they want.

Case Study: Julia's Story

As Julia's kids grew up, they grew less willing to spend any
time with their bedridden uncle, John. Julia felt guilty about it.
Every time Julia visited him, he would ask where the children
were. Julia felt she had to lie each time, saying they were away
with the school, or busy with their homework, or had a special
project which kept them away.

"Look, he's getting old, and I don't know how much longer he might be around," she told them. "He's lonely and looks forward to seeing you. Remember all the things he did for you when you were small? He was always babysitting, and spoiling you. He never had much money, but he always spent what he had on you."

Julia's kids however, were often completely unresponsive and would use emotional blackmail on Julia. "But, Mum, he can never hear what we're saying anyway, he's so deaf," said Bernard, fifteen. "And it's boring at his place. There's nothing to do. I don't get to see my friends much anyway. Surely I deserve to have some fun? You don't want me to be miserable do you?"

Katie, sixteen, was also a blackmail expert. "C'mon, Mum," she'd say. "You know how much homework we get at school, surely you don't want us to fail our exams? I wanted to come with you this morning, but I've got this big geography essay to do. The marks I get for it will count towards my final results. If I don't do well, I could be in big trouble. Besides, you shouldn't be using emotional blackmail on us. It's not fair. We don't want to go. End of story."

Children can be absolute masters of the art of manipulation. Parents who routinely try to emotionally blackmail their children must always be ready to have the tables turned on them.

In this scenario, Julia felt powerless, and tried to exert moral and emotional pressure on her children. Instead of reasoning calmly and coolly with them or simply instructing them to do what she thought was right, she used emotional blackmail. The kids then did exactly the same because they had learned how the game is played.

*Adults who use emotional blackmail
raise children who are even better at it.*

One day, we were watching a busker on the streets of London. At the end of his act, he turned to the group of spellbound children who were watching him and called out, "Hey, kids! If your parents won't give you £1 to put in my hat, it means they don't love you!" He raised £18.

The more anyone gives in to emotional blackmail, the more it will become a pattern that dictates the future of a relationship. The closer the relationship, the greater the sense of guilt, and guilt is the most powerful tool of the blackmailer.

Case Study: Stephen's Story

Stephen was married to Camilla for five years before they separated by mutual agreement. Well... Stephen thought it was mutual agreement. Although Camilla had agreed to the split at the time, she never really thought that Stephen would go through with it. She simply assumed that, after a couple of weeks on his own, he'd return to her, begging to be allowed to move back in.

Stephen never returned. Instead, he worked much harder and longer hours, and buried himself in his job. Camilla secretly believed that he'd never be able to keep up the pace, and would realize, sooner rather than later, how empty and pointless his life was without her. But then he met another woman.

Camilla was beside herself with rage. She regularly phoned Stephen's mother to keep in touch with his life. She knew his mother loved her like a daughter and was devastated when the couple split. When his mother started talking about the new woman in Stephen's life, Camilla saw red. She started calling Stephen at odd times of the day and night, saying she'd made a huge mistake and wanted to meet him to talk about things.

Reluctantly, Stephen agreed to meet. Camilla was humorous, charming and warm – just like she'd been when they'd first met. But Stephen had moved on. He still liked Camilla and felt genuinely fond of her but no longer felt an emotional bond.

He listened to her talking about how much she missed him, but said he was sorry, he'd met someone else, and he hoped Camilla would be happy too.

But Camilla didn't get the message. She would call him in tears and beg him to visit. If ever he came, she'd weep and say she felt her life was over without him. He felt helpless in the face of her tears. He'd try to comfort her. Then she called and threatened suicide.

Stephen didn't know which way to turn. Luckily, his new girlfriend, Chrissie saw what was happening and took charge of the situation. She persuaded Stephen's mother to call Camilla's family and tell them she was worried about her state of mind, and could they look after her? Chrissie told Stephen to write Camilla a letter, telling her firmly that he was sorry, but it was over. There's no way he'd consider returning to her.

Like most women, Chrissie could see the emotional blackmail being played by Camilla and knew Stephen was an unsuspecting victim. Chrissie's quick thinking saved Stephen from being trapped in a relationship he no longer wanted. If Chrissie hadn't stepped in, he may have drifted back to Camilla, even though he hadn't wanted to. He'd been extremely frightened by her suicide threat, and felt he would have been responsible if she had gone ahead. He simply hadn't realized she was deliberately using emotional blackmail to win him back, and had no real intention of ever harming herself.

Stephen and Chrissie married the next year. Camilla is still there on the sidelines, visiting his mother regularly and chatting about 'the good old days' of their relationship. But no one really takes much notice of her. They all feel sorry for her, but wish she'd move on and get a life of her own.

Guilt puts the victim under huge pressure. No one wants to become too cynical about other people, but it's important to stand up for what you want. Stephen knew he didn't want to go back to Camilla, and should have taken his cue from that. Men are not used to dealing with their own emotions, and have little idea about how to deal with emotional women.

Men like direct arguments and debate about which sports team is the best, which political party has the right policies to run a country, and which beer gives the mildest hangovers. Men deal with facts, data and concrete realities. When others – usually women – confront them with emotions, most men just can't cope. Women know this, and use it to their advantage. Yet men can still be emotional bullies to get what they want. This tends to work best when the women in their lives are the sensitive, quiet types who are used to giving in to a domineering man.

Case Study: Irene's Story

Irene had a beautiful nature. She was calm and compassionate and cared about people, never putting her needs above those of others. She was a generous, happy and loyal person. But she didn't see herself this way. She would often give in to others' demands or fail to assert herself, just to keep the peace. Irene's husband Bob, however, was very demanding and jealous and always wanted things his way.

One day, Bob announced he wanted to buy a new boat. He told Irene his old one wasn't fast enough, big enough, easy enough to handle and lacked the technology he wanted. He'd been looking around and said he could get exactly what he wanted for a reasonable price.

When he told her the price, she almost passed out. "We can't afford that at the moment", she said. "We've just paid the children's school fees and you promised that I could have a new car at the end of the month because mine is a wreck and keeps breaking down all the time."

Bob was furious. "There you go again, always thinking of yourself," he said. "Me, me, me, that's all you care about. Doesn't it every cross your mind that I have needs too? I work hard all week to earn enough money to keep this family. I'm constantly under stress and my Saturday fishing is the only chance I get to relax."

Bob gave Irene a hard time for the next three days. Irene felt drained. Eventually, she decided to try a compromise. "Bob, I was thinking about the boat and maybe if I bought a smaller used car, and you put the purchase of a new boat off for twelve months, we could manage both in the long run."

Bob was unmoved. "No," he replied. "The boat will be more expensive next year and besides, it's a good idea to get a boat *this* summer. We'd be able to spend more time with the kids because they could water-ski off it. We need to keep the kids occupied at weekends or they'll end up in trouble."

Irene was distraught. "But, Bob, we can't afford it right now. There are so many other things that need doing around the house." Bob was unresponsive. "I can't believe this, Irene," he said, his voice growing angry. "Surely you care about our children? You're the one who's always worrying about where they are and what they're doing. I never thought I'd see the day that you'd start depriving them of time we could all spend together as a family. They need this boat too!" After two more days of tension, Irene felt she couldn't bear the situation any more. She knew Bob could drag it out indefinitely, and the kids were becoming more and more upset by the tension in the house. Finally, Irene worked out a solution. She would go back to work fulltime and everything would be OK.

Bob bought his boat – and now he wants a marina berth for it. He knows he'll get it because he'll use the same tactic again.

Irene was as much a victim of blackmail as anyone who receives a ransom note, or direct threats. The essential ingredients of criminal blackmail and emotional blackmail are exactly the same.

The victim: Irene's sense of obligation to her family, her love of the children and her desire to keep a happy home were her weaknesses

The blackmailer: Bob knew all Irene's secrets and feelings because of their intimate relationship

The demand: Irene would agree to the purchase of a new boat

The threat: the guilt of contributing to the deterioration of her husband's health; letting her children fall into bad company because of her selfish and self-centred attitude; the continuation of the dreadful tension at home

The resistance: Irene's attempt to explain that Bob's demand was not practical; she offered an alternative

The compliance: Irene eventually gave in

The continuity: Bob's continued blackmailing tactics for a marina berth because he knew they would work

Emotional blackmail destroys a victim's self-image. If they continue to yield to the blackmailer, they will eventually lose their self-confidence and forever be robbed of the ability to assert themselves. They will become plagued by self-doubt, fear and guilt, and this allows the blackmailer to make ever more outrageous demands.

How To Handle An Emotional Blackmailer

Emotional blackmailers usually appear to be strong and resolute. Even though they give the impression that they know what they want and they are prepared to do what they have to do to get it, this is rarely the case.

Blackmailers are usually just bullies. They have a poor self-image and can't handle rejection. They lack the self-confidence to discuss their situation and consider the options, and are desperately frightened of losing what they already have. They'll usually accuse their victims of being selfish, uncaring or self-centred – all the qualities they themselves possess. In many ways, they are like naughty children. They make their demand and, if it is not satisfied immediately, throw a tantrum. Every time a parent gives in to a tantrum, they are sowing the seeds of an emotional blackmailer.

*Always remember – emotional blackmailers
are like bullies or naughty children and
should be treated accordingly.*

If you feel that you are the victim of an emotional blackmailer, it is important for you to decide whether you are prepared to go along with the situation or whether you're going to do something about it. People will always treat you the way you allow them to treat you. If you are a victim, it's because you have allowed it. But just as a blackmailer's behaviour has been learned over a period of time, so it can be modified over time. This behaviour modification needs commitment and time, so you must be prepared for a rough patch and the long haul.

The first thing to realize is that the blackmailer needs your agreement for something, otherwise they would not be asking for you to allow them to do whatever it is they'd like to do. In reality, therefore, it's you who has the upper hand. Without your consent, the blackmailer feels powerless. The only way to lose your power is to show weakness. Don't plead with them not to be so difficult and don't accept any blame for the situation. Don't try to understand how the blackmailer feels. Always remember that it's *you* who is being blackmailed and what is important is how *you* feel. Never try counter-blackmailing.

When a blackmailer's demands, threats and accusations start to flow, it is essential that you have a stock of readymade responses. These may not come to you naturally so practice them until they become part of you.

What You Can Say To A Blackmailer

"Well, that's your choice."

"I'm sorry you choose to feel that way."

"Obviously you're angry, let's discuss it when you're not upset."

"Well, your opinion differs from mine."

"I can see you're not happy, but that's the way it is."

"I think that needs a lot of thought. Let's talk about it later."

"We see things differently."

"You may be right. Let's consider it for a while before we make a decision."

"Obviously you're disappointed, but it's not negotiable."

Refusal to weaken or negotiate immediately is likely to bring on a period of silence or sulking from the blackmailer. This is often the point where the victim gives in. The situation must eventually be resolved – but this should only be when the blackmailer is ready to discuss the situation maturely and rationally. During a blackmailer's period of silence, don't complain about the problem, as this will let the blackmailer know that you're frustrated and this is what gives them their power. Just say, "I'm willing to talk about it when you are."

Avoid counter threats, insults or
attacking a blackmailer's vulnerabilities.

The blackmailer will feel powerless and desperate but still needs to save face, so 'stroke' them for their otherwise good points. If it comes down to a compromise, set your boundaries and stay steadfastly within them. If the blackmailer is making you feel uncomfortable, refuse to go along with whatever they're saying.

....

Don't fight or argue with blackmailers – train them.

....

Using the responses we have discussed, you can modify a blackmailer's behaviour. Blackmailers respect people who stand their ground.

When The Blackmailer Is Also In The Dark

Sometimes a blackmailer might not even realize what they're doing. South African journalist Charlene Smith wrote a powerful book about the night she was raped in her own home and how she hounded the authorities to pursue her attacker. At that time, South Africa had the worst rape statistics in the world, with a woman being raped every 26 seconds. Rape was the most taboo topic in the country and few people, particularly the female victims, had the courage to speak out about what was happening.

In her book, she talks about the terrible effect it had on her, how she finally emerged all the stronger, and how she became a touchstone for so many other women who went through the same trauma. One woman who called her, however, received little sympathy. This woman had given up college as a result of her rape, had demanded her husband buy a house in another area, and stopped caring for their three children and their home. Her children cared for themselves, the house became neglected and her husband tore himself apart with grief and frustration because he was unable to help her recover. When she contacted Charlene, she was stunned by the writer's attitude. Charlene bluntly told her how she was using emotional blackmail to make her family suffer, just as she had suffered. "Mary's addiction to self-pity made her the slave of her attackers," wrote Charlene in *Proud Of Me*. "She copied their abusive behaviour in a different way. Their blows were obvious, the blows she administered to her family were far more deadly, but not apparent to the naked eye."

> Victims can unwittingly find themselves passing on the consequences of emotional blackmail to other family members and friends.

The woman probably was not aware that she was emotionally blackmailing her family. It was easy to fall into the role of the blackmailer, particularly as her husband and kids felt unable to protest or fight back. They were overwhelmed with feelings of guilt about the rape having been their fault. What if the husband had been home that night? What if the kids hadn't gone out? Maybe the rape would never have happened. Guilt is often the most powerful weapon in the arsenal of the blackmailer. It can leave their victims paralysed.

In this position, it's much better for the blackmailer's victims to go outside the home and seek help. A trusted friend of the woman was approached to intervene. A good counsellor, psychologist or psychotherapist could also be called. Sometimes, someone who is beyond the emotional range of the blackmailer, and unencumbered by the emotional baggage, is needed to help break the cycle of self-pity and eventual self-destruction.

When Blackmail Becomes A Life Sentence

When you surrender to the emotional blackmailer's initial threats, an unpleasant cycle may develop that will become progressively more difficult to stop. The blackmailer could eventually ruin the victim, emotionally, psychologically and financially.

A woman we know was badgered by her fiancé into co-signing a joint loan contract for him. He begged her to act as co-guarantor on a loan for a new car that he needed for work and, he said, he simply didn't have the right credit rating to get it alone. At first, she resisted. "But why not?" he asked her. "We're talking about spending the rest of our lives together. If you don't feel you can trust me over a simple loan, we might as well call the whole thing off now!"

The argument dragged on for days. "If you *really* loved me, you'd do this simple thing for me," he said. "It's not as if I'm asking you to apply for a loan just for me. We're doing it together, and it will be for both our futures." He used "After all we've been through together, it's the least I'd expect" as his final weapon to force her to sign. Eventually, blinded by romance and fearful of losing him, she agreed to sign along the dotted line. Later, when she'd discovered he was actually an incompetent, hopeless liar who couldn't stick at any one job for more than two weeks, and who owed money all over the country, it was too late.

By giving in to the blackmailer, she ended up saddled with a massive debt that she's still paying off by installments. As for her fiancé, he's long gone. And, sadly, she's now suspicious of any man who approaches her.

When a blackmailer uses withdrawal of love as the threat, many women can become easy targets.

Long-term scars can also be inflicted by parents. In farming communities, particularly, parents can put intense pressure on their oldest son – or youngest son, if he turns out to be more compliant – to stay at home, and take on the family farm. But he may have wanted a different future for himself. He may have wanted to travel, to go into business on his own, learn a trade or enrol in acting school. If he gives in to emotional blackmail he will always feel trapped and resentful towards his parents.

Emotional blackmail of daughters tends to take a different form. We've all heard of women who have spent their lives caring for an elderly parent, forgoing their own happiness out of a sense of obligation, with a frail mother or father determined to load them with guilt should they ever think of leaving to build a life of their own.

Emotional blackmail, wherever it occurs, is unpleasant and nasty. When you've played the role of the victim once, you can be trapped into playing it forever and you stand little chance of finding the happiness, love and joy of living a life free of emotional guilt. So if you cry, be sure it's for the right reasons.

Chapter 4

WOMEN'S TOP SECRET POINT-SCORING SYSTEM

How a man's week gets ruined

Like most men, Andy had never heard about women's secret point-scoring system. He thought he was just holding up a picture for Justine.

To the rest of the world, Mark and Kelly had the perfect life. Mark had a great job, they had a lovely home, their three kids were all happy and well-balanced, and they took a holiday abroad every year.

Behind closed doors, however, their relationship was in trouble. Even though they really loved each other, they were both confused, upset and desperate about the fights they seemed constantly to be having. Kelly seemed to be angry all the time, while Mark was bewildered – he just didn't understand what was happening.

The problem was that Mark, like most men, was completely unaware that Kelly was using a special female scoring system to rate their marriage.

When the subject of a trial separation came up one night, they both agreed to consult a relationship counsellor. Kelly was happy about going to a counsellor. Mark agreed, but secretly felt they should be sorting things out themselves. This is what they said to the counsellor:

Kelly: "Mark's a workaholic. He forgets about me and the kids, and he never does anything for us. It's as though we don't exist. It's business, business, business, with us somewhere on the bottom of his list of priorities. I'm sick of being both mother and father to the children. I need a man who wants me, looks after me and participates in the family without me having to nag him to do so."

Mark: (amazed) "I can't believe what you're saying, Kelly... What do you mean I don't look after you and the kids? Look at our beautiful home, the clothes and jewellery you wear, the excellent school the kids go to... I provide all this for you and the kids! Yes, I do work hard so we can all live this way and have the nice things we want in life.

I work my butt off every week for you and you never appreciate it! You just nag...

Kelly: (angrily) "You just don't get it do you, Mark? I don't think you ever will! I do everything for you... I cook, clean, wash, organise our social life and make sure our family is taken care of... All you do is work. When was the last time you emptied the dishwasher for me? Do you even know how to put a load of washing on? Tell me when you last took me out to dinner for a treat? Tell me the last time you said you loved me..."

Mark: (shocked) "Kelly... you know I love you..."

Most men are totally unaware that women keep a point score on their partner's overall performance in a relationship. Most men are oblivious to the fact that this scoring system even exists and can fall foul of it without ever understanding where they've gone wrong. The number of points a man accrues from his partner directly affects the quality of his life at any time. Not only do women keep score, they also own the scoreboard! When a man and woman decide to live together, they never discuss the finer detail of what each will contribute to the relationship. Each silently assumes the other will continue giving what they have been giving, will behave in the way their parents did, or will conform to the kind of stereotypical roles that have men mowing the lawn and women cooking the meals.

Men See Only The Big Picture

Men prefer to stand back and see the 'big picture' and make a smaller number of big contributions than be bogged down with a series of what seem like smaller, less important ones. For example, a man may not often present his partner with a gift but, when he does, he brings a big one. Women's brains, on the other hand, are organised for fine detail and they make a wider range of smaller decisions on the many intricate facets of a working relationship. A woman will allocate one single point for every individual thing a partner does in the relationship regardless of size, and two or more points for an intimate act of love.

If a man buys his partner a single rose, for example, she'll give him one point. If he buys her a bunch of six roses he still only gets one point. But if he bought her one rose every week for six weeks, then he'd score six points. A single rose is clearly for her, whereas a bunch of roses could be perceived as being a decoration for the home. Regular gifts of a single rose show she's always uppermost in his mind.

Similarly, if a man paints the house, he gets one point. If he picks up his dirty clothes or tells her he loves her, he also gets one point each. In other words, the points are given for the number of actions taken, not for the size, quality or outcome of a single action. If he buys her a car or the diamond ring of her dreams he'll certainly score additional points at that time. But 95% of all points awarded in a relationship are for everyday things that do or don't happen. It truly is the thought that counts with women.

Women allocate one point per action or gift, regardless of its size. If men ran a point-score system they'd allocate points relative to the size of the action or gift.

Most men are completely unaware of how women score points because men simply do what they do in a relationship and don't consciously consider keeping score. For women, score keeping is done subconsciously, not consciously, and all women intuitively understand how it works. This difference becomes the cause of many misunderstandings between men and women.

Women are great scorekeepers and have long memories that can accrue points for years. They will keep doing things for a man because they assume that, eventually, the score will be evened out. They silently assume their partners will soon be grateful and return their support.

Women keep score
and never forget.

A man has no idea of when the score in the relationship is uneven. A woman can let it get to 30 to 1 before she complains about it. She then accuses him of doing nothing and he feels surprised and upset by her accusations. He had no idea there was any problem. For if a man kept a scoring system, he wouldn't let it get to this stage. Once he felt the score was 3 to 1 he would complain about his giving more and he'd want the score evened up.

If a man kept score, he'd believe the bigger the action or the larger the gift, the more points should be scored. He'd see working five days a week as scoring at least thirty points but, from her standpoint, it would only register five points – one point for each day he works. As most women know, men have always believed size matters.

For women, it's not size that
matters, it's frequency.

Our Experiment With Brian And Lorraine

Brian was a finance broker who worked long hours seeing clients and building his business. His wife Lorraine kept house and cared for their two kids. They described themselves as a happy, normal couple. We asked them to keep a scorecard daily for 30 days of the contributions they believed they made to their relationship, and to allocate the number of points they believed should be received from the other. One point would be allocated for a minor contribution and a maximum of 30 points for a major contribution to the relationship. They should also record penalty points for things their partner did that irritated them. They were not to discuss with each other how, or when, points were allocated, or which activities had scored points, if any.

Here's a partial summary of some of their results after the 30 days. You'll notice that neither recorded many penalty points. We suspect there were two likely reasons for this: couples who live together develop the tendency to ignore or filter out each other's bad points and, when couples are doing a test like this, they're often on their best behaviour.

How Brian Scored The Month

Brian's Activity	*What He Scored*	*What She Scored*
Working 5 days a week	30	5
Driving to mother-in-law	5	1
Assembling child's model airplane	5	1
Barbecuing for friends	3	1
Investigating noises late at night	1	2
Topping up oil in car	2	1
Cleaning leaves from gutter	3	1
Take family to Pizza Hut	2	1
Washing the car	2	1
Working late one night	5	1
Balance pH in the pool	2	1
Taking kid to the football	3	2
Reading *Which Computer* magazine	1	0
Remove dead rat from garden	2	1
Getting paint for garage	2	1
Planting a bush	2	1
Driving family on weekend	3	1
Supergluing her broken shoe	3	1
Bought flowers/chocolate & wine	10	3
Hang wall painting	2	1
Take out garbage	1	1

Adjust door handle	1	1
Telling her she looked beautiful	1	3
Mow lawn	3	1
Fix kid's bike	2	1
Reconfiguring stereo speakers	4	1

Things Lorraine Scored That Weren't On Brian's List

Giving me his coat when it was cold	3
Dropping me at front door because it was raining	2
Opening the car door for me	2
Warming the car before I get in	2
Sharpening carving knife	1
Putting Mum's number on speed dial	1
Open tight jar	1
Complimenting me on my cooking	3

Things Brian Could Have Done To Earn More Points

Picking up his wet towel	1
Peeling vegetables	1
Putting the kids to bed early	2
Talking to me instead of watching TV on arrival home	5
Listening to me without interrupting with solutions	6
Calling to say he'd be home late	3
Organising a weekend away for just the two of us	10
Offering to clean kitchen	2
Turning TV down to talk to me	2
Calling to say 'I love you'	3
Make the bed	1
Shaving before sex	1
Give head & foot massage	3
Kiss me	1
Kiss me without groping	3
Not flick remote control	2
Hold hands in public	3
Make me feel more important than the children	3
Go shopping with me	5

Give a romantic card	4
Dance in the kitchen	2
Unpack dishwasher	1
Show interest when I talk	3
Take dirty clothes to laundry	1
Tell me he misses me	3
Put toilet seat down	1

These lists points out several things: first, because men have spatially oriented brains they allocate more points than women for physical and spatially related tasks. For example, Brian gave himself five points for helping his son construct a model aircraft but Lorraine only saw it as earning one point. For him it had been a difficult but skilful task and he was proud of what he had achieved; for her it had been playing with a toy. Women usually award a man one point for each domestic task he performs but are more likely to allocate more points for small, personal or intimate tasks than for large tasks. For instance, when Brian complimented Lorraine for a meal she cooked one evening, she gave him three points but he was totally unaware he'd scored any at all. In fact, he couldn't remember saying it and didn't write it on his list. It's not that he forgot about it; it simply never occurred to him that complimenting a woman's cooking was a good point scorer. When he bought her a bunch of flowers, chocolates and champagne he thought he'd earned at least ten points – one third of his personal score for working five days a week – because they were expensive, but she only gave him four points. Brian had earned significant points for small acts like 'giving me his coat because it was cold' without him realising that this small act would have scored points. He just thought he was 'looking after her'.

....

"Why don't we try changing positions tonight?"
he asked. "Good idea!" she said, "You stand at
the kitchen sink and I'll sit on the sofa and fart."

....

Brian thought the more he worked, the more points he scored, but working extra hours actually meant he had less time at home to do small things, so he lost points. He thought he was earning extra money for a better life and she would admire him for it; in fact, she thought he cared more about work than about her. Working late scored five points per night in his opinion, but Lorraine only gave it one. If he had called her from work to say he loved her and missed her, and called again when he was nearly home, he would have scored at least three points. Like most men, Brian was oblivious to the fact that little things mean a lot to a woman, despite having often heard it from his mother and grandmother.

How Lorraine Scored Her Month

The list of Lorraine's personal activities was four times longer than Brian's. She had written out every activity in detail but only allocated low scores to most. Vacuuming, grocery shopping, watering plants, banking, pet care, paying bills, sending birthday cards, planning family events, bathing children, reading to them or disciplining them scored one point each. Repetitive actions such as picking up clothing or wet towels left on the floor, washing clothes, cooking or making beds all scored one point each time she did them. Brian never saw Lorraine's routine because he was mostly at work so he gave her an overall score for her efforts – 30 points; the same score he gave himself for working 50 hours a week. Lorraine had scratched his back one night for which he awarded her three points and she initiated sex on two occasions; that scored her 10 points each time.

Penalty Points

Penalty points are deducted whenever one partner does something that frustrates or annoys the other.

Penalty Points Lorraine Gave Brian

Criticizing me in front of friends	-6
Farting during dinner with friends	-10

Leching after other women at a shopping centre   -5
Insisting on sex when I didn't feel like it   -6

Penalty Points Brian Gave Lorraine
Talking to me while I watch TV   -2
Saying 'No' to making love   -6
Nagging   -5
Talking about too many things at once   -3

*"I don't nag. I continually remind him,
otherwise he'd never get things done."*

Brian's complaints were about things Lorraine did or didn't do
for him while Lorraine's complaints were more about things
Brian did in public. These lists also show how, when a man
wants sex but a woman doesn't, the amount of resentment felt
on both sides is the same.

*"What do you mean, leching?" Brian
protested. "She was obstructing my view!"*

At the end of the experiment, Brian had given himself an average weekly score of 62 points. He gave Lorraine a weekly
average of 60 points, so he felt happy the relationship score
was evenly balanced. Lorraine had scored herself an average of
78 points but had only given Brian a weekly average of 48
points.

Lorraine And Brian's Reactions
Lorraine felt the score was weighted 30 points a week in
Brian's favour. This explained a resentment simmering inside
her for the past year. Brian was devastated at the result. He had
been proceeding in the relationship as if everything was just
fine and had no idea how Lorraine was feeling because she
never said anything about it. He felt Lorraine had been a little

distant from him since their last child was born a year earlier and thought it was because she had more to do and must have been stressed. To make things easier for her, he began to work longer hours at night to give her space and so he could bring her home more money.

For Brian and Lorraine, this experiment was an eye-opener. What had begun as a simple fun test to show how men and women score points differently had headed off a potentially disastrous situation. Lorraine was at home feeling cheated and resentful and Brian was working longer hours, thinking he was doing what she wanted him to do.

Solution For Women

Women should accept that men's brains are programmed to see the big picture, and that men believe they get more points for doing bigger things. That way, they won't feel resentful if the score is balanced in his favour. They should also encourage a man to do the smaller things they like in a relationship, and reward him when he does them.

> *All men are the same. They just have*
> *different faces so you can tell them apart.*
> MARILYN MONROE

Men are not programmed to offer help, support or advice unless someone specifically asks for it because, from a male viewpoint, this is seen as saying he thinks the other person is incompetent. That's the way it is in the male world – they wait for you to ask. If you don't ask, they'll assume the score is even, so the relationship must be in good shape. Men have short memories.

They will forget the positive things they did for you last week but also forget the positive things you did for them. Women always remember. Never assume a man understands how women score points; it's a concept they, their fathers, brothers and sons never knew existed. Many things men do are not counted on their lists because they do them without thinking they would have scored points.

Solution For Men

Not only do women keep score, they accumulate points over long periods and never forget. She will say no to sex today because you yelled at her mother two months ago. When a woman feels the score is balanced in your favour it's unlikely she'll even mention it. When it's in deficit, she will become distant, angry and your love life will fade. If this happens, the man must ask her what she wants him to do. Remember that a woman scores one point for each activity a man performs and he receives better scores for small things involving emotional support. Bringing flowers, complimenting her appearance, picking up after himself, helping with the dishes and using breath freshener count as much, sometimes more, than bringing home a pay cheque or painting the house. This is not to say a man should necessarily work less hard. But if he maintains an awareness of how his partner considers these matters and makes the effort to do the small things, the quality of his life will dramatically improve.

Take The Test Now

With your partner, score and record all your contributions to your relationship for ten days just as Brian and Lorraine did. Evaluate the results, and you can use them as a template to approach your relationship in ways that will give you more happiness than you ever imagined. A score difference of less than 15% shows a fairly even relationship where no one feels resentful or used. A difference of 15%–30% shows enough misunderstanding to cause tension, and more than 30% means someone feels unhappy in the relationship.

The partner with the negative score needs to balance their contribution by doing things their mate likes to even the score and reduce tension.

Summary

Earning a lot of points takes no more effort than you are currently putting into your relationship. It's simply a matter of understanding how the other person measures things and changing your approach. The scoring system used by the opposite sex is not better or worse than yours, it's just different. Women understand it, but most men are oblivious to it until it's pointed out. When we asked Brian and Lorraine to participate in the experiment, Lorraine understood exactly what we wanted. Brian's response was, "Huh? Point scoring? What's that about?" Like most men, he never knew women kept a score sheet. When a man and woman are arguing, her most frequently used line is, "After all I've done for you! You're so lazy you never do anything to help me!"

Take the point-scoring test from time to time as your relationship takes different directions to be sure the score is even. A couple will score things differently when they have limited responsibilities than when they have a mortgage, three kids and a dog.

Finally, one of our male readers who took the test sent us the following examples of how a woman can award or deduct points to your love scorecard on a daily basis.

Dear Barbara and Allan,

Taking this test has completely changed my relationship with my girlfriend. We now get on better than any time in our three years together and I'd like to share my experiences about how women score points.

Thank you

Happy Jack

Everyday Domestic Duties

You take out the rubbish	+1
You take out the rubbish at 4.30am as the truck pulls away	-1
You load the dishwasher whenever you dirty a dish	+1

You leave dishes in the sink	-1
You leave them under the bed	-3
You leave the toilet seat up	-1
You leave the toilet seat up in the middle of the night (and she's pregnant)	-10
You pee on the seat	-5
You completely miss the toilet	-7
You replace the toilet-paper roll when it's empty	0
When the toilet-paper roll is empty, you resort to Kleenex	-1
When the Kleenex runs out you hobble, pants down, to the next bathroom	-2
You don't air the bathroom	-1
You make the bed	+1
You make the bed, but forget to add the decorative pillows	0
You throw the bedspread over crumpled sheets	-1
You fart in bed	-5
You make sure there's plenty of petrol in the car for her	+1
There's barely enough petrol left to make it to the nearest petrol station	-1
You check out a suspicious noise late at night and it's nothing	+1
You check out a suspicious noise late at night and it's something	+3
You smash it with a six iron	+10
It's her father	-10

Social Events

You stay by her side during the whole party	+5
You stay with her for a while, then go and chat with an old school pal	-2
Named Charlotte	-9
When mingling, you hold her hand and gaze at her lovingly	+4
When mingling, you introduce her as "the trouble and strife" and pat her on the rear	-5

Gifts

You buy her flowers, but only when it's expected	0
You don't buy her flowers when it's expected	-10
You buy her flowers as a surprise	+5
You give wild flowers you've hand picked yourself	+10
She smells them and gets stung by an African tsetse fly	-25

Driving

You lose the directions on a trip	-4
You lose the directions and get lost	-10
You get lost in a bad part of town	-15
You meet the locals up close and personal	-25
She finds out you lied about having a black belt	-60

Chapter 5

SOLVING THE SEVEN BIGGEST MYSTERIES ABOUT MEN

The men were talking about their last fishing trip.
The women were talking about other things.

Following the success of *Why Men Don't Listen and Women Can't Read Maps*, we were inundated with letters and emails from women asking us for more information about the differences between the sexes. Here are their seven most commonly asked questions:

1. Why don't men know much about their friends' lives?
2. Why do men avoid commitment?
3. Why do men feel the need to be right about everything?
4. Why are grown men so interested in 'boys' toys'?
5. Why can men only seem to do one thing at a time?
6. Why are men so addicted to sport?
7. What do men really talk about in the rest room?

The problem for women is that they try to analyse a man's behaviour from their own female standpoint. As a result, male behaviour can simply be baffling. But the truth is that men are not illogical; they just operate differently to women.

1. Why Don't Men Know Much About Their Friends' Lives?

Julian hadn't seen Ralph for a year so they agreed to spend a day together on the golf course. When Julian arrived home that evening, his wife Hannah was eager to hear how he got on:

Hannah: "How was your day?"
Julian: "Good."
Hannah: "How is Ralph?"
Julian: "Good."

Hannah: "How does his wife feel after coming out of hospital last week?"

Julian: "I don't know – he didn't say."

Hannah: "He didn't say? You mean you didn't ask?"

Julian: "Well, no, but if there was a problem, I'm sure he would have told me."

Hannah: "So… how's their daughter going with her new husband?"

Julian: "Ah… he didn't say…"

Hannah: "Is Ralph's mother still having chemotherapy?"

Julian: "Umm… I'm not sure…"

And so on. Julian knew how many shots they'd each taken to get round the course, he remembered the trouble in the bunker, the hole-in-one he almost hit and the joke about the nun and the rubber chicken, but he knew practically nothing about Ralph's wife, children and family. He knew about Ralph's problem fighting the local council over his building plans, the make and model of the car Ralph was thinking of getting, and Ralph's latest overseas trip to close a business deal. But he knew absolutely nothing about Ralph's youngest daughter who was now living in Bangkok, or that Ralph's brother had been diagnosed with Parkinson's disease or that Ralph's wife had been nominated as Citizen of the Year in their local community. Instead, he had a new repertoire of great jokes.

A man will know every good joke his friend has told him but not be aware that his friend has split up from his wife.

If a man goes for a drink with his friends for an hour or more after work, women are invariably amazed that he comes home knowing little to nothing about anyone's personal life. That's because men use all these activities as a form of fire-gazing. They can spend hours together fishing, golfing, playing cards or watching football, without saying much. When they do talk, it's about the facts – results, solutions or answers to questions – or to trade information about things and processes. But they rarely discuss people and their emotions. Men have 'bottom line' brains that are generally not aware of feelings or emotions.

A study by the University of Leeds delved into the reasons men go to a bar for a drink after work –

Why men go for a 'drink'
9.5% go to drink alcohol
5.5% go to meet women
85% go to relieve stress

Men relieve stress by disengaging the brain and thinking about something else. That's why, when men go for a drink, it's called a 'quiet drink' – there's no necessity to talk if you don't want to.

If a man is with his friends and not talking, it doesn't mean they've had an argument; he's just fire-gazing.

Men don't expect other men to talk much and they never insist on having a conversation. When one of them is fire-gazing with a drink in his hand, other men intuitively understand, and allow him to carry on. They never force him to talk. Nobody says, "Tell me about your day... Who did you meet and what were they like?" When they do talk, men discuss work, sport, cars and spatially related things. They take turns at speaking because their brains are organised either to speak or to listen. Unlike women, they can't do both.

Solution
Men find it hard to understand why a woman wants to know all the details about the lives of friends and acquaintances

because if his friend wanted him to know anything, then he'd tell him. It's not that a man is not interested in his friends, he just wants to know the bottom-line facts and outcomes. The only time a man talks to others about close personal details is if he is unable to solve a problem and then, as a last resort, he will ask his friend for advice.

So, if you want information about the health, career, relationships or whereabouts of your family members or those of your social circle, never rely on men to know the answers; ask women. Men meet others to discuss results and solutions and to relieve stress. They rarely ask about personal matters.

2. Why Do Men Avoid Commitment?

> **Commitment**: *verb, female:* A desire to get married and raise a family; *verb, male:* not trying to chat up other women while out with one's wife or girlfriend

Case Study: Geoff and Sally

Jodie thought Geoff and Sally would make a great couple so she arranged for them to go on a blind date.

They had a wonderful night, exchanged phone numbers and planned to meet again. The next day, Sally called Jodie and thanked her for introducing them and said she really liked Geoff and wanted to get to know him better. That night, Geoff also called Jodie and said the same about Sally.

When Geoff hung up, Jodie immediately rang Sally and repeated what Geoff had said. This was the signal that Sally needed to start the process of getting to know Geoff and to start a relationship so, next weekend, she invited him to go to the beach with her and then to dinner. Geoff happily accepted. They went out together for the next three weekends and would see a movie together once or twice during the week. For Sally, the time that had passed signalled that they were now in a relationship. She was not dating anyone else other than Geoff, even though they had never discussed having an exclusive relationship.

Geoff's story

A month had passed but Geoff had absolutely no idea he was supposed to be in a relationship because it had never been discussed. This is how it is with the male brain. It does not understand the concept of a relationship the way women do.

Geoff decided to take Mary to his best friend's birthday party. Mary was always the life and soul of any gathering – a real fun person – and he hadn't seen her for months. At the party they were having a great time when Geoff spotted Jodie. He immediately went over and introduced her to Mary. Jodie seemed a bit frosty towards them both, and Geoff sensed that she didn't like Mary. This puzzled him because Mary was a fun person and everyone liked her. But he didn't give it second thought.

Jodie's Story

Jodie was shocked that Geoff had not taken Sally to the party. Instead, he had brought some loudmouth tart named Mary. Jodie knew that, rather than Sally finding out through gossip, she'd have to be the one to tell her, and she wasn't looking forward to the task. Predictably, it didn't go well. When Sally heard about the party, she broke down in tears because she'd thought she and Geoff had been getting on so well. Sally called Geoff and asked him to come and see her that evening. He sensed something might be wrong, but had no idea what it might be.

The Showdown

Geoff arrived looking forward to seeing Sally again, hoping she might have cooked his favourite meal. When she opened the door, however, he could see she'd been crying and was angry with him. "How could you do this to me?" she whimpered, "... and in front of our friends, too! How long have you been seeing her? Do you love her? Are you sleeping with her? Answer me!!" Geoff couldn't believe his ears. He was speechless.

He spent the next three hours trying to sort this problem out with Sally, whatever the problem might be. He explained he never realised that they were an exclusive couple – he'd thought Sally was probably seeing a variety of guys, not just him. This was the first time they had discussed their feelings and emotions, and both realised that they were heading in completely different directions.

Sally wanted a commitment from Geoff. But Geoff was not ready to give it yet. He wanted his freedom. They decided they would remain friends but not be lovers any more... well, that's what Sally decided. Geoff thought she probably had PMT and would get over it by the weekend...

Women are frequently mystified by the way a man can be committed with an almost religious fervour to a sports team, but rarely seems to be able to invest anything like the same amount of emotional energy in a relationship. A man will often hold back his emotions and feelings with the woman he loves, but can become visibly emotional and passionate when his favourite team is playing – especially if they're losing. How can he be so steadfastly dedicated and loyal to a bunch of thickset, not particularly bright, transitory sportsmen whom he's never met and who couldn't care less about him, but not have anywhere near the same apparent devotion to her?

For almost all of human existence, males have been polygamous for survival reasons. Men were always in short supply because so many were killed while hunting or fighting, so it made perfect sense for their survivors to adopt the widowed females into their harems. This would also give the men a greater opportunity to pass on their genes. From a species survival standpoint, it made sense for a male to have ten or 20 females, but made no sense for one female to have ten or 20 males as she could only bear one offspring at a time. Only 3% of animal species, such as foxes and geese, are monogamous. Each sex is the same size and colour and you usually can't tell which is which. The brains of most other male species, including humans, are not hardwired for monogamy. This is the reason men will put off making a commitment to one woman for as long as possible and why so many men have difficulty being monogamous in a relationship. We differ from other species however, in that our advanced brains have developed large frontal lobes that let us make conscious decisions about what we will or won't do, so it's never enough for cheating men to protest that they couldn't help themselves. They always had a choice. For a woman, being committed, at least until her offspring are self-sufficient, is hardwired into her psyche.

....

If you want a committed man
— look in a mental hospital.
MAE WEST

....

Women understand that if another woman has been 'going out' with a man for a while and they are both not dating anyone else, a relationship exists. But for most men, like Geoff, this is an alien concept. When Sally wailed, "What was he thinking?" the answer is: he wasn't thinking anything at all.

What Most Men Think

It's a universal theme that a man's male friends will joke that his permanent relationship with a woman or marriage is a clear sign that the unfortunate man's life, as he knows it, is almost over. "Once you're committed, she'll have you by the balls," they'll laugh. "Say goodbye to half your house and 90% of your sex life!" they'll chuckle. And then there's the warning, usually from single men, "You'll need permission to sneeze now that she's giving you the handcuffs." One of the most common practical jokes played on a bridegroom-to-be is for his mates to write the word HELP on the soles of his wedding shoes. Most men will avoid committing to a relationship as they feel a woman will take away their freedom and they will become weak and powerless. A man's response to these jibes is often not to discuss commitment with a woman or even to do the complete opposite of what she wants.

While many men claim that commitment means they'll lose all their freedoms, it's hard to work out which precise freedoms they're talking about. When you do pin them down, they talk about the freedom to come and go as they want, not to talk if he doesn't feel like it, never to have to explain their actions or justify their behaviour, and to have as many women as they want. At the same time, however, they want love, nourishment and lots of sex. In short, they want it all – and how many men today could possibly claim they've ever had it all, quite apart from having lost it all? This way of living might have once existed in the ancient harems of Arabia and is still practised in some primitive cultures, but most men today stand little chance of ever even sampling such living conditions.

The only way to live a life of complete freedom is to live alone on a desert island where there are no rules. Being in a relationship is like getting a driver's licence. If you want to be a motorist you must learn the road rules and follow them – otherwise you'll always be a pedestrian. A relationship is simply a negotiation with rules – if you want love, friendship, sex and a person who will nurture you, you must offer something in return. You can't have your cake and eat it too. What women expect in return is love, devotion and loyalty. The last thing on their minds is taking away a man's freedom.

Solution

The concept of being in a potentially permanent relationship didn't even occur to Geoff. When a woman suspects a man is a commitment-phobe, she needs to clearly point out to him that he is actually in a relationship. For example, she can make a joke about how, now he's in a relationship, she's happy to make him a cup of coffee, or she can talk about how great it is having sex and then waking up together since they're in a relationship. She has to learn to be direct and upfront, rather than coyly just hoping her man will take the hint. Because then it's odds on, like Geoff, that he still won't get it. It's not only that men aren't mind readers, it's just that most of them are not very sensitive to a woman's state of mind. Remember, men evolved hunting animals and fighting enemies, not trying to understand them or be sensitive to their emotional needs.

So, never assume that you are in a relationship without discussing it with the other person. Men can't read minds so a woman should ask them how they feel about her and where they want the relationship to go. Men are direct and will let a woman know if they want it to be an exclusive relationship or not. Men see being direct as a sign of respect so, if a woman wants a commitment, she should ask for it, rather than just expect it.

There are however, limits on the number of times anyone can bring up the subject. It's a sad reflection on any partnership when a woman is driven to saying, "Can you please drop our two kids off at school, now that the two of us are in a relationship?"

3. Why Do Men Feel The Need To Be Right About Everything?

To understand this characteristic of modern men, we need to look at the way they were raised as boys. Boys were expected to be tough, never cry and be good at everything they did. Their role models included Superman, Batman, Spider-man, Zorro, Tarzan, James Bond, Rocky and the Phantom, all of whom were solitary males who never cried over problems, but went about finding solutions instead. And, naturally, they rarely failed in the task. They occasionally had a sidekick who was usually a smaller, lesser male, very rarely a woman. If a female assistant ever made an appearance, she was much more trouble than she was worth. Batgirl, for example, was always being rescued by Batman, Superman regularly saved Lois Lane from certain death, Tarzan spent much of his time swinging through the jungle to keep Jane out of trouble, and the Phantom would probably have been streets ahead without

Dianna causing problems. Those superheroes sometimes seemed to prefer having a horse or dog as a partner because animals are loyal, reliable, never answer back or prove the hero wrong. Like most traditional male stereotypes in books and movies, boy's heroes were rarely wrong and never showed weakness or emotion. There was never a Mrs Batman or a Lady Zorro. The Lone Ranger was never a man who preferred a crowd. Cartoons still depict the male tough guy as a huge creature who has muscles which make him look like a condom full of walnuts, he has a deep, raspy voice (high testosterone) and the heroine is still usually a Barbie doll type with anatomically impossible breasts.

> *"I married Mr Right, I just didn't know his first name was Always."*

By the time a boy reaches manhood, he is conditioned to feel that not being able to do something, or solve a problem, means he is failure as a man. This is why, when a woman questions what a man says or does, he acts defensively. When a woman says, "Let's stop and ask directions," he hears "You're hopeless. Let's find another man who knows more than you." When she says, "I want to call a mechanic to fix the car," he hears "You're useless. I'll find another man who can solve the problem." He might not hesitate to give a woman a cookbook for her birthday but, if a woman were to give him a self-development book as a gift, he'd be absolutely indignant. He'll assume she's trying to tell him that he's not good enough as he is. Even going to a relationship seminar or to a counsellor is tantamount to a humiliating admission that he's wrong, and most men become defensive or aggressive at the very suggestion that it might be necessary. Men find it difficult to say, "I'm sorry," because to do so is to admit he is wrong.

Case Study: Jackie and Dan

Jackie wanted to stop work and become a mother but Dan felt they were not yet financially ready. This soon became a major bone of contention between them, and they argued about it regularly. Very soon, it began to put their relationship under strain. One day, Jackie announced to Dan that she had consulted a financial consultant to work out their economic situation. Dan couldn't believe his ears: Jackie wanted to someone else to sort out their problems! Obviously, Dan thought, she didn't think he was capable of doing the sums himself. Their arguments escalated – and, three months later, they separated.

Jackie felt she was helping Dan and easing the pressure on him by calling in a financial consultant. She expected him to be happy that she was taking responsibility for getting someone to do the groundwork to plan financially for their baby. Dan saw it quite differently. In his eyes, she had revealed that she thought he was wrong about their monetary situation, and had called in an advisor to show up his incompetence.

Don't You Trust Me?

The common expression of men whose actions are challenged by a woman is: "Don't you trust me?" When you hear this phrase you can be sure you've just insulted his masculinity. If he's lost and trying to read a map and she says, "Let me look at the map," he assumes she thinks he's incapable. His response is, "Don't you trust me to get us there?" If he's tired of the neighbour's dog barking at night and says he's going next door to sort it out, and she pleads with him not to in case it causes trouble, he says, "Don't you trust me to handle it properly?" If they're at a party and she warns him that a certain woman guest has a reputation as a man-eater and he should avoid her, he says, "Don't you trust me?" In each of the circumstances, her response is always the same: "I was only trying to help!" She felt she was showing him she loved him and cared for him, but he saw her as telling him he was wrong and unable to work things out for himself.

> *A man equates being given advice by a woman as saying he is wrong and that she doesn't trust him.*

He accuses her of always trying to control him. He feels so strongly about it that even she starts to wonder that maybe she is a controlling type.

Solution

A woman should avoid any approach to a man that will make him feel he's wrong. Instead, she should talk about how she feels, as opposed to how wrong he is. For example, instead of saying, "You never know where you're going and we're always late!" she could say, "You're doing a great job, darling, but these street signs are so confusing. Me – I'd feel so much better if we stopped and asked a local person if they know which is the right turn-off." In other words, he's not to blame.

When a man gets it right, the woman should praise him. When they arrive at their destination, she should say "Thanks, darling. You did a great job of getting us here." Better still, buy him a Satellite Navigation System – that way he'll always get the right answer.

4. Why Are Grown Men So Interested In 'Boys' Toys'?

For our friend Gerry's birthday, we gave him a motorised paper stapler that was the size of a miniature television set. It had a see-through plastic case so you could watch all the wheels and dials moving inside. It looked like something out of the Space Shuttle. It took three AA batteries that needed replacing every week and yet all it did was put a staple into a piece of paper – just like any other stapler. Gerry, however, was overjoyed when we gave him this gizmo, not because it was a stapler, but because it had lots of wheels and dials that went round and round, was lit up by flashing lights, and made real motor sounds. Gerry told us that sometimes when he gets up in the early hours of the morning to go to the bathroom downstairs, he passes the stapler sitting on the table and can't resist putting 4 or 5 staples into a sheet of paper just so he can watch the wheels whizz round. When his male friends visit him, they all stand around and take turns at putting staples into paper, laughing with delight. Any woman who visits doesn't give it a second glance. They're amazed that anyone could become so excited about such an overpriced piece of equipment that performs the most menial task in the home. But this male behaviour is the equivalent of a woman paying an inflated price for a cuddly teddy bear with oversized eyes and a small nose that was made in Brazil because she "…just couldn't resist it."

It's easy to explain why the sexes react so differently to such things. Below are the scans showing the areas of the brain that light up when a person is using spatial ability. The activated areas are the dark sections. The spatial part of the brain is the area used for estimating speeds, angles and distances – it's the hunting brain.

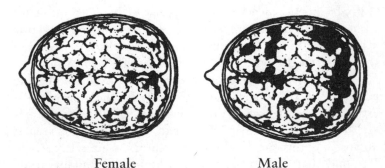

Female   Male

Areas of the brain used for driving a car, kicking a football, reverse parking and operating mechanical things – Institute of Psychiatry, London, 2001.

Because of the spatial arrangement of the male brain, men and boys become addicted to anything that has buttons, a motor or moving parts, makes sounds, has flashing lights and runs on batteries. This includes any type of video game or computer software, hand-held GPS navigation units, robotic dogs that act like real dogs, electrically opening curtains, speedboats, cars with complicated dashboards, whipper-snippers, guns with night-vision scopes, nuclear weapons, spacecraft and anything that comes with a remote control. If washing machines came with a remote control, men would probably even consider doing the laundry.

Do-It-Yourself Projects

The entire DIY business is aimed at the spatial area of the male brain. Men love the challenge of assembling classic sailing ships, toy train sets, model aircraft, Meccano sets, computer tables, bookcases or anything that has a set of instructions, however indecipherable they may be. Boys go to toy stores. Men go to DIY stores, hardware shops and car yards where they can find things to make or build or watch work, and thereby satisfy their spatial urges. Boys instinctively believe that as soon as they sprout hair on their chins they will wake up next morning able to completely strip down a car engine and put it all back together.

In the home, men's spatial urges can be frustrating for women because an average man has a nine-minute attention span and will often leave unfinished projects from one end of the house to the other. They regularly don't get around to fixing certain things that are broken but become angry and possessive if you suggest someone else finishes the job. For example, if a toilet is not working in the home, a woman may say, "Let's call a plumber." To a man, however, this is seen as an attack on his spatial ability. He can fix it himself, he says. Not only that, a plumber charges outrageous amounts to do what is clearly a simple job.

Calling a plumber without first consulting the man
of the house can be taken as a major insult.

So late Saturday afternoon (after the game), the man who's refused a plumber's help to fix the dysfunctional toilet, turns the water off at the mains and then dismantles the mechanism. He discovers what seems like a worn washer and heads for the DIY shop. He wanders around the shop for about 45 minutes, looking at all the great spatial toys he could own, road tests an electric sander or two, tries out a pneumatic drill and eventually finds what looks like similar-sized replacement washer. He then goes home to discover that it's the wrong size, but he can't put the old washer back in because he can't find it. The DIY store is now closed and he can't turn on the mains water until the tap is fixed, so no one can now have a shower or use the toilet.

Many women simply don't understand that most men would rather saw off their right leg than admit that they can't fix something. To do so would be admitting he is deficient in the number-one-male-brain skill area – spatial ability and problem-solving. If his car is making a strange noise he will always lift the bonnet and take a look, even though he has no idea what he's looking for. He's hoping the problem will be something obvious like a giant armadillo eating the carburettor.

A woman should never call a plumber, builder, financial expert, computer technician, armadillo catcher or any spatially-qualified male without first consulting the man in her life as he will think she feels he's not spatially-competent. Instead, she should tell him what is needed, ask his opinion and give him a deadline. That way, if he calls a plumber, he can feel he has solved the problem himself.

The only difference between men and
boys is the price of their toys.

Most new business start-ups are now initiated by women but 99% of all patents – of 'boys' toys' that is – are still registered by men. There's a lesson in this: always buy a man a spatially-related toy as a present. Never give him flowers or a nice card; they won't mean a thing to him.

5. Why Can Men Only Seem To Do One Thing At A Time?

In *Why Men Don't Listen and Women Can't Read Maps*, we presented an in-depth study into why male brains are so singularly focused: what we describe as 'monotracking'. We received such an overwhelming response to this section we will summarise it again here. Most women can't understand why men only seem to be able to do one thing at a time. A woman can read while listening and talking, so why can't he? Why does he insist on turning down the television when the phone rings? Women of the world lament in unison: "When he's reading the newspaper or watching TV, why can't he hear what I've just said?"

The reason is that a man's brain is compartmentalised and specialized. In simple terms, it's as though he has little rooms throughout his brain and each room contains at least one main function that operates independently of the rest. The cord that connects his left and right brain hemispheres, the *corpus callosum*, is, on average, 10% thinner than a typical woman's, and carries about 30% fewer connections between left and right. This gives him his 'one-thing-at-a-time' approach to everything he does in life.

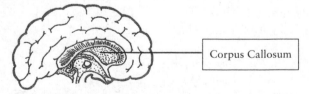

Men's brains are 'compartmentalised' and have up to 30%
fewer connections between hemispheres than women's brains.

While this single-minded, focused approach to everything may seem limiting to women, it allows a man to become a dedicated specialist or expert on one subject. 96% of the world's technical experts are male – they are excellent at performing that one skill.

Understanding the male 'one-thing-at-a-time' mentality is one of the most important things a woman can ever learn about men. It explains why a man turns the radio down when he reads a map or reverse parks a car. If he is driving around a roundabout and someone talks to him, he often misses his turn-off. If he is working with a sharp tool and the phone rings, he may injure himself. Take an MRI scan of a man's brain when he's reading, and you'll find he is virtually deaf. Remember: you should never talk to a man while he's having a wet shave – unless you mean to hurt him!

A man is twice as likely as a woman
to be involved in a car accident
while talking on a mobile telephone.

A woman's brain is configured for a multi-tasking performance. Most women can do several unrelated things at the same time, and brain scans reveal a woman's brain is never disengaged, it's always active even when she is asleep. This is the main reason that 96% of the world's personal assistants are women. It's as if she is somehow genetically related to the octopus. She can talk on a telephone, follow a new recipe and watch television at the same time. She can drive a car, put on make-up and listen to the radio while talking on a hands-free telephone. But when a man is following a recipe and you want to talk to him, it's advisable to go out for dinner that night.

The best strategy is to only ever give men one thing at a time to do if you want a successful, stress-free outcome. In business, discuss one point at a time and stick to the point until the men at the meeting are happy with the solution before moving to the next point.

And, most importantly, never ask a man questions during lovemaking.

6. Why Are Men So Addicted To Sport?

For thousands of years, men went hunting in packs with other men while women would gather food and raise children. Men ran, chased, stalked and used their spatial skills to catch food but, by the end of the eighteenth century, advanced farming techniques rendered this dynamic ability almost redundant. Between AD 1800 and 1900, men invented almost every modern ball sport in existence today as a substitute for their hunting activities. As children, girls have dolls as practice for childrearing and boys kick and chase balls as 'hunting' practice. As adults, women trade their dolls for children, but men still kick balls. So in reality, nothing much has changed in a hundred thousand years – men still hunt and women still raise children.

By being a dedicated follower of his favourite sports team, a man can once again be a member of a hunting pack. When he watches his heroes on the field he fantasises he's making the shots himself and scoring the points. Men can become so emotive when they watch football that they feel as though they are actually playing in the match. Their brains estimate the speeds, angles and direction of the ball and they scream with delight whenever a 'kill' is made.

Sports allow a man
to be part of a hunting pack.

They verbally abuse the referee (even though the referee can't hear them) when they disagree with a call – "You call that a foul?! You idiot! Buy yourself some glasses!!!" They can memorise the scores and recall, in vivid detail, goals scored in games played years ago and can come close to tears when discussing what the player should have done and outcomes that might have been. For example, after England won the 1966 World Cup against Germany, there was barely a single man in Britain who couldn't recite the names of the players, the goals they almost kicked and the tactical errors that had happened. This is a formidable skill, but they still don't know the names of their nieces, nephews, next-door neighbours or what date Mother's Day is celebrated.

> *Men can feel overcome by emotion*
> *when watching sport but seldom*
> *in an emotional relationship.*

Driving a car is almost entirely a spatial skill. Speeds, angles, cornering, gear changes, merging and reverse parking is male heaven. Men are so obsessed with driving they will watch other men on television driving racing cars in circles for hours on end. Men watching a boxing match will double up and actually seem to feel the pain when a fighter is felled by a blow beneath the belt.

Men can be so obsessed with watching sport that they also love to watch or participate in any pointless challenge. These may include drinking competitions where the winner is the last man standing, a 'Fat Belly' tournament where men with huge beer bellies charge at each other, a bicycle race on ice, or an event which involves building strange aircraft which men strap to their backs and jump off a bridge into a river to see what happens. Predictably, women rarely have any interest in these types of 'sports'.

> *"My wife said if I didn't stop being so obsessed*
> *with Manchester United, she'd leave me.*
> *I'm really going to miss her."*

The world has become a confusing place for men – their primary brain skills have become largely superfluous and women are attacking them from every direction. Men no longer have clear specifications of what is expected of them or any clear role models to follow. Sport has always been a consistent activity where a man can again feel part of a team; no one tries to change him or criticise him and he can feel successful when the team wins, a feeling he may no longer get through his work. This explains why men who work in repetitive or mundane careers are the biggest followers of sport but those who describe their work as exciting and fulfilling are the least interested. It is also why a man will buy a new set of golf clubs instead of a much-needed dining room table, and prefers a season's football pass over a family holiday in France.

Solution

If your partner is obsessed with a sport or hobby, you have two choices. First, get involved. Learn about his interest and become knowledgeable about it. Go to an event with him and you will be surprised how many other 'sports widows' also go and enjoy the social aspects of sporting functions. Even if you still don't find it interesting, all the others there will be impressed with your understanding and you can make many new friends.

Second, use his sports obsession as a positive opportunity to spend time with your friends or family, go shopping or start a new hobby of your own. When there is a big sporting event, make it a special occasion for him. Let him see how much you appreciate its importance. Don't fight or compete with a man's sport or hobby. Join him, or use the available time to do something positive for yourself.

7. What Do Men Really Talk About In The Rest Room?

Let's first answer the universally asked male question: "What do women talk about when they go to a public rest room together?"

The answer is, everything and everybody. They talk about how they like that venue compared to others they've visited, they discuss clothing they and others are wearing – "Did you see that woman in the purple dress? I'd never be caught dead in that!", who the nice men are, who they don't like, and any personal problems they or their friends may be having. When fixing their make-up, they'll discuss application techniques and different types of products, and will share cosmetics with others, including strangers. Any woman who looks upset is given group therapy... and heaven help the man who upset her! Women will sit on the toilet and talk to other women through the wall, they will ask strangers to pass toilet paper under the gap, and it's not unknown for two women to use the same cubicle so they can continue their conversation. One nightclub in Birmingham, England, has even installed extra-large cubicles in the ladies' rest room and each has two toilets for deep and meaningful conversations.

> **Women's rest-rooms are networking lounges**
> **and counselling centres where you can**
> **meet new and interesting people.**

So, back to the question: What do men talk about in a public rest room? The answer is – nothing. Absolutely nothing. They don't talk. Even if he's in there with his best friend, talk is still kept to a minimum. And a man never talks to another strange man in a public toilet. Never, ever, under any circumstances. They will certainly never talk to other men if they're sitting on the toilet and never meet another man's gaze. Never. In the toilet cubicles, men prefer floor-to-ceiling walls to limit inter-action with their neighbours, while women prefer large gaps so they can talk and pass things to each other. You'll rarely hear a fart in a woman's rest room but, if it does happen, the culprit will hide in the cubicle until the witnesses have left. A man's rest-room can often sound like the Fourth of July and the man who drops the loudest fart will emerge victorious from the cubicle.

Here's a letter from one of our male readers, demonstrating the point about the kind of hush reigning in the men's rest room:

> "I was driving North on the Motorway when I pulled in at a rest stop to use the men's room. The first cubicle was occupied so I went into the second. I was barely sitting down when a voice from the other cubicle said, "Hi, how are you?" Like all men, I never start a conversation with a stranger or fraternize in men's rooms at a rest stop, and I still don't know what got into me, but I answered with an embarrassed "Not bad!"
>
> The other guy said, "So... what are you up to?"
>
> I was thinking, "This is bizarre" but, like a fool, I answered, "Same as you... just travelling North!"
>
> Then I heard the guy say nervously, "Listen... I'll have to call you back, there's an idiot in the other stall who keeps answering my questions!"

Men also have a territorial ritual they indulge in when choosing a urinal. If there are five urinals in a row and the first man comes in to use one, he'll choose the one furthest from the door, so he's away from newcomers. The next arrival will choose the urinal furthest from the first man, and the next man will choose the one midway between the other two. A fourth man will usually choose to use a cubicle rather than stand beside a complete stranger who might look at him. And men always look silently directly in front and never talk to strangers. Never. Men's motto is 'Death before eye contact.'

For a man, standing beside other men in a public toilet is like standing in a lift with your willy out.

Chapter 6

THE OTHER WOMAN – HIS MOTHER

It wasn't until their wedding night that Jane realised Martin, age 36, still let his mother buy his underwear.

There were two women who came before King Solomon, dragging between them a young man who had agreed to marry both of their daughters. After listening to their stories, the king ordered the young man to be cut in half, so they could each have their share.

"No!" exclaimed the first woman. "Do not spill blood! Let the other woman's daughter marry him." The wise king did not hesitate. "The man must marry the other woman's daughter," he said. "But she was willing to see him cut in two!" exclaimed the king's court. "Yes," said King Solomon, "that shows she is the true mother-in-law."

Enter the Dragon

Mothers-in-law probably inspire more jokes than any other group of people on earth. They are constantly the butt of humour by comedians, between men, and in TV sitcoms, consistently characterised as witches, battleaxes or shrews. Remember, it was one of the founders of modern Russia, Lenin, who, when asked what should be the maximum penalty for bigamy, replied: "Two mothers-in-law".

> *"My mother-in-law called by this morning. When I answered the door she asked, "Can I stay here for a few days?"*
> *"You certainly can," I replied – and closed the door.*

> *What's the difference between a mother-in-law and a vulture? The vulture waits till you're dead before it eats your heart out.*

But while mothers-in-law do indeed prove a problem in many people's marriages, with up to a third who break up blaming the mother-in-law for the rift, it's not usually the woman's mother who causes most of the problems. Our research finds, time and time again, that it's the man's mother who is the real danger. His mother-in-law may provoke the most public complaints, but these are usually more tongue-in-cheek than protesting about some real problem.

> *"I received an email today advising that my mother-in-law had passed away and asking whether to arrange a burial, a cremation or embalming. I replied, "Be sure – arrange all three."*

Difficult mothers-in-law aren't a major problem for most men. Even for the legendary Giovanni Vigliotti of Arizona, who enjoyed 104 marriages between 1949 and 1981 in his own name and 50 aliases, those 104 mothers-in-law were far less of a problem than the 34 years in jail he received as a result.

A man's mother-in-law might irritate him, nag him and exasperate him, but most men don't usually dislike them. Mother-in-law problems don't dominate men's lives.

There's an old Polish proverb: "The way to a mother-in-law's heart is through her daughter." Most men realise this. What most women's mothers want, more than anything, is to see their daughters happy. And if the men in their lives make them happy, they're unlikely to cause problems.

If they're going to have problems with their in-laws, it's far more likely to come from their father-in-law refusing to let go of his cherished 'princess'. There simply aren't many father-in-law jokes – they're just not a laughing matter.

His Mother – Her Burden

The real dramas in most families come from the man's mother, the female partner's mother-in-law. Research carried out by Utah State University showed that in over 50% of all marriages there were real problems between the daughter-in-law and her husband's trouble-making and recalcitrant mother.

While not all mothers-in-law deserve this fearsome reputation, to many daughters-in-law a meddling, possessive and intrusive mother-in-law who won't cut the umbilical cord with her son can be soul-destroying. For her, mother-in-law crises often seem unmanageable and unsolvable, and can cause misery, anguish and, ultimately, the threat of divorce.

> *A man met a wonderful woman and became engaged.*
> *He arranged to have dinner with his mother that*
> *evening so she could meet his new fiancée. When he*
> *arrived at her home, he took three women – a blonde,*
> *a brunette and a redhead. His mother asked why he*
> *had brought three instead of just one. He said he*
> *wanted to see if his mother could guess which woman*
> *was her future daughter-in-law. She looked at each*
> *one carefully and then replied: "It's the redhead."*
>
> *"How did you work it out so quickly?" he asked.*
>
> *"Because," she replied, "I can't stand her."*

They're Not All Bad

Of course, not all mothers-in-law live up to the dreaded reputation of wickedness. While the Utah State University research shows that approximately 50% of mothers-in-law are seen as troublemakers, the other 50% must be either neutral at worst or loving, helpful and generous members of the extended family. And, often, mothers-in-law are blamed for the shortcomings and emotional problems of their sons or daughters-in-law.

Case Study: Anita and Tom

They had only been married six months when cracks started to appear in their newfound happiness. Anita felt Tom was becoming impossible to live with. He dropped his clothes anywhere he liked and threw his wet towels on the floor. Tom turned every room into a pigsty. It drove Anita to breaking point.

Anita: "Tom, you're such a pig – I just can't live with you any more!"

Tom: "No – you're the problem, you're just so fussy you're driving me insane! It was never like this when I lived at home. My mother never complained about me or about anything I did!"

Anita: "Good – let's talk about your mother. After living with you for six months I can't believe that she raised you – she must have spoilt you. You believe that women should do all the washing, cooking, ironing, cleaning and work full time – in fact, you don't have respect for women at all. Your mother has created a monster and I'm not going to stand for it any longer."

Tom: "What's it got to do with my mother? Why can't you just stick to the point and stop blaming everybody else except yourself?"

Many mothers ruin their sons for the next women in their lives. They mother them, cook, clean, wash and iron for them. They believe they are showing their sons love with these acts, but they are actually causing problems for their sons in later life when they develop relationships with women. The sons, in the end, find it hard to do the things their mothers did for them.

It's a tough one for the female partner in a relationship to deal with but, instead of criticising his mother, it's actually far more effective to train him to do what she wants him to do, and stop blaming his mother. He is now an adult and must be responsible for his own actions.

These problems can be very complex, for we have a three-way relationship, which can vary from being one in which all three people seem to be emotionally well-balanced, independent, unselfish and caring, to one where one, two or all three individuals may be motivated by jealousy, possessiveness, dependence, immaturity, selfishness or emotional instability.

Why Being a Mother-in-Law Can be Tough

It's important to bear in mind that mothers-in-law are in a difficult position because the daughters-in-law usually have a close bond with their own mothers and will regularly discuss with them, in detail, every little thing. A mother wants to be involved in her children's life. It's normal that a girl will rely more on her own mother than on her mother-in-law. This can cause jealousy on the part of her partner's mother. Mothers-in-law are always thinking about what their sons are doing, especially if he is their only child and their life is boring. Is he eating properly? Is the house clean enough for him? etc. etc. But sons rarely talk with their mothers about anything. Consequently, a mother-in-law will rarely get much information and begins to feel excluded from her son's new family and may think the only way she can be included is to force her way in by being constantly present. During courtship, a man's girl-friend will often work hard at building a relationship with his mother because it is a good strategy to keep her onside. When marriage makes things more permanent, however, it almost becomes like two women fighting over one man.

But for every problem there is a solution. What is needed is the willingness to solve it. The son and daughter-in-law must tackle the situation openly and maturely.

Case Study: Mark and Julie

Mark and Julie decided to get married. Because of a disagreement, Julie and her mother Sarah had not spoken for three years. This meant that Julie relied more and more on Mark's mother Fran to help her choose her wedding dress, the wedding menu and all the normal arrangements – all the things Julie would have done with her own mother had circumstances been different.

Yet, just before the wedding, with the help of Mark, Julie located her mother and they patched up their relationship. Fran was suddenly not needed any more and felt left out in the cold. She felt used and abused.

A mother-in-law is often left out after marriage unless she has developed a strong relationship with her daughter-in-law. If the daughter-in-law is close to her own mother she may forget that her husband's mother is as important to the family unit as her own mother. Our lives are becoming busier and busier and there is less and less time for our immediate family, let alone our extended family; less time for human contact. We use email for business to reduce the need for human contact but for the older generation the telephone or a face-to-face meeting is what they know. It can be very difficult for our generation to handle our parents and both sides need to be understanding and come up with solutions if everyone is going to be happy. The parents need quality time and the children need time for their immediate family. Where, in the past, extended families all lived in the same house, now we may live in another village, another town or even another country. Making the effort is part of family life.

In India and parts of Africa, a woman who marries 'divorces' her own parents and lives with her husband's family and calls them mother and father. In many countries, in-law relationships are clearing defined and often enshrined in explicit arrangements. But in Western culture, the relationship between the man and the woman takes precedence over all else – and the in-laws become the butt of the jokes.

Case Study: Bernadette, Richard and Diana

Bernadette's perspective

Bernadette was in her early forties when her husband left her. "Good riddance!" she told her friends. He drank too much and never really cared about his family. But she still had her son Richard. He was an honest young man of 22, and he would look after her.

Bernadette thought that Richard wasn't interested in girls. She had provided him with every care, comfort and emotional support, what could he possibly see in another woman? Those airheads he occasionally dated were obviously just for sex. She felt Richard realised that just as she had raised, cared and loved him since his birth, it was now his responsibility to look after her.

Diana's perspective

> *Adam and Eve were the happiest and*
> *the luckiest couple in the world, because*
> *neither of them had a mother-in-law.*

Diana liked Richard as soon as she met him. While they were courting, however, she felt it strange that he didn't take her home to meet his mother until after they had announced their engagement. Bernadette wasn't particularly welcoming, but Diana just thought she needed time to adjust. She laughed off her remarks that perhaps they weren't ready yet for marriage, and that they could change their minds any time in the lead-up to the wedding.

When the ceremony finally took place, Bernadette was extremely badly behaved, and told everyone she didn't think it would last.

It wasn't long before Diana realised she had inherited the mother-in-law from hell. The problems started immediately after Diana and Richard returned from their honeymoon. Bernadette would call in most days, completely unannounced.

Diana tried to be friendly but she soon tired of being told by Bernadette how to cook Richard's favourite food and how he liked the house kept. Bernadette found fault with almost everything that Diana did. Before long, when Richard wasn't around, Bernadette would openly insult her, but deny it if ever Diana brought it up with Richard, and accuse her of trying to cause trouble between her husband and his mother. Diana began avoiding her mother-in-law, but instead Bernadette would phone every night and talk endlessly with her son. She would ask when he was coming 'home' to paint the house, weed the garden, fix the leaky tap, talk over a problem or take her shopping. Her requests seemed endless. Richard was now at her beck and call, regardless of Diana's needs. Bernadette had effectively replaced her husband with her son.

How many mothers-in-law does it take to change a light bulb? One. She just holds it up and waits for the world to revolve around her.

Two years later, Diana gave birth to a son, Travis. Bernadette was soon physically back in Diana's life every day, helping with the baby. Bernadette knew it all and took over. Instead of teaching Diana about motherhood, she criticized her constantly. Bernadette became obsessive with Travis, picking him up and holding him every minute they were together. Diana started to feel excluded. Bernadette was taking her baby from her and the child would love Bernadette more than his mother, she thought. Diana felt trapped and miserable. Bernadette always dropped in uninvited and unannounced and regularly criticized and insulted Diana.

Diana tried time and again to discuss the problems with Richard but he felt that Diana was simply being possessive and that his mother was only trying to help. He also felt that it was his responsibility to look after his mother's needs. Richard felt that Diana was being selfish, jealous and immature.

Eventually, Diana tired of the arguments and fumed in silence.

Richard's perspective

Richard missed his father after the divorce but things were definitely quieter around the home. His mother always told him that his father was good for nothing and it was now up to him to be the man of the house. His mother lavished him with care and affection, cooked his favourite meals, made his bed, picked up and cleaned up after him and never let him wear the same item of clothing twice without washing and ironing it.

She never criticized him; in fact she felt that everything he did was absolutely wonderful. The only problem Richard had was that whenever he brought a girlfriend home, their relationship soon cooled off after meeting his mother. But when he met Diana, he knew he was in love. He decided to keep Diana away from his mother as much as possible.

After Richard and Diana married, Bernadette was always around, helping out, but Diana seemed so jealous about his relationship with his mother, it got to the point where his mother stopped coming round. Instead, he would see her at weekends when he would help out around her house. He did have one problem with his mother, though. She would ring him every night and talk endlessly on the phone just when he started to relax for the evening. But then, he thought his mother must be lonely, living on her own, and he did have a responsibility to her.

What's the difference between in-laws and outlaws? Outlaws are wanted.

When Travis was born, Bernadette was the first to help out, always there, washing baby clothes and caring for Travis.

Bringing up a child was all new to Diana. His mother's advice was invaluable. But Diana seemed completely unwilling to take advice. She became possessive of Travis and was always arguing with Bernadette and complaining endlessly to Richard about his mother. He loved Diana but she was driving him nuts with her emotional outbursts. Having a typical problem-solving male brain, Richard thought he should not have to work hard all day then come home to solve arguments between his wife and his mother. He began to think that life would be less complicated if he was single again.

Mother- and daughter-in-law must forge a bond if their lives are to work. Women did this naturally for survival in the cave and need to do it now for survival in the modern world, for a stress-free life and to avoid dragging men into the problems. Women need to sort this relationship out between themselves without getting their husbands/sons involved. Men may actually enjoy the attention of having two women fighting over them and while this continues it feeds their egos. The wife needs to be clever enough to take control of the situation and ensure that problems are dealt with strictly between her and her mother-in-law. When this works it is a win-win situation. The last thing a woman needs is her mother-in-law complaining about her to her husband; she really needs an rather than an enemy.

This drama is not uncommon. It is played out in families the world over. In some countries the problems are worse than others. In Russia, where young married couples live with parents because apartments are rarely available, a strong culture of mother-in-law hatred has arisen. In Spain there is a disease known as Suegritis, an illness said to be caused by mothers-in-law. There is a carnival whistle known as Masasuegras, meaning 'kill mother-in-law'. In the Indian capital Delhi, there's actually a jail wing specifically for mothers-in-law, arrested for demanding excessive dowries from their daughters-in-law, and breaking up marriages. It is constantly under threat from overcrowding.

In Spain and Italy, a mother-in-law can be sued for damages

for ruining a marriage. In Lutz, Florida, a wife who could no longer cope with her husband defending his mother drugged him and had an hilarious cartoon of his mother's crabby face tattooed on his cheek. Her husband left her and filed for divorce – then sued her for damages. In Australia, a woman was told by a pharmacist that a photo of her mother-in-law was not considered enough authority to sell her arsenic.

Jewish mothers-in-law come in for even more ridicule. In the American documentary *Mamadrama*, their embrace is described as "loving in the way that a bear hug is loving; it'll crush you to death".

What's the difference between a Rottweiler and a mother-in-law? Eventually, the Rottweiler lets go.

The mother-in-law/daughter-in-law problem may exist from the very beginning and, sometimes, the hostility is quite open. When Sylvester Stallone announced he was going to marry his pregnant girlfriend Jennifer Flavin, his mother told the world, "He shouldn't walk down the aisle with that girl. Jennifer is in love all right, but with the idea of being important. I think there's a mean streak in her." It should have been a clue when she once declared: "In my eyes, no woman's good enough for Sylvester. I'll lie down and die for him."

In many cases, however, when the three people involved try to find an acceptable solution and reach an accommodation, it doesn't work. If problems are cropping up early on in a relationship, then the daughter-in-law, by necessity, has to be the one to try and build bridges. She has to realise that time is limited between the courtship and marriage and, while all her attentions have been focused on her primary relationship, it's likely that, if she invests no time at all in the relationship with her potential mother-in-law, there will be a negative dividend. She should try and spend some time with her alone, so the mother-in-law sees her as an individual in her own right, rather than as simply the spouse. Strengthening that relationship on a one-on-one basis will lead to fewer problems when there are more people involved.

Later on in a marriage, if problems have been allowed to take root, however, it's actually very difficult to settle on a workable agreement between three people, each of whom have different agendas and priorities. One side will rarely yield to what they perceive as an alliance between the other two. At this stage, therefore, the problem must be solved by the two most affected parties – the son and the daughter-in-law.

The first questions that they need to answer are:

Do they both recognize that a problem exists?
Do they want a happy, loving and long life together?
Do they want to solve the problem?

If the answer is 'No' to any one of these questions, marriage guidance counselling is recommended. If the answer is 'Yes', the husband and wife should sit down and commit to paper exactly what they feel the problems are.

In the case study above, for example, Diana could write:

Bernadette calls around unannounced, which means we have no privacy and our plans are constantly upset.
Bernadette phones every night, just as we're trying to enjoy quiet family time.
Bernadette demands too much attention from Richard, so he does not spend enough time with his family.
Bernadette is nosy. She wants to know everything and be involved in all our activities.
Bernadette is always critical and has no respect for my ability, and is domineering, expecting Richard to obey her like a child.

Richard, on the other hand, could write:

My mother is lonely and it's up to us to comfort her, but Diana doesn't care.

My mother doesn't have a man around the house to do odd jobs and Diana doesn't understand that it's my responsibility as her son to help her out.

My mother tries to help Diana, but Diana refuses to share Travis, or accept valuable child-rearing advice.

My mother makes me feel guilty when I don't comply with her requests.

I don't understand why everyone is angry all the time, when all I want to do is get along with everyone.

The problem, then, is Diana's and Richard's. Bernadette does not have the problem. She has been allowed to maintain her control of Richard and through him she controls Diana, and Travis. Richard has never severed the umbilical cord between him and his mother. He hasn't really left home 'yet' and has not matured.

....
The best time to cut an umbilical cord is at birth.
....

Diana is also an unwitting participant here. She has helped become the architect of her own misery. She did not set limits on Bernadette when she saw problems first emerging. She has, in effect, let Bernadette rampage boundlessly through her marriage and family.

Setting Boundaries

Setting boundaries means deciding ground rules and drawing lines others are asked not to cross. Boundaries were not laid down by Richard and Diana when they first married.

This is a very easy trap for young people to fall into. They are inexperienced and have usually lived within other people's boundaries. They are not assertive and usually feel that other family members are only trying to help with their advice.

Setting boundaries and being assertive are two vital lessons that young married people must learn. When boundaries have been set, everyone knows how far they can go. They know that if they step outside the boundaries, they will invite trouble. Within their marriage, Diana and Richard would have boundaries, lines that cannot be crossed even with each other, so why not have boundaries for Bernadette too?

Diana claims that Bernadette drops in uninvited and unannounced. So Bernadette needs training in crossing the boundary of privacy. She must be told that it would be appreciated if she would telephone before she came around. It should be explained that she and Richard need private time to relax or work on projects together and that unannounced calls often prove inconvenient. Understandably, Bernadette will feel rebuffed and hurt, but that's her problem. It must be pointed out that they don't love her any less but these are the boundaries. Bernadette will eventually get over it and adjust.

The problem of Bernadette wanting Richard to work around her home is also a boundary problem. Richard does have a responsibility to help her but an agenda needs to be agreed by Diana. The three of them should talk it through at a time when emotions aren't running high. It might even be a solution to talk to a handyman in the area, and give Bernadette the phone number. Richard and Diana could even offer to pay his bill for a year as a combined birthday and Christmas present. Diana could offer to participate to help Bernadette feel part of the family.

> *My mother-in-law and I were happy*
> *for 20 years. Then we met.*

With regard to rearing Travis, Bernadette has again crossed an unset boundary. The problem will become significantly less when visits are only made by arrangement. Diana must be assertive. She needs to thank Bernadette for her concern but state that she and Richard have agreed on a programme of development for Travis and they intend to follow it.

Richard should limit his mother's phone calls to a specific time agreed with Diana, say, ten minutes. Richard should then tell his mother he has things to do and say goodbye.

Most importantly, however, he needs to help his mother develop her own interests outside his family. This could include such activities as lawn bowls, a reading group, becoming a hospital volunteer, joining a retirees' club, taking a course, or helping at an organisation like Meals-on-Wheels. Both Richard and Diana should encourage her to get out more, and be prepared to support her emotionally during this stage. They should also be ready to take a real interest in her 'new' life until it assumes a momentum of its own.

If you could convince your mother-in-law to walk 10 miles a day, after just one week she'd be 70 miles away.

Every single one of Diana's problems can be solved by setting out boundaries and insisting they be observed. It's not easy. Bernadette will be upset initially, and will probably lash back with guilt claims and emotional blackmail such as:

> *"After all I've done for you!"*
> *"Who else do I have to turn to?"*
> *"You don't care about me any more."*
> *"When I'm dead and gone you will be sorry."*
> *"You're selfish – just like your father."*
> *"I feel so alone now."*

Such tactics, however, will only work if you let them. You *know* you're right to be doing what you're doing, you've talked it through thoroughly, you've examined all the possible responses and you're ready to deal with them. People can only succeed in making you feel guilty if you agree to accept that guilt.

Mother-in-law: an anagram of Woman Hitler.

The next stage of Bernadette's response may be a withdrawal of assistance, i.e. babysitting. She may even threaten disinheritance. These reactions are to be expected, but if Richard and Diana want to live an independent, mature and happy life, they must assert themselves. Diana and Richard should not try to explain or justify their decisions; just restate that is the course they have chosen to take.

All through this process, they must remain caring and supportive of Bernadette. It might be tempting to cut her off, particularly if the backlash is sharper than they imagined, but they shouldn't. They need to keep her updated on family progress but still encourage her to forge a life of her own. If they tackle their boundary-setting exercise with Bernadette using empathy and love, a sound adult and enjoyable relationship will ultimately, inevitably, grow.

And, at the end of the day, if all these efforts do not solve the problem, move to another town.

Chapter 7

WOMEN'S SECRET WAYS WITH WORDS

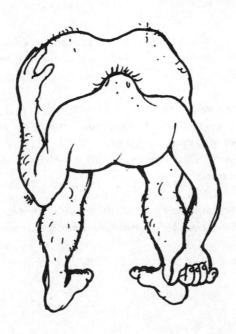

When women tried to communicate with
him, Trevor simply buried his head.

An archaeologist was digging through some rubble at an ancient site when he stumbled across a dusty old lamp. As he was rubbing off the dust, a genie popped out. "You have freed me!" cried the genie. "I will grant you a wish."

The archaeologist thought for a moment, then replied, "I wish for a bridge with a highway between England and France!"

The genie rolled his eyes and muttered, "Hey, I just got out of this lamp and I'm cramped and tired. Do you have any idea how many miles it is between England and France? That's an engineering impossibility! Make another wish!"

The man pondered a little, then said, "I wish I could understand how to communicate with women."

The genie paled and asked, "One lane or two?"

I f you are male, this is one of the most important chapters you will read in this book. It's very likely that you may be sceptical about some of the things you are about to read so we suggest you confirm each point with any woman in your immediate vicinity.

For over a decade, we have collected and recorded responses to surveys about how men and women communicate, and we have drawn on the science of human behaviour to explain their differences. Most importantly, we have developed strategies for dealing with these differences.

We have researched men of many nationalities and races. As a result, we are able to reveal for the first time the intriguing logic behind the five most asked questions these men had about the way women communicate. These secrets are a source of both amusement and confusion for most men but, for those who acquire knowledge of them, a new level of relationship with the opposite sex is attainable. Here are the questions.

1. Why do women talk so much?
2. Why do women always want to talk about problems?
3. Why do women exaggerate?
4. Why do women never seem to get to the point?
5. Why do women want to know all the little details?

1. Why Do Women Talk So Much?

The enormous capacity women have for chatter is one of the most difficult concepts for most men to understand. In *Why Men Don't Listen and Women Can't Read Maps* we covered this phenomenon in detail and will give a brief summary of it here.

Women evolved in a group situation with other women and children all staying close to the cave. The ability to bond and to build close relationships was paramount to each woman's survival. Men evolved silently sitting on a hill, searching for a moving target. When women engaged in any activity together, they would constantly chatter as a means of bonding. When males were hunting or fishing, no one talked for fear of startling the prey. When modern man goes fishing or hunting he still doesn't say much. When modern women go gathering (shopping) they still constantly chatter. Women don't need a reason to talk and don't need an end goal. They talk to make a connection with each other.

Here are the MRI brain scans of men and women in conversation with each other. The dark areas are the activated parts in the brain.

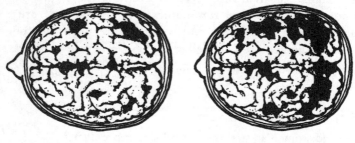

Male   **Female**

Speech and language areas of the brain, Institute of Psychiatry, London, 2001.

These brain scans show how a woman's brain is highly utilised in speech and language functions. In *Why Men Don't Listen and Women Can't Read Maps* we showed how a female brain can effortlessly output 6,000–8,000 spoken words a day. Contrast this with a man's maximum output of 2,000–4,000 a day and you can see why women's capacity for talk causes so many problems for couples. A working man can exhaust his word output by mid-afternoon then arrive home to a woman who may still have 4,000–5,000 words to go! Two women can spend all day together and then easily talk for another hour on the telephone. A man's response to this is, "Why didn't you tell her all that when you saw her?"

"I hope I haven't talked too much!"

Having a brain that is not strong in speech and language skills largely accounts for the notable gender distinctions in rates of certain speech problems: males outnumber females by about three to four times for stuttering, and 10 times for severe dyslexia.

Men's brains are configured for problem solving and to continually come up with solutions. Men use speech and language to communicate facts and data. Most men will "only speak if they have something to say", that is, when they want to communicate facts, data or solutions. This creates serious problems when communicating with women because women's 'talk' is completely different. Female 'talk' is used as a form of reward and to bond with another person. Put simply, if she likes or loves you, if she is agreeable to what you are saying or wants you to feel accepted and significant, she will talk to you; if she doesn't like you, she won't talk.

> *Men's brains are solution-oriented.*
> *Women's brains are process-oriented.*

One man will only talk to another man about personal problems if he feels the other man could have a solution. As we explained earlier, the man who is asked feels honoured that his opinion is being sought and will offer solutions. When a woman talks, however, she mainly does it to bond with the other person and solutions are not required. Unfortunately, a man thinks a woman is discussing her problems because she doesn't know how to deal with them, so constantly interrupts her with solutions.

No wonder a woman will claim a man is constantly cutting her off and not letting her state her own point of view. From a woman's standpoint, his constant offers of solutions make it appear as if he always wants to be right and that she's always wrong. When a woman, on the other hand, shares her emotions or problems with someone, she is showing she trusts that person because of the confidences she's sharing.

> *When she's sharing personal confidences with you*
> *she's not complaining — it means she trusts you.*

The reverse is also true – if she doesn't like or love that person, is not agreeing with what they are saying, or she wants to punish the person, she'll stop talking. Silence is used as a form of punishment and is an effective tactic when used on other women. This tactic doesn't work on men – men feel the added 'peace and quiet' is a bonus. So when a woman threatens, "I'll never talk to you again!" it should be taken seriously – but not literally.

> *Women use silence to punish men.*
> *But men love silence.*

If a woman wants to punish a man, the easiest way is to talk to him non-stop and keep changing the subject.

Solution for men
Understand that the main purpose of a woman's 'talk' is to talk. Her goal is to feel better by talking about her day and to bond with you – no solutions are required. All you need to do is listen and encourage her. The content of a man's talk is not important, it's his participation that counts.

Solution for women
Set a time with a man when you want to talk and tell him you just want him to listen without offering solutions. Don't give a man the silent treatment and then feel upset because he hasn't noticed you're not speaking to him. He enjoys this quiet time because he can relax. If you have an issue with him, be direct about it.

2. Why Do Women Always Want To Talk About Problems?

Women live an average of seven years longer than men, mainly because of a better ability to cope with stress. When a man wants to forget about a stressful day, he can do so by thinking or doing something else. His mono-tracking brain allows him to concentrate on the news, television, watering the garden, surfing the Internet or constructing a model ship, to the exclusion of his problems. By concentrating on one thing at a time other than his problem, he can forget about it. A man under stress who doesn't preoccupy himself with another activity will stop talking and sit alone on his rock trying to find a solution to his problem. The danger is his that stress is being internalised and may result in stress conditions such as diarrhoea, constipation, stomach ulcers or a heart attack – hopefully not all at the same time. Women deal with stress by talking about their problem over and over, backwards and forwards and from every angle, without reaching any conclusions. Talking about their problems is how they relieve their stress. If a man talked like this, other men would assume he was incapable and was asking for solutions... which they would promptly offer.

Case Study: Lisa, Joe and the Midnight Argument

When Lisa and Joe first moved in together, they argued a lot. Frequently, the arguments would drag on dramatically, way past midnight. The problem was Lisa had been raised to believe a couple should never sleep on an argument. They should kiss and make up before they went to bed. So she'd talk, talk and talk about the problem they'd been arguing about – until it started another argument. Joe couldn't handle it. He'd much rather have an argument, go to sleep and forget it.

Lisa wanted to reduce her stress level and was eager for them to reach a mutually satisfactory decision; Joe felt they just kept on going over and over the same points. He was completely talked out by the end of the day and was content to let their disagreement lie.

> *My husband and I decided never go to sleep*
> *until we'd resolved an argument.*
> *One night we stayed awake for six months.*
> PHYLLIS DILLER

To men, it's a mystery why women like to talk through an argument, especially late at night. The female brain is, however, a communications computer that is process-based. Women like to talk through every aspect of their actions and their feelings. Men are more likely to recoil at such a prospect. Men prefer to have an argument, and then leave it alone. Men like to go off to their rock, and think about something else.

> *There are two theories to arguing*
> *with women. Neither one works.*
> RODNEY DANGERFIELD

Women want to make the peace and smooth out any disagreements. They believe talking can make everyone feel better. Men believe talking can usually make things far worse.

Solution

When a woman is talking through a problem and may not appear to make sense, remember that she needs to go through the process of talking to feel better. Listen with compassion and tell her you're always there to listen when she needs you. This is much easier than trying to fix problems that don't exist and it scores you lots of points.

> *Things women wish men knew, Number 105:*
> *Anything a woman said six or eight months ago*
> *is inadmissable in a current argument.*

If you can't respond immediately, gently ask a woman if she could leave the subject and pick it up another day when the heat has subsided from an argument. Say, "Sorry, darling, but I can't get my head around this problem at the moment. Could we talk about it tomorrow/at the weekend/next week, when I've had a chance to think it through?" This approach is far more likely to work than saying nothing, and hoping the woman will simply run out of things to say. She won't.

3. Why Do Women Exaggerate?

Both men and women exaggerate. The difference is that men exaggerate facts and data while women exaggerate emotions and feelings. A man might exaggerate the importance of his job, the size of his income or the fish he caught, his car's performance or how many good-looking women he's dated. Women will exaggerate how they and others were feeling about a personal issue or about what someone said. Women's brains are focused on people and they fantasise about life and relationships far more than men and exaggeration about these things makes for more interesting conversations.

Exaggeration makes conversations about relationships much more interesting and exciting.

Women's exaggeration of words and emotions is commonplace and is perfectly acceptable to other women when they talk among themselves and is part of the social fabric of being a woman.

Most women love to daydream about a handsome knight galloping up on a white horse to carry them away, even though they invariably end up falling for the red-haired, freckled-faced computer technician holding a beer, whom they met at the White Horse Inn on Saturday night.

A sociological study has verified that a woman's ultimate fantasy is having two men at once. In this fantasy, one man is cooking, the other is cleaning.

Here are some common examples of female exaggeration:

"I've told you a million times to pick up your wet towels."
"You always expect me to do all the housework and look after the kids at the same time."

"When I saw her wearing that dress, I thought I'd die!"

"You do this to me every time."

"I'll never speak to you again!"

For a man, a woman's exaggeration can be frustrating because his brain relies on facts and data for understanding and he decodes words literally. For example, if he disagrees with her in front of friends, she may later say she says, "You're *always* putting me down and *never* let me have my own opinion! You do this to me *all the time*!" He's likely to take it literally and argue that he *doesn't* do it *every time* and defend himself with examples. "That's not true!" he protests, "I didn't do it last night and haven't done it for months!" She rejects his response and recalls the times, places and dates where he committed the same offence. He walks away feeling hurt and indignant. But whether or not he committed the offence is irrelevant. All she wanted him to do was to demonstrate, in front of their friends, that he cares about her. She was exaggerating her emotions and he was arguing against what he thought were facts and data.

I feel like a million — but one at a time.

MAE WEST on men

Despite women's capacity for talking, when it comes to communication women also rely on body language to send and receive information. Body language reveals a woman's emotional condition and accounts for 60%–80% of the impact of most female conversations. From a male viewpoint, women often seem to be waving their arms about and using a wide range of facial expressions and gestures when they talk, including speaking on the telephone. Tone of voice conveys what she means and women communicate with a range of five tones — men can only identify three. Words account for a mere 7% to 10% of the impact of her message. Consequently, the words are not critical to their conversation because most of their messages are non-verbal. It's perfectly OK for women to use words that don't even match the conversation. For women, emotions and feelings are what matter and body language and tone are the main channels for this communication.

How A Woman Can Delude Herself

When a woman repeats a scenario to herself in her head, it may seem that her recollection is real. This letter from Jessica shows how it happens:

Luke and I decided to meet at our favourite restaurant for dinner on Saturday night around 6pm.

Luke went to the football with his mates that day, and I had a wonderful fun time with the girlfriends I hadn't seen much since Luke and I became an item. We spent all day shopping, having lunch and coffees and talking about every little thing.

Time soon got away from me and I was a little late getting to the restaurant. I knew it would be a romantic dinner; I felt excited and was really looking forward to seeing Luke.

When I arrived, he was just sitting there, staring out of the window. I apologised for being late and told him what a great day I'd had with the girls and showed him what I had bought. I gave him a special gift – a beautiful set of gold cufflinks to go with his dinner suit. He mumbled "Thanks," put them in his pocket and just sat there saying nothing.

He was in such a strange mood, I thought he must be punishing me for being late by not talking to me or making a fuss of me. The dinner conversation was really hard work, and not very interesting. It seemed like he was a million miles away. We decided to have coffee at home.

The car trip home was quiet and now I knew that we had a serious problem. I sat there racking my brain, trying to work out what it could be, but decided to wait until we got home to bring it up. I had some suspicions but didn't want to say anything yet.

When we got home, Luke went straight into the living room, turned on the TV and stared blankly at it. His eyes seemed to say it was over between us. I started to realise something I'd thought about for some time was true – he must have another woman, he's thinking about her and doesn't want to tell me or hurt me. It was also becoming clear who it was too – Debbie, that trollop with the mini-skirt at his work! I've seen the way she sways her hips whenever she walks past him and he must think I'm an idiot not to have noticed how he looks at her and gives her that stupid little smile. They must think I'm blind! Well, I sat there on the lounge with him for about 15 minutes until I couldn't stand it any longer. I went to bed. Ten minutes later, Luke also came to bed and surprised me by cuddling me. He didn't resist my advances and we made love. But then he just rolled over and went to sleep. I was so upset and stressed that I lay awake for hours and finally cried myself to sleep. It felt like the end was coming.

I promised myself that tomorrow I'd confront the situation and demand he tell me the truth. Who is this other woman? Does he love her or is it just a fling? Why can't men just be truthful? All I know is I can't live my life like this any longer...

What Luke was really thinking that night:
England lost. Had a great bonk though...

Solution

If you're a man, understand a woman's need to exaggerate emotional conversation and not take her literally. Never call her a 'drama queen' or correct her in front of others. Simply take a step back and try to listen to her real feeling without telling her what she should think or say. A woman, however, needs to realise that men take things literally and she should stick to the facts and limit exaggeration – especially in business, where it can be confusing and costly.

4. Why Do Women Never Seem To Get To The Point?

To men, women often seem vague or to beat around the bush rather than getting straight to the point. Sometimes a man feels as if he is supposed to guess what she wants, or that he is expected to be a mind reader. This apparent vagueness is known as indirect speech.

This letter from a male reader shows how it can make men feel:

My wife has elevated indirect speech to an art form. Yesterday, for example, she was puttering around in the kitchen and said, "At the staff meeting today, my supervisor said, 'Don't eat the salami.' "

"What?" I exclaimed, "What did she say about salami?"

"Not her, you," she replied in an exasperated tone, "I don't want you to eat the salami. I'm saving it."

I stood there with that dumb look on my face, trying to locate the transcripts of our conversation in that dusty filing cabinet in my head, while she casually picked up where she had left off, telling me what her supervisor had actually said.

She does this constantly. I have to insert bookmarks into the stream of words so that I can identify which thread of the conversation she's currently severing. She can keep 4 or 5 different lines of thought going simultaneously with casual ease, while I struggle to keep up. Her girlfriends all seem to follow it, but it gives my two sons and I brain damage. How can such an intelligent woman be so scatterbrained when she talks?

"Would you like to see a movie tonight?" she asked. I was impressed she'd asked but said "No" – I had things to do in the garage. It was almost an hour before I realized she wasn't talking to me. I asked if there was a problem, she said "No", but still remained quiet. When I pressed her about it she yelled, teary-eyed, "You never take me to the movies!" Hang on – I thought it was me who was invited to go, not her!

Today, as I carried a load of laundry into the garage, I said, "I need to go to Hardware House later."

I busied myself in the garage for 30 minutes or so, during which time I started a load of laundry, moved some boxes, and cleaned off a shelf. I made a mental checklist of things to do later in the day, after I returned from Hardware House. When I re-entered the house, she looked up from her work and asked,

"Why?'"

"Huh? Why what?" I asked.

"What do you need?"

"I don't need anything! What are we talking about?"

"If you don't need anything, why are you going to Hardware House?" she demanded, arms crossed in that unmistakable what-are-you-trying-to-pull posture that most married men recognise.

Hey, that conversation was a long time ago, and I've already loaded up my conversation buffer with a half dozen things to talk about and, as far as I'm concerned, Hardware House is old news. But to my wife, it was never settled, so it stays on top of the stack, where she assumes I am also keeping it.

By the time we get things straightened out, she's convinced I don't listen, and I'm half convinced she's right. I'll try to figure it out later, right after my salami sandwich.

Frustrated Raymond

When a woman talks she often uses indirect speech. This means she hints at what she wants or infers things. Raymond's wife was also multi-tracking, so he got completely lost.

Women's indirect speech has a purpose – it builds relationships and rapport with others by avoiding aggression, confrontation or discord. From an evolutionary point of view, being indirect allowed women to avoid disagreement with one another and made it easier to bond by not appearing to be dominant or aggressive. This approach fits perfectly into a woman's overall approach to preserving harmony.

When women use indirect speech with other women there is seldom a problem – women are sensitive to picking up the real meaning. It can, however, be disastrous when used on men. Men use direct speech and take words literally. As we've said, men's brains evolved as single-focused machines because of the demands of hunting. They find women's lack of conversational structure and purpose very disconcerting, and accuse women of not knowing what they're talking about. They respond by saying things like "What's the point here?",

"Where is this conversation going?" and "What's the bottom line?" Men then proceed to talk to a woman as if she is a mental patient in an institution or will cut her off saying, "We've been over this a dozen times", "How much longer will this take?" and "This conversation is too much hard work and isn't going anywhere!"

Indirect Talk In Business

When a woman uses indirect speech in business, it can prove problematic because men may have difficulty following a multi-tracked, indirect conversation. Men need to be presented with clear, logical, organised ideas and information before they will make a decision. A woman can have her ideas and requests rejected purely because her male boss didn't have a clue what she really wanted. Marie was the classic victim.

After six months of negotiations, Marie finally won the chance to present her company's new advertising program to a big financial client. The audience would be eight men and four women, the account up for grabs was worth $200,000, and she had 30 minutes to sell her story. She knew she'd only have one shot at the title. On the day, Marie arrived perfectly dressed in a tailored, knee-length business suit, her hair was up, she wore light natural make-up and she had practised her Powerpoint presentation to the point where she could deliver it in her sleep.

As she started into her presentation, however, she noticed how blankly the men were regarding her. She felt they were judging her critically and, assuming they were losing interest, she began to multi-track her presentation to try to spur their interest by going back to previous slides, talking indirectly and trying to show how one related to the other. The women were giving her encouragement by smiling at her, using various facial expressions and making listening sounds like, "Uh huh" "Right!" and "Mmmm" and generally looking interested. Marie was excited by the women's feedback and started pitching her story to them, unintentionally ignoring the men. Her entire presentation became a juggling act. She finished and departed, convinced she'd done a great job and eagerly waited for the company's response.

Here's the conversation that took place between the male executives over coffee after Marie had gone:

Marketing Director: "Do you guys have an idea what the hell she was talking about?"
Chief Executive: "No... she lost me. Tell her to send the proposal in writing."

Marie had multi-tracked her presentation and used indirect talk with a group of men who didn't have a clue what she was talking about or what related to what. The women executives were happy with the presentation and had participated by asking questions but no man wanted to raise his hand and admit he didn't understand. A woman needs to understand that if a man doesn't follow what she's saying he'll often pretend he understands rather than look like he's stupid.

> *When a man can't follow a woman's business talk,*
> *he often pretends to understand.*

Women often expect the males in their lives will understand, decode and follow indirect speech. But men simply don't get it.

Regardless of a man's age, a woman still needs to talk with direct speech. Give him timetables, agendas, bottom line answers and deadlines. Women need to be direct with men in business and give them one thing at a time to consider. Marie is still waiting for an answer...

Indirect Talk At Home

When a woman says...	She really means...
We need to talk	I'm upset or have a problem
We need	I want
I'm sorry	You'll be sorry
It's your decision	As long as I agree
I'm not upset	Of course I'm upset!
You'll have to learn to communicate	Just agree with me
Do you love me?	I want something expensive
You're being really nice tonight	Is sex all you ever think about?
How much do you love me?	I did something you won't like
Be romantic, turn out the lights	I have flabby thighs

Case Study: Barbara and Adam

Barbara was going shopping with friends and wanted her 16-year-old son Adam to clean the kitchen. "Adam would you like to clean the kitchen for me please?" she asked. "Uh... yeah..." was his mumbled response. When she returned from their trip with her friends, the kitchen still looked like a bomb had hit it. In fact, it was in worse shape than before she'd gone out. She was fuming. "But I was going to do it before I go out tonight!" he complained. The problem here rested with Barbara. She had used indirect speech and assumed that Adam would realise that when she returned home with her friends, the kitchen would need to be clean. She asked, "Would you like to clean the kitchen?" No teenage boy would 'like' to clean the kitchen and neither did Adam. A direct request with a deadline like, "Adam, please have the kitchen cleaned before I get home from shopping at midday" would have ensured a more successful outcome.

---

*Boys don't 'like' to do household chores –
they need to be directly instructed to do them.*

That night, she said to Adam, "I'd like you to study for an hour before you go to bed." This indirect approach will work with girls but is lost on boys. A boy's brain hears that his mother would like him to do it but he has not actually been instructed to do it, so he doesn't. If she found him listening to the radio or watching TV instead, an argument might take place. A direct instruction with a time limit is the only realistic way to handle males.

"Adam, I want you to study in your room for an hour and I'll come in and say good night before you go to bed." With direct instructions there is little room for miscommunication and males appreciate clear directions. Many women are concerned that direct speech is too aggressive or confronting. When used with another female, that would be true. For males however, direct talk is perfectly normal because that's how they communicate.

Solution

For women: indirect speech is used by females to bond with other females. Use only direct speech with males. It may seem difficult at first but with practice it will give you the results you want and you'll have fewer disagreements with the males in your life.

For men: if a woman is talking and you're having difficulty following the plot, just sit back, listen and go for the ride without offering solutions. At worst, give her a time limit – "I'd like to watch the 7pm news, darling, but you've got my full attention until then." When you do this she will usually talk herself out and feel happy and relaxed, without you having to do a thing.

One of our readers sent us the *Dictionary of Women's Indirect Terms* that occur during their regular arguments

'**Fine**' A woman uses this word at the end of any argument where she believes she's in the right but needs him to shut up. A man should never use 'fine' to describe how a woman looks. This may cause an argument that ends with the woman saying, 'Fine!'

'**Five minutes**' This is about half an hour. It is equivalent to the five minutes a football game is going to last before a man says he'll take out the rubbish.

'**Nothing**' This means 'something'. 'Nothing' is usually used to describe the feeling a woman has when she feels like choking a man. 'Nothing' often signifies the start of an argument that will last 'Five minutes' and end with the word 'Fine'.

'**Go ahead**' (with raised eyebrows) This is a dare that will result in a woman getting upset over 'nothing' and will end with the word 'Fine'.

'**Go ahead**' (with normal eyebrows) This means 'I give up' or 'Do what you want because I don't care'. You'll usually receive a (raised eyebrows) 'Go ahead' within a few minutes, followed by 'Nothing' and 'Fine' and she will talk to you in about 'Five minutes' when she cools down.

Loud Sigh This means she thinks you're an idiot and wonders why she is wasting her time standing here and arguing with you over 'Nothing'.

'**Oh?**' As the start of a sentence, 'Oh' usually signifies that you are caught in a lie. For example, 'Oh? I talked to your brother about what you were doing last night' and 'Oh? I'm expected to believe that am I?' She will tell you that she is 'Fine' as she is throwing your clothes out of the window but don't try to lie more to get out of it, or you will get a (raised eyebrows) 'Go ahead'.

'That's OK' This means she wants to think long and hard before paying you back for whatever you've done. 'That's OK' is often used with 'Fine' and used in conjunction with a (raised eyebrows) 'Go Ahead'. At some point in the near future when she has plotted and planned, you are going to be in big trouble.

'Please do' This is not a statement, it is an offer for you to talk. A woman is giving you the chance to come up with whatever excuse or reason you have for doing whatever you have done. If you don't tell the truth you'll get a 'That's OK' at the end.

'Really?' She is not questioning the validity of what you are saying, she's simply telling you she doesn't believe a word. You offer to explain and get a 'Please do'. The more you tell her your excuses the louder and more sarcastic her 'Reallys' become, peppered with lots of 'Ohs', 'raised eyebrows' and a final 'loud sigh'.

'Thanks a lot' A woman will say this when she is really cheesed off with you. It signifies you have hurt her in some callous way, and will be followed by the 'loud sigh'. Don't ask what is wrong after the 'loud sigh', as she will say 'Nothing'. The next time she'll let you be intimate with her will be 'One Day'.

5. Why Do Women Want To Know All The Little Details?

Josh was reading the newspaper one evening when the telephone rang. He answered it, listened for about ten minutes giving occasional grunts, said "Yeah – OK. See you..." then hung up and continued reading.

"Who was that?" his wife Debbie asked.

"Robert, my old school pal," he said.

"Robert? You haven't seen him since high school! How is he?"

"He's fine."

"So... what did he say?" she asked.

"Nothing much...he's going well... he's fine," Josh responded in that annoyed tone men have when trying to read the newspaper.

"That's all he had to say after 10 years? He's fine?" she demanded.

She then proceeded to cross-examine him like a lawyer, getting him to repeat the conversation over and over until she got the full details. From Josh's standpoint the conversation was over and didn't need any more discussion. But Debbie wanted to know every detail.

As far as Josh was concerned, the story was simple – Robert had left school at age 15 and worked as a male escort to support his deserted mother who'd had a nervous breakdown after discovering that her husband was transsexual and was going to run off with her brother. After she had committed suicide, Robert became a drug addict to help cope with the pain and later got a job as a sword swallower with the Moscow Circus. After losing his testicles in a freak accident, he joined the French Foreign Legion and later became missionary in Afghanistan but was arrested for teaching Christianity then freed after he agreed to be a slave for the Taliban. He escaped one night by floating undetected in the tank of a sewerage truck and is now back in town with his new wife, a former lesbian prostitute-turned-nun who wants him to move to Africa to set up a leper colony – which he plans to do now that he's been released from jail having had his murder charge over-turned. He and his seven adopted Brazilian children have now become vegetarians and Jehovah's Witnesses and he says he's never felt better... he's just fine.

For Josh it was all straightforward. The bottom line was that Robert was fine – Josh didn't see the point in regurgitating the whole story. But no, Debbie had to nag him about every little detail, didn't she...

This conversation highlights a basic brain difference between men and women. For men, the details are irrelevant.

A woman thinks when a man doesn't talk much it means he mustn't love her because, for her, words are used to bond. A man thinks a woman talks too much and is trying to interrogate him.

Women Are Programmed To Search For Details

As the nest defender of the human race, a woman would make sure she had a close circle of friends who would look after her if the men didn't return from hunting or fighting. Her group of friends was like her insurance policy. Her survival depended on her ability to bond with others in the group and this meant knowing every little detail about the condition of each group member and their families and being actively interested in them for group survival.

When a discussion takes place between a man and a woman after a social function, the woman will know what each member of her social group or family is doing, their dreams and goals for the year, the state of their health and condition of their relationships. Women also know where their friends are going on vacation and how well their children are doing at school. The men will know what new 'boy's toys' the other men have bought, will have thoroughly examined Bob's new red sports car, discussed where the good fishing spots are, decided how terrorism should be defeated and how England beat Germany in the football... oh yeah... the joke about the guy ship-wrecked with Elle Macpherson. But they know little about the personal lives of anyone at the function – the women tell them all about it on the way home.

It's not that women are trying to be nosy...well, yes it is... long-term survival is hardwired into their brains so they want to know how each person in their group is doing and how they can help.

Solution

If you are a man, understand that the need for a woman to know personal details and information is for the survival of relationships and is hardwired into her psyche. So when you talk with a woman, try giving her more details than you would normally consider giving. Put on your joggers, take her for a long walk and just let her talk. This way, you'll get plenty of exercise.

Remember, you don't have to concentrate or come up with any answers – no effort is required on your part. If you are a woman, understand that too many details drive men insane and bore them to death. In business meetings, cut to the chase, be precise and succinct. At home, tell a man when you want to talk, give him a time-frame and tell him he doesn't have to offer solutions, just listen. And don't keep asking, "Are you listening to me?" or "What's the last thing I said?"

Chapter 8

WOMEN'S SEX
APPEAL TEST

Which way do you make men run?

AFTER MARRIAGE

BEFORE MARRIAGE

How to attract a man.

Take The Test

When a man's eyes meet yours across a crowded room, what exactly will his response to you be? It's something that women have wondered about since Adam first bumped into Eve: when a man first notices you, what will be his first impressions? Most women would like to know how attractive they are to men, so we've created this test to show you just how well – or otherwise – you rate. The test is based solely on your physical shape, appearance and presentation. It's a guide to the impact you will or won't have on a man when he first sees you, and is based on the responses of the male brain to certain female shapes, ratios, colours, sizes, textures and body language signals. The impact of personality traits on attraction will be discussed later. This test is like a man is evaluating you in a photograph. The questions are not in a predictable sequence, so you can't cheat.

1. **Which of the following best describes your body?**

    a. Thin/straight
    b. Athletic/toned
    c. Heavy/pear

2. **On a first date, how would you dress to try and impress a man?**

    a. Wear trousers or a long skirt, but dress elegantly
    b. Go casual, not too dressy, with comfortable shoes
    c. Dress smartly, with a short skirt and high-heeled shoes to show off the legs

3. **If we looked in your wardrobe, what type of shoes would we mostly find?**

   a. High heels or strappy stilettos
   b. Trendy shoes with a medium heel
   c. Low heels or flat shoes, but stylish

4. **If you could buy any new outfit regardless of price, which of the following would you choose?**

   a. A long, flowing outfit that hides all problem areas
   b. A short, tight-fitting, low-cut outfit that shows off my assets
   c. A trouser suit, tailored and elegant

5. **Measure your waist and hips and calculate your hip-to-waist ratio. Divide your waist size by your hip size. For example, if your hips are 40 inches and your waist is 30 inches, then your ratio is 75%.**
   Your ratio is:

   a. Over 80%
   b. 65% to 80%
   c. Under 65%

6. **When you're chatting to an attractive man who makes you go weak at the knees, what position do you take?**

   a. Try and get him to sit down so he doesn't notice my body
   b. Stand close to him with my legs uncrossed
   c. Play with my hair, lick my lips, tilt my hips and caress my body to get his attention

7. **If you asked a stranger to describe your bum what would they say?**

   a. Wide load
   b. Flat, thin or athletic
   c. Rounded/peach-shaped

8. **If you run your hand over your stomach how does it feel?**

   a. Tight/muscular
   b. Smooth/flat
   c. Lumpy/round

9. **When dressing for a night out with the girls, how would you dress?**

   a. Wear loose clothes to give no hint of the body underneath
   b. Wear a push-up bra or show some cleavage
   c. Wear tailored, close-fitting clothes to show off body shape

10. **Describe your make-up:**

    a. All the latest fashion colours and styles
    b. I prefer the natural look
    c. My face is my palette, and I need a lot of make-up, whatever time of day, to look my best

11. **If Picasso were to paint you, how would you look?**

    a. Thin/angular/muscular
    b. Plenty of curves
    c. Round

12. **If you were asked to pose for *Vogue* magazine, what pose you would take?**

    a. Pull your hair up on top of your head and look back over your shoulder
    b. Arch your back, tilt your hips, place your hands on your hips and pout
    c. Push your bottom out and bend forward, blow a kiss to the camera

13. **How would someone describe your neck?**

    a. Long, thin or tapered
    b. Average length and thickness
    c. Short, thick and strong

14. **Asked to describe your face, your friends would say:**

    a. Elegant/strong features
    b. Babyish face/big eyes
    c. Plain but warm

15. **You're going to a candlelit dinner and want to look sexy. Which lipstick would you choose?**

    a. Neutral/natural-looking colour
    b. Bright red
    c. The latest fashion colour

16. **You are being dressed for the Oscars. You can wear any pair of earrings you want. You choose:**

    a. Diamond or pearl studs
    b. Mid-size earrings with any beautiful stone
    c. Long dangly earrings with lots of diamonds

17. How would a man describe your eyes?

a. Large/child-like
b. Almond-shaped
c. Smaller/narrow

18. Look at your nose in a mirror. How would a cartoonist draw it?

a. Larger
b. Small, button-like
c. Average

19. My hair is:

a. Long
b. Mid-length
c. Short

20. How would you describe your appearance ?

a. Casual
b. Sexy
c. Elegant

Your Score

Question 1	Question 2	Question 3
A=5 points	A=5	A=5
B=7 points	B=3	B=3
C=3 points	C=7	C=1

Question 4	Question 5	Question 6
A=1 point	A=5	A=1
B=5 points	B=9	B=3
C=3 points	C=7	C=5

Question 7	Question 8	Question 9
A=3 points	A=5	A=1
B=5 points	B=3	B=5
C=7 points	C=1	C=3

Question 10	Question 11	Question 12
A=3 points	A=5	A=3
B=5 points	B=7	B=5
C=1 point	C=3	C=1

Question 13	Question 14	Question 15
A=5 points	A=7	A=3
B=3 points	B=9	B=5
C=1 point	C=5	C=1

Question 16	Question 17	Question 18
A=1 point	A=9	A=5
B=3 points	B=7	B=9
C=5 points	C=5	C=7

Question 19	Question 20
A=5 points	A=1
B=3 points	B=5
C=1 point	C=3

Now total your scores up and see where you stand on sexuality.

100 points or more

The Sex Siren

When men see you, they're hooked, ready to be reeled in. Builders stop work and whistle at you. You really know how to walk the walk of sexuality and should never be short of a date. Men love to watch you and will approach you. You know how to sell yourself and use your body language to control men. The next chapter will show you why what you are doing gets a result and will give ways of improving your score. Take a sexuality bow.

66 to 99 points

Miss Elegance

The majority of women fall into this section. This means you have reasonable success at getting men to fall for you at first sight. Builders will notice you if they've stopped for lunch. If you are between 78 and 99 points, you only need to work on a few areas to knock them in the aisles. If you're in the 66 to 78 range, you should know that if you work harder on your physical appearance, you'll have even more dramatic results. The next chapter will show you what to do to make sure that men are attracted to you at first sight.

Up to 65 points

You're One Of The Boys

Builders tell you dirty jokes. You probably believe that personality is more important than appearance and you're right to some extent. But the problem is: how do you attract the right man in the first place in order to dazzle him with your wit and charm? You can improve the way you present yourself without having to compromise your beliefs. Joining a gym to improve your body shape, for instance, will increase your attractiveness to men, but will also make you feel much fitter and healthier and give you a greater zest for life. The male factor could just be an added extra! You can also camouflage your physical imperfections by dressing to enhance your good points. You may say you're not interested in a man who's so shallow as to be hypnotized by physical appearance. The problem with that, however, is that even the most intellectual and sensitive of men are at the mercy of their biology, at least at first. Men can't help being attracted to the obvious feminine signals. Why not work with this – however much you may dislike it – to improve your appearance, and end up with a greater range of men to choose from? The next chapter will show you how to improve your attractiveness and explains why so many men zoom in on women with IQs lower than their shoe size, and don't give you a second glance.

Chapter 9

WHAT MADE ROGER RABBIT'S EYES POP OUT

The Power of Female Sexual Attraction

"I'm not bad... I'm just drawn that way..."
Jessica Rabbit.

Case Study: Kim And Daniel's Story

Kim and Daniel had been dating for a year and decided to get married. They both loved their relationship and each thought the other was the perfect partner. Daniel loved the way Kim was always well groomed whenever they were together and her appearance was a constant reminder that he had made the right choice. She told him that she loved dressing for him and loved the adoring way he looked at her whenever she entered the room. Four years into their marriage, Kim changed. She didn't seem to care much about the way she looked at home or when they were out with friends. Kim felt she was a married woman now and didn't need to impress anyone any more and thought grooming was a waste of time, money and energy.

At home after work she would usually wear her pink chenille dressing gown and slippers, no make-up and her hair was rarely brushed. Daniel thought maybe she was just having a hard time at work and that soon she would start making an effort. It began to irritate him that she made the effort to be presentable at work, but at home, she'd look an absolute mess. Before long, however, she started to go out with their friends looking like a wreck, too. She stopped wearing make-up, never shaved her legs and wore outfits Daniel said made her look like her mother. Daniel began silently to simmer. This kind of behaviour said to him that he and his friends weren't important enough for her to put in any effort.

Men being visual creatures, Kim's appearance became a real turn-off and he began to avoid approaching her for sex. For the first time in their marriage, cracks were starting to appear and Daniel began noticing other women. At his office, many of the women wore tailored outfits and most were perfectly groomed and made up. They would flirt with him, which built his own self-esteem, and also highlighted the contrast with the way Kim looked when he came home.

He decided to approach the situation head on and told Kim how he felt. At first, Kim was angry and couldn't understand why he couldn't love her the way she was. Obviously, she thought, he was much more shallow than she'd ever realised. Daniel could not articulate why he felt this way and felt guilty for having even mentioned it.

Six months later, Daniel left Kim and now lives with Jade from his office. Kim mixes with a new social group of women who think all men are bastards.

Like it or not, the way we physically look affects our ability to attract, and keep, a partner. People we meet form up to 90% of their opinion about us within the first four minutes, and our physical desirability is assessed in less than ten seconds. In this chapter, we will examine the ingredients that cause men and women to look desirable and be drawn to each other. This is not to say that because you don't look like Cameron Diaz or Brad Pitt, you can't do well with the opposite sex. But by understanding how the process of attraction works, and then employing some simple strategies to use it to your advantage, you can easily become more alluring. Those ancient biological gender signals we'll now explain operate on an subconscious level, and we just cannot help responding to them. This is a principal strand of evolutionary psychology, which says that, in each of our brains, there are residual behaviour patterns and responses formed by the pressures of our ancestors' lives. Evolutionary biology takes a direct, sometimes quite unappealing, approach to sexual attraction.

So, which has the most potent power – beauty and physical attraction, or personality and intelligence? In this chapter we'll examine both. To do this effectively, we've put aside the theory of romantic love, political correctness and personal niceties in order to be as objective as possible.

The Theory Of Beauty

There's a reason why flowers are pretty. Flowers are colourful in order to be attractive in the green sea of a forest. Flowers communicate information about themselves to animals and insects, telling them where there is a source of food and about their condition.

Humans also find flowers beautiful. This response evolved to enable us to evaluate the necessary information about the plant and flower for our own survival. We needed to know if a fruit was green, ripe, sour, poisonous or dangerous. And exactly the same process applies to human beauty.

Every person gives off certain signals, both tangible and imperceptible, that may make them desirable to a potential mate. They are coded messages transmitted and then received back, which tell another person how suitable they might be for our purposes. For a man, attraction occurs on a biological level, when a woman displays attributes that may allow him to successfully pass his genes on to the next generation. For a woman, an attractive man is one who, on a biological level, can provide food and safety for her during the process of child rearing, which explains why women are generally attracted to older men.

Women like older men because they have more experience and greater access to resources.

For both sexes, responses to these primeval attraction signals are hardwired into the brain. Beauty and sexual attraction are both essentially the same thing, with the word 'beautiful' originally meaning 'sexually stimulating'. Our evolution shaped our brains so that good looks were a sign of being healthy and relatively disease free, and the biological purpose of beauty is to attract for purposes of reproduction.

To tell a person they are beautiful or attractive is to say, in the basic biological subtext, that you want to have sex with them.

What Science Shows

Research (Eagly, Ashmore, Makhij and Longo) has shown how we automatically assign positive traits like honesty, intelligence, kindness and talent to good-looking people and we make these judgements without being aware of it. Toronto University analysed the results of the 1976 Canadian federal elections and found that attractive candidates received two and a half times the votes given to unattractive candidates (Efran and Patterson). Follow-up research with voters found 73% of voters strongly denied that a candidate's appearance could have influenced their choice and only one in eight voters was prepared to even consider that a candidate's appearance could have affected their vote. This means they made their votes on a subconscious level without even knowing it.

Attractive people get better jobs, higher pay, are more believed and are allowed to break rules more often than their less attractive counterparts. Bill Clinton proved it.

It may be politically correct to deny the impact of attractiveness on our decision making but, whether we like it or not, evidence continues to confirm it as true and that our brains are hardwired to react to another's physical appearance. The good news is that you have control over many of the factors about how you look and can alter things if you want. You can choose to make yourself attractive.

Women's Bodies – What Turns Men On Most

The preferred 'look' in the nineteenth century for women in the Western world was a pale complexion, slight rouge on the cheeks and an overall air of feminine delicacy and fragility. The 'look' for today emphasizes youth and health, and beauty contests were created purely to encourage an image of desirability that reflects a woman's health.

Brain researchers at Massachusetts General Hospital showed photos of 'beautiful' women to heterosexual men and found that these images switched on the same parts of the brain that are activated by cocaine and money.

In the next two chapters you will learn the results of 23 major studies and experiments showing what men and women find attractive in each other's bodies. Based on these results, we have given each body part an attractiveness priority rating, and will explain why that particular body part makes its impact.

Almost every study into attraction in the last 60 years reaches the same conclusions as the painters, poets and writers over the past 6,000 years – a woman's appearance and body and what she can do with it is more attractive to men than her intelligence or assets, even in the politically correct twenty-first century. The twenty-first-century man wants the same immediate things in a woman as his forefathers but, as you will see, a man's criteria for a long-term partner aren't the same thing.

A wife is sought for her virtue,
a concubine for her beauty.
CHINESE PROVERB

What makes a man attractive to a woman, however, is dramatically different and we'll cover this later. It's important to understand that a woman's body has evolved as a permanent, portable sexual signalling system, which is purpose-built to attract male attention.

> *Men prefer looks to brains because most*
> *men can see better than they can think.*
> GERMAINE GREER

Bear in mind we are first analysing only the physical characteristics and geography of the body as if we were evaluating a potential partner in a photograph. These are the things that draw you to someone before you hear them speak or know who they are, and at the end of this chapter we will discuss the non-physical factors relating to how we choose our partners. We will first analyse body language signals below the neck and then we'll group all facial cues together toward the end of the chapter. Male turn-ons numbers two, seven, eight and nine will be discussed at that time.

Men's Turn-ons In Priority Order:

1. Athletic Body Shape
2. Sensual Mouth
3. Full Breasts
4. Long Legs
5. Rounded Hips/Small Waist
6. Hemispherical Buttocks
7. Attractive eyes
8. Long Hair
9. Small Nose
10. Flat Belly
11. Arched Back
12. Arched Vulva
13. Long Neck

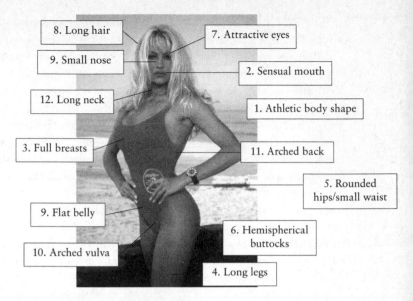

Labels on image:
- 8. Long hair
- 7. Attractive eyes
- 9. Small nose
- 2. Sensual mouth
- 12. Long neck
- 1. Athletic body shape
- 3. Full breasts
- 11. Arched back
- 5. Rounded hips/small waist
- 9. Flat belly
- 6. Hemispherical buttocks
- 10. Arched vulva
- 4. Long legs

Turn-on 1: Athletic Body Shape

Top of the attraction list for men is a woman with an athletic-looking body. A strong, fit body is a sign of health and signals a woman's ability to successfully bear his children, flee from danger and defend offspring if necessary. Most men prefer a heavier woman to a leaner one because additional fat is an aid to successful breast-feeding. Few women know that one of the world's greatest sex symbols, Marilyn Monroe, was a size 16 and had very beefy legs. As far as men are concerned, no undernourished waif could ever become a real sex symbol.

Turn-on 3: Full Breasts

The breasts of the woman at her sexual and reproductive peak – in her late teens and early twenties – are men's favourites. These are typical of the breasts seen in men's magazine centrefolds, on erotic dancers and in advertisements that trade on sex appeal.

The bulk of a breast is fat tissue that gives it the rounded shape and is not involved in milk production. Women without children have pink nipples, mothers have darker brownish nipples and monkey females don't have any breasts at all. Primate breasts rise and fall dramatically with pregnancy but human female breasts tend to be permanently enlarged and only change a little during pregnancy. Most of the time they serve one clear purpose – sexual signalling. When humans walked on all fours, it was round, fleshy buttocks that played the main role in attracting males, who mounted their mates from the rear. Ever since humans began to walk upright on two legs, however, breasts have become larger in order to attract a male who was approaching from the front.

Low-cut dresses and push-up bras emphasize this signal by creating cleavage, which mimics the rear view of a woman's buttocks. Some women are horrified when they first hear about the significance of the cleavage, while others use it to optimal advantage.

Take the breast test

Few men can tell the difference between a close-up photograph of a cleavage and of a bum.

Which are breasts and
which are buttocks?
Can you tell the difference?

Zoologist Desmond Morris discovered that one in two hundred women have more than two breasts, a hangover from the days when humans, like many other primates, had bigger litters of offspring and needed greater feeding facilities. A third breast can even be seen on the statue of Venus de Milo, above her right breast near the armpit.

*Why do men have difficulty making
eye contact? Breasts don't have eyes.*

The nipple is surrounded by a pink/brown patch called the areola and contains small glands, which emit a scent during sexual activity that impacts on the male brain. This would explain why a man loves to spend so much time with his head buried in a woman's breasts.

All research surveys show men love breasts in most shapes and sizes. It doesn't matter whether they are the size of a small lemon or look like watermelons – most men are keenly interested in them all and love cleavage.

Turn-on 4: Long Legs

The sight of a woman who has legs seemingly up to her armpits always creates a lasting impression on men. The principle behind a woman's legs as a sexual signal is simple. The more leg a man can see, and the longer her legs are, the sexier she looks to him because it draws attention to the area where her left and right legs meet. Conversely, if a woman's sexual organs lay under her armpit, her legs would hardly attract a second glance. Instead, he'd notice what beautiful biceps and triceps she had! As it is, you never hear a man tell a woman she has beautiful long arms. Babies are born with legs that are short relative to body size and the leg/body length ratio does not alter much in young children. When a girl reaches puberty, however, her legs undergo rapid lengthening as hormones flood her body and change her into a woman. Her extra-long legs become a powerful non-verbal signal telling males she is sexually maturing and is now capable of childbearing. This is why long legs have always been associated with potent sexuality.

For a woman, it's a ladder in her stocking.
For a man, it's a stairway to heaven.

Finalists in the Miss World and Miss Universe contests have longer legs than the average woman, Barbie dolls have artificially lengthened legs, and stocking manufacturers can increase their sales by displaying them in photographs, or on shop dummies of women with much longer legs than nature ever bestowed. The mothers of teenage girls often complain their daughters wear skirts that are too short, but this impression is often created by the girl's disproportionately long legs. By age 20, her overall body growth has caught up, making her legs appear up to 10% shorter than they were at puberty.

Most women unconsciously understand the dynamics behind extra-long legs and quickly learn as teenagers how this works, often wearing high-heeled shoes to make their legs look longer, and short dresses, even in cold weather. They ignore the discomfort of heels that can, in the long-term, cause spinal damage, or the risks of pneumonia, merely to look attractive to men. Men love high heels on a woman because it gives back her teenage, highly fertile-looking legs. They enhance a woman's sexual shape by lengthening her legs, arching her back, forcing her buttocks to protrude, making her feet appear smaller, and thrusting her pelvis forward. This is why the shoe with the highest heel, and the stiletto with bondage straps, is by far the most efficient sex aid on the market.

Most men also prefer women with rounded, thicker legs over those with thinner, muscular legs, because additional fat highlights the sex difference between male and female legs, and is an indicator of better lactation. He likes her legs to look athletic but is turned off if she looks like she could play for England in the World Cup.

Studies have revealed the shortness of a woman's dress and the height of her heels varies with her menstrual cycle. She will unconsciously select more revealing dresses and higher heels when she is ovulating. Maybe that's a good lesson for parents: lock up your daughters between the fourteenth and eighteenth day after their period!

Turn-on 5: Rounded Hips/Small Waist

For centuries, women have put up with corsets and all manner of waist-shrinking contraptions to achieve the perfect hourglass figure. At times, they even suffered deformed ribcages, restricted breathing, compressed organs, miscarriages and had ribs surgically removed in the quest for irresistible femininity. During the nineteenth century, a woman would wear a bustle to highlight the size of her hips and buttocks to signal her potential to successfully give birth. A corset would further

Preparing for a girls' night out in 1890.

emphasize her hips and reduce and flatten her stomach to show she was not pregnant and, therefore, available. During the nineteenth century, the ideal waist size for a girl was when her age matched her waist in inches.

I decided to get into shape.
The shape I chose was round.
ROSEANNE

A woman in excellent health and most capable of successfully bearing children has a hip-to-waist ratio of 70%, that is, her waist is 70% the size of her hips. Throughout recorded history this is the ratio that has proved the most dramatic male attention-grabber. Men begin to lose interest when the ratio exceeds 80% and, for most men, the greater the ratio – either up or down – the less attentive he will be. Women whose ratios exceed 100% attract little interest as this kind of ratio shows fat distribution around the womb and ovaries and is a non-verbal indicator of lower fertility. Mother Nature deposits excess fat away from the vital organs and that is why there is no fat around the heart, brain or testicles. Women who have a hysterectomy often accumulate fat deposits around the belly like men because they no longer have reproductive organs.

Professor Devendra Singh, an evolutionary psychologist at the University of Texas, studied the physical attractiveness of Miss America beauty contestants and *Playboy* centrefolds over a period of 50 years. He found that the weight of the ideal sex symbol had gone down an average of 13 pounds during that period but the hips-to-waist ratio of around 70% had not changed. He found that the ratio that holds the greatest sex appeal for men is between 67% and 80%.

Tight corseting and hip pads are still used by women in some countries but simply standing in the Hip-Tilt position is more than enough to emphasize a 70% hips-to-waist ratio and attract male attention.

> *A beautiful woman is wheeled, on a trolley, into the*
> *anaesthetist's room of a local hospital before she under-*
> *goes surgery. When the nurse leaves her, she lies waiting*
> *under a sheet that barely manages to conceal her curva-*
> *ceous figure. A young man in a white coat approaches*
> *the woman, pulls up the sheet and starts examining her*
> *perfect, hour-glass shape. He then fetches another man*
> *in a white coat. That man comes over, pulls aside the*
> *sheet and looks closely at her naked body. When a third*
> *man starts to do the same, she grows restless. "I'm glad*
> *you're seeking a second and third opinion to be*
> *absolutely sure," she says, "but when will I have my*
> *operation?" The first man shakes his head. "No idea,"*
> *he says, "but we'll be finished painting this room soon."*

Professor Singh conducted a test using images of women who were underweight, overweight and of average weight and showed them to groups of men who were asked to rate them in terms of their attractiveness. Women of average weight with the ratio of around 70% were found to be the most alluring. In the overweight and underweight groups, the women with the narrowest waist got the vote. The experiment's remarkable finding was that men gave the 70% hip-to-waist ratio the highest rating even when the woman's weight was quite heavy. This explains the enduring popularity of the hourglass figure, and why Coca-Cola replicated it in their bottle shape to appeal to wartime soldiers. The nineteenth-century artist Auguste Renoir was famous for painting chubby women who looked like prime Weight Watchers candidates, but a closer examination reveals most of them had the key hips-to-waist ratio.

Turn-on 6: Hemispherical Buttocks

Men find rounded, peach-shaped buttocks most attractive. Women's buttocks store large amounts of fat for use in breast-feeding and as an emergency food storage in lean times, similar to a camel's hump. Stone Age sculptures and paintings abound with images of women with huge protruding rears, a condition known as steatopygia, which is still seen in some southern African tribes. Protruding rears is an ancient signal of female sexuality that was so honoured in Greece that a temple was built to Aphrodite Kallipygos, 'the goddess with the beautiful buttocks'.

The nineteenth century was a time when women were expected to keep their entire bodies covered in public. Young women wanting to capture male attention could recreate the appearance of a large rear with the wearing of a bustle. When excess fat became unfashionable toward the end of the twentieth century, because of its connection with overindulgence and poorer health, young women began to have 'bum-tucks' and liposuction to reduce buttock size. Wearing designer jeans has also become popular as they highlight the buttocks and give them a firm, rounded look. High-heeled shoes make the wearer arch her back, push out her buttocks, and make her wiggle when she walks which invariably draws male attention. Marilyn Monroe reputedly chopped two centimetres off the heel of her left shoe to emphasize her wiggle.

A nineteenth-century woman wearing a bustle, and an African beauty with the real thing. Modern women find it hard to believe that a large protruding rear has always been an attractive attribute – and still is in some African countries.

Turn-on 10: Flat Belly

Women have more rounded bellies than men, and a flat, smooth belly sends out a clear signal that they're not pregnant, and therefore available to male suitors. This is why gymnasiums and yoga classes everywhere are packed with women doing abdominal exercises, trying to achieve that perfect ironing-board stomach.

Belly-dancing classes abound but few participants have any idea of its erotic history.

Belly-dancing has recently made a popular reappearance as a form of exercise, although few women have any idea of its origins. It was originally performed by harem girls for their masters and was used by the dancer to bring the master to orgasm by sitting on him and performing a series of muscular gyrations and thrusts. Hawaiian and Tahitian pelvic dancing has similar origins and these dances survive today under the genteel guise of 'traditional folk dancing'.

Turn-ons 11 & 12: Arched Back and Vulva

Curves and arches indicate femininity and fertility, while geometric and angular shapes shout masculinity. Men the world over, therefore, love curvy women. A woman's upper back is narrower than a man's, her lower back is wider and her lower spine is more arched than his. Extra arching in the back

makes the buttocks protrude and thrusts the breasts forward. Ask any woman to assume a sexy standing posture and her first position will usually be an exaggerated back-arch and hip-tilt with one or both arms placed on her hips to take up more space and so be more likely to attract attention. If you're sceptical about this, ask any woman to stand and do her best to act sexy. Go on – try it right now.

Turn-on 13: Long Neck

Male necks evolved as shorter, thicker and stronger structures than female necks to protect against being snapped during hunting or battle. This left the longer, thinner, tapered female neck as a powerful signal of gender difference, which men kiss and love to see adorned with jewels, and cartoonists exaggerate to highlight femininity. It's also the part of the body where 'necking' takes place between lovers.

In several Southern and East African tribes, like the Ndebele, Zulu, Xhosa and Masai, young girls wear silver rings around their necks, adding and adjusting the rings as they grow into womanhood. The rings elongate the neck, which, in those cultures, is a sign of great beauty. The neck rings weigh down the head and deform the collarbone so the neck can be diverted downward to an angle of 45 degrees. If the wire necklaces were removed, the elongated neck would not be able to support the head and the neck would break.

Both Nefertiti and Olive Oyl were adored for their elongated necks and, even today, catwalk models have longer necks than the average woman.

Happiness, to this woman from the Karen tribe in Burma, is knowing you look your best.

How The Face Attracts Attention

Our magnetism to attractive human faces seems to be built into our psychology and does not depend upon our cultural origins. Preferred features in females are small faces with short chins, delicate jaws, high cheekbones, full lips, and eyes that are large in proportion to the length of the face. Overall, we love a wide smile and a vulnerable air. Generally, races the world over prefer faces which are most suggestive of being suitably fit for healthy reproduction. And for a woman's face to be universally classified as 'pretty' the formula is clear – it must be childlike.

The most attractive women are those with baby faces.

These signals trigger massive paternal reactions in the brains of men and confer a powerful desire to touch, embrace and protect. In women, it is the maternal reaction that makes them impulsively buy soft toy animals that use these 'baby releaser' responses.

A baby's face has the same built-in signals that are used to sell stuffed toy animals at inflated prices to customers, especially women.

Research shows the most appealing face to men is that of a girl aged twelve to fourteen, as this combines the vulnerability of youth with the pubescent appearance of sexual maturity. For women, this can cause enormous anxiety about ageing. Consider how many women now make use of cosmetic surgery to try to cling on to, and later regain, their youthful appearance. Cosmetic surgeons even sometimes use templates of baby face shapes in their work on women.

Turn-on 2: Sensual Mouth

Humans are the only primates with lips that sit on the outside of the face instead of inside the mouth. Zoologists believe a woman's lips evolved as a mirror of her genitals because they are the same size and thickness and, in an aroused sexual state, both expand as they fill with blood. This is known as 'genital echo', a reaction that transmits a powerful signal to male observers and that first evolved when we began to walk upright. Lipstick was invented in the first beauty parlours 6,000 years ago, being used by the Egyptians as a permanent display of a genital echo. And it only ever came in one colour – red. This is why men like their women to wear lipstick and eye make-up as both artificially send off the signal that she is interested in him or turned on by him. Wearing bright red lipstick is one of the most sexual signals a woman can use, and is always the colour of choice for any woman posing as a sex symbol.

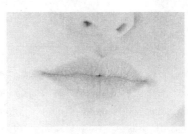

> *A woman's face is a canvas upon which,*
> *daily, she paints a portrait of her former self.*
> PICASSO

A state of arousal or remarks about a woman's sexuality can cause a flushing in the capillaries of her cheeks known as blushing and rouge effectively recreates this effect. Face powder gives the skin a smoother, flawless appearance, which imitates youth, good health and good genes.

For thousands of years, the length of a woman's earlobes has been taken as an indicator of her sensuality, a connection that still exists in parts of Africa and in Borneo, with the Kelabit and Kenyah tribes. Modern women make the same impact by wearing long dangling earrings. Our computer image tests show the longer a woman's earrings dangle, the higher male respondents rate her sensuality.

The Kelabit women of Borneo have stretched earlobes and are considered attractive, but other women achieve the same effect with long earrings.

Feminists may say these are all very good reasons never to wear cosmetics or earrings, but it is important for a woman in a relationship to understand the effect these signals have on men and exploit them for romantic encounters. By the same token, a woman who wants to be taken seriously in a business setting should wear less eye make-up and more subtle lipstick. Too much of either has the potential to turn male clients on in the wrong way and can cause rivalry in female clients.

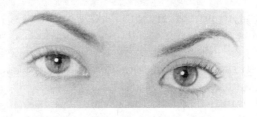

Turn-on 7: Attractive Eyes

In almost every country, large eyes are considered attractive. Make-up achieves the effect of enlarging the eye and recreating an infantile look. If eyes look larger relative to the lower face, they will inspire protective feelings in men. When a woman finds a man attractive, her pupils dilate, and mascara, eye shadow and eyeliner all artificially create a permanent state of looking interested. Contact lenses give the illusion a woman's eyes are glistening and have dilated pupils which explains why, as we reported in *Body Language* (HarperCollins), photographic experiments show a man finds a woman 'strangely attractive' when she wears contact lenses. Overall, men show a slight preference for women with lighter ,coloured eyes, with infantile blue eyes topping the list for Caucasian men.

Modern women started to use cosmetics in the 1920s as they began entering the workforce in larger numbers. Since then, the female cosmetics and toiletry industry has become worth, globally, more than US$50 trillion a year – and all with the purpose of creating the illusion of facial sexual signals. Female celebrities who are photographed without their make-up are routinely paraded triumphantly on the covers of women's magazines to make other women feel better about themselves. Sadly, however, we have become so unused to seeing bare faces that some women believe they are ugly without make-up, and use it as a mask to hide behind rather than a simple aid to making their faces even more enticing and mysterious. Men are more attracted to a woman who wears natural looking make-up than one who looks as if she applied it with a brick-layer's trowel.

Turn-on 9: Small Nose

A small nose is also reminiscent of childhood and brings out protective, parental feelings in men. Cartoonists exploit this to great effect by creating cartoon characters with large eyes and tiny button noses to win the hearts of their audiences.

Bambi, Barbie and Minnie Mouse all had small noses.

You'll never see a female model with a big nose. Plastic surgeons usually alter noses to form an angle of 35–40 degrees to the face, giving it that childlike appearance. Male actors are also now paying out for nose reduction operations in line with the new androgynous image of the twenty-first-century male.

Turn-on 8: Long Hair

If a person's hair was never cut, it would grow to 110 centimetres. The lifespan of a single hair is six years, we lose 80–100 hairs a day and, unlike other animals, we don't moult. Blondes have 140,000 hairs, brunettes 110,000 and redheads 90,000. Blondes have the edge in other ways too. Women with blonde hair have higher oestrogen levels than brunettes, something that men seem to pick up on. They decode them as being more fertile, which immediately attracts them – the *real* reason that blondes have more fun? Blonde hair is also a strong visual cue to a woman's youth as it darkens after childbirth, and genuine blondes also have blonde pubic hair.

Real blondes are like a good shirt –
the collar should always match the cuffs

For thousands of years, long hair has been a badge of femininity. While there are no detectable anatomical differences between male and female hair, we have been wearing it differently since Saint Paul the Apostle declared in a speech to the Corinthians that men should wear short hair as glory to God while women would wear long hair as glory to man. Today, 2,000 years later and in an age largely marked by equality between the sexes, this custom is  still generally in place everywhere. Fashion may come and go but overall, men still wear it short; women wear it long.

We conducted a poll of 5,214 British males asking whether long or short hair was more sexually attractive on women. The results were predictable: 74% found women with long hair more sexually attractive; 12% voted for women with short hair; and the rest had no preference. In ancient times, long, shiny hair indicated a healthy, well-nourished body and told the health history of its owner and her potential fitness to produce offspring. Long hair was seen as giving a woman a sensual allure while short hair was seen as giving her a more serious approach to life. The lessons to be learnt from this are clear – a woman should wear long hair when she wants to attract men, and wear it short or keep it up for business meetings. In serious business, a sensual appearance can be a liability to a woman in a position of power, or in a male-dominated industry. For instance, Pamela Anderson and Anna Kournikova, while two of the most popular women on the planet, will never make President!

The Connection Between Attractiveness And Pornography

Looking at pornography is almost entirely a male activity, with 99% of pornographic websites on the Internet aimed at men, and most images of naked men are aimed at gay men. Women need to understand that men are searching the Internet for the shapes and curves that appeal to the male brain. When a man looks at a pornographic image of a woman he never wonders if she can cook, play the piano or strives for world peace. He is attracted solely to curves and shapes and the hint of any imagined possibility she could carry his genes. It never occurs to him to wonder whether she might have a nice personality.

Past generations of men also liked to feast their eyes on erotic pictures of women, then via paintings. Artists who sculpted, sketched or painted images of naked women were almost entirely men.

Men love the Renaissance period of art – and it has nothing to do with all those statues of naked women. Honest.

Many women insist that modern men who wax lyrical about the artistic value of Old Masters' paintings of naked women are simply there for the porno value. Remember, Jessica Rabbit was only a pencil drawing – lines on paper – but the effect of the shapes caused millions of otherwise intelligent men to drool. For men, it's all about shapes.

Hentai Cartoons

Big money is being made from using all the information above about female attraction signals to create what are called Hentai cartoons, which originated in Japan. These are hard-core pornographic images presented in a cartoon-strip or comic-book form and all contain the female body-language signals we have discussed. The eyes of the females depicted are always dilated and are two to three times the size of the mouth, the nose is tiny, the lower face small and the hair is long, often in a ponytail tied back with ribbons.

A typical Hentai cartoon is packed with all the signals that appeal to the male brain, including childlike facial features, long neck, 70% hips-to-waist ratio, pubescent breasts and flat belly. In this cartoon, the legs are elongated to an impossible 63% of overall body height.

These cartoons portray a fully mature female body with the face of a ten to twelve-year-old, and have an estimated audience of over 30 million men.

How A Woman's Clothing Impacts On Men

In discussing the impact of a woman's appearance, it's important to understand the history behind dressing. For centuries, the purpose of a woman's dress has been to catch the eye of a potential suitor by emphasizing her feminine attributes.

Before the Women's Movement began in the 1960s, women dressed for the reason they always had: to attract men and to outdo other women. Feminism told women that dressing to appeal to men was no longer important – her internal beauty now counted more than her appearance, an idea that appealed to millions of women everywhere. They believed they could now be free of the oppressive obligation of always having to look good for men.

Styles like punk and grunge appeared as a form of defiance to the male-attracting dress and to show the world that men and women could now be equal in the way they looked. This anti-attractiveness dress code evolved to the point where, by the 1990s, fashion models began to have unfeminine, emaciated-looking bodies, wore black lipstick and even sported dark rings under their eyes as though they were on drugs. Such a look had very little appeal to men. Heterosexual men rarely watch fashion shows but, when a Miss Universe competition is held, over 70% of those who watch are men who want to look at women displaying signals that stimulate ancient reactions in the brain.

The only fashion shows many men will actively enjoy are swimsuit parades.

Modern women have two basic types of dress code: business dress and non-business dress. Business clothing can give her an equal footing to compete with males and other females in the business 'hunting' stakes and, secondly, enables her to outdo other women by displaying the success, power, importance and desirability of the wearer.

The key to successful business dress is simple. How does the person you want to influence expect you to look? What, in their opinion, should your cosmetics, jewellery, hairstyle and clothing look like to ensure you will be perceived as credible, trustworthy and reliable in business? If you are in an industry where you need to sell your technical or management expertise to men, most of the attraction signals we have discussed would be inappropriate. If however, you are in the business of selling a feminine image such as hairdressing, cosmetics or fashion clothing, many of the signals we've discussed can be used to great effect.

Cosmetic Surgery

An increasing number of people are today choosing cosmetic enhancement (enhancement sounds better than surgery) to improve their appearance. In America alone, over one million people opt to go under the knife every year. The main reason people elect to have such procedures performed is to boost their confidence and self-image by improving the way they can emit the kind of signals we've discussed here. Celebrities are the most frequent patients.

Michael Douglas had his eyes tightened, Pamela Anderson had her breasts enhanced. Michael Jackson and Cher had everything done – and both, as a consequence, should be sure to stay out of the sun and away from hot radiators! It may be that the world's sexiest woman is hiding under a burqa somewhere in Afghanistan, but we'll never know because, according to what we see and hear, being sexy goes with designer clothes, nutritionists, make-up artists, body coaches, choreographers, clever photography and plastic surgery.

Michael Jackson still says he didn't alter his appearance.

Cosmetic enhancement is not new. Centuries before liposuction and breast implants there were padded stockings for the man whose calves were too skinny, a 16-inch iron corset for the lady who wasn't skinny enough, and bustles to give a woman wider hips and rear. Even King Henry VIII wore a codpiece – which literally translated means 'scrotum bag' – to enhance his small, syphillis-ridden manhood. He wore it to compete with the codpiece-wearing French royalty, but his was studded with jewels and emblems.

Like Henry VIII, Don Carlos of Spain wore a codpiece so big it entered the room before he did.

In a typical week, an average person is exposed to over 500 images of 'perfect' human beings in magazines, in newspapers, on billboards and on television. Most of these images are the result of technology, like airbrushing, enhanced make-up, computer artwork and special lighting effects, and rarely do they show a real person.

If you have acne scars, a birthmark or feature you really don't like, you may want to consider cosmetic correction and most people who have these surgeries report they are happy with the result.

Do not read women's magazines,
they will only make you feel ugly.

The most common cosmetic operation in Japan is having the eyes widened to look like Caucasians. Japanese people have three eyelids against a Caucasian's two, and the surgery removes the third eyelid and opens the eye.

It is important, however, for everyone to understand that cosmetic surgery won't make you a better person, make you more loved or even take away your problems in life. Correspondingly, anyone who judges you by your appearance has a low self-image problem themselves, and is not the kind of person you want to be associated with.

The Other Side Of Attraction

Why Men Don't Listen and Women Can't Read Maps documents the results from 15,000 men and women who were asked what they looked for in a partner.

Here are the lists:

What men look for

A. On first sight
1. Good looks
2. Shapely body
3. Breasts
4. Bum

B. In a long-term partner
1. Personality
2. Good looks
3. Brains
4. Humour

List A shows what we already understand – men are visual beings and like to look at attractive women. Most women understand this, and scientific research proves it again and again even though it may not be 'politically correct' to acknowledge it. Most feminists abhor the thought of a woman being judged on her physical appearance and describe men as superficial and shallow. But that doesn't change the fact that men have an overwhelmingly visual response to women on their first approach. The items on list A are certainly visual and if you are into one-night stands, will certainly do the trick. But not so on list B, where 'good looks' is the only visual item men looked for in a long-term partner.

> *Sexual attractiveness is 50% of what you've got and 50% of what others think you've got.*
> ZSA ZSA GABOR

This survey reveals two things. Firstly, men focus on visual images on their first meeting with a woman, and her overall presentation is more important than whether she has a good body. This means that the way a woman dresses, her make-up, presentation and grooming scores her more points than if she is carrying a few extra kilos, has a few pimples or small breasts. Secondly, in a long-term partner, a man is more interested in a woman's overall personality, intelligence and sense of humour than her body but 'good looks' is still high on his list. The good news is that you largely have control over most of your appearance and you can change things to suit yourself.

> *As a woman, having a sense of humour doesn't mean you tell jokes. It means you laugh at his jokes.*

Because visual cues are so important to a man, he unconsciously uses what a woman does or doesn't do with her appearance as a measure of her respect and feelings for him. He thinks if she spends time on her appearance it means she wants him to be attracted to her. One of the biggest complaints made by men in divorce proceedings is that after they were married their wives let their entire appearance go down the drain. They feel that she used her appearance to attract them and then felt it was no longer necessary after marriage. Most men are disillusioned by a woman who only dresses for her work colleagues. A woman however, finds it difficult to comprehend how a man can think this way because she will love him no matter how he looks.

Solution

Your appearance affects how others will respond to you and treat you. It also affects your own self-image and behaviour. Your grandmother may have said, "People should never judge a book by its cover" but the reality is: they do. Most of the elements of your appearance are, to a greater or lesser extent, within your control. Most colleges have courses in grooming and deportment that teach you how to walk, sit, talk, dress, apply make-up and so on. The bookstores are full of publications on how to do the same. Large department stores often offer a free make-up service to teach customers how to choose and apply cosmetics, and clothing stores will happily show you how to select and wear clothing. A good hairdresser can be sought to recommend how best to wear your hair, your dentist can correct your teeth and lingerie parties will show you how to best display your physical assets.

Your weight is completely under your control too, so see a nutritionist to teach you good eating habits and join a health club to get into the shape you want. If you think it's absolutely necessary, shout yourself a nose job or enhance your breasts for your birthday. In the twenty-first century there is no longer any legitimate reason not to look the way you want.

> *"Will you still love me when I become*
> *old and grey?" she asked.*
> *"Not only will I love you," he said, "I'll write to you."*

We are not suggesting that a woman should become as obsessed with her appearance as many women do, but it is important to put some effort into how she looks and to make the most of what she has. As Helena Rubinstein said, there are no ugly women, only lazy ones.

> *There are no ugly women, only lazy ones.*
> HELENA RUBINSTEIN

Most importantly, you can make yourself more attractive by learning new skills and knowing more about life. Everyone is attracted to the person who can converse on a wide range of interesting topics.

When you look at all current Top 40 pop songs on any list in the world you'll discover that the records which are most popular and sell the most are usually not written and sung by the world's best musicians. They are the products of people who worked out what the customer wanted, wrote lyrics and music to a proven formula and then went out and sold it like crazy. The world's best musicians are unknowns sitting at home waiting to be discovered. Being popular and attractive works exactly the same way.

Men may rave about pert breasts and women about iron biceps but research shows that, ultimately, long-term relationships have more to do with mind than matter. The key ingredient is the inner glow that comes from confidence – sexual, emotional and professional. In other words, become a really interesting person and they won't notice your physical shortcomings.

Summary

It's a fact that a woman's appearance can attract or repel a man at any time during their relationship. Many women become infuriated about this. They believe it's unjust that if a man has grey hair or wrinkles he is seen as distinguished and wise, while she is seen as simply being old. But that's a fact of life. It's also a fact that sometimes there is bad weather with thunder and rain, yet there's absolutely no point getting upset about it, calling it unfair, saying it's unjust or holding a rally. The weather is the weather – it doesn't matter what you think about it. When you accept that, you can prepare for it by having an umbrella, coat, hat, gloves or sun lotion. That way, you can go out in the weather, enjoy it and have a good time. There is no point in staying indoors and complaining about what you can't change. And so it is with the way men think. Don't fight them, manage them.

If you're unhappy with any aspect of the way you look, change it.

Chapter 10

MEN'S SEX APPEAL TEST

Do women see you as a stud or a slug?

What happens to men who
drink milk instead of beer.

How do you rate with women in the attraction stakes? Do women find you compulsive – or repulsive? Compelling or repellent? Take this test now to find out exactly how you rate with women. In the next chapter you'll discover the secrets about what women really look for in a man. This test is based on the physical and non-physical points you score each time a woman meets you and will tell you how well you fare. Once you've done this test, ask a few of your female friends to rate you on the questions, and discover how your results compare.

Take The Test

1. You are appearing on the TV programme *Blind Date* and the female contestant asks you to describe your body type. How would you answer?

    a. V-shape
    b. Rectangular
    c. Round

2. I believe a man should be:

    a. 100% monogamous
    b. Committed, but occasional flings can enhance a
       permanent relationship
    c. Commitment-free – open relationships will be the way
       of the future

3. If you asked women to describe your bum, they'd say:

a. Wide load
b. Small and tight
c. Thin or flat

4. How much hair do you have?

a. About half (eg. receding hairline)
b. Most of it
c. Bald or shaved

5. You ask several women to describe your mouth. What's their answer?

a. Happy
b. Neutral or down
c. Kind/gentle

6. What sort of sense of humour do you have?

a. I'm hopeless with humour
b. I can be the life of the party
c. I have to work at it

7. How would a woman describe your eyes?

a. Distant/cool
b. Fun/mischievous
c. Kind/gentle

8. Look in the mirror. Describe your chin and nose:

a. Average, they seem to fit the face
b. Strong nose, protruding jaw
c. Smaller nose and chin

9. Your thighs are:

 a. Muscular/angular
 b. Long/lean
 c. Round

10. Your income is:

 a. Below average, but I prefer to work part-time
 b. Average for my age and experience
 c. Significantly above the average

11. Measure your waist size and divide it by your hips then multiply by 100. For example, if your waist is 36 inches and your hips are 42 inches then your ratio is 85.7%. Your ratio is:

 a. 100% or more
 b. 85-95%
 c. Less than 85%

12. If a woman ran her hand over your belly, what would she feel?

 a. A barrel or the Michelin Man
 b. A six-pack
 c. A flat surface

13. Does size matter? I believe women think penis size is:

 a. Not important
 b. Relevant
 c. Very important

14. **You've been invited to a party and you've heard there will be a lot of women there you'd like to impress. How do you dress?**

    a. Tailored pants and shirt, polished shoes
    b. Tracksuit with running shoes
    c. Jeans and shirt with casual shoes

15. **If a woman was feeling upset, sad or anxious:**

    a. It's unlikely I'd notice it
    b. I'd know it immediately
    c. If I talked to her for a while, I'd probably become aware

16. **Socially I usually wear a:**

    a. Beard
    b. Clean shaved face
    c. 3-day growth

17. **How broad is your subject range?**

    a. I know a lot about people, places and things
    b. I have a reasonably good spread of topics
    c. I'm an expert in my own area

Your Score

Question 1	Question 2	Question 3
A=7 points	A=9	A=3
B=5 points	B=1	B=7
C=3 points	C=0	C=5

Question 4	Question 5	Question 6
A=3 points	A=3	A=1
B=5 points	B=1	B=9
C=4 points	C=5	C=4

Question 7	Question 8	Question 9
A=1 point	A=3	A=5
B=4 points	B=5	B=3
C=5 points	C=1	C=1

Question 10	Question 11	Question 12
A=3 points	A=3	A=1
B=5 points	B=7	B=5
C=9 points	C=5	C=4

Question 13	Question 14	Question 15
A=5 points	A=5	A=1
B=3 points	B=1	B=9
C=1 point	C=3	C=7

Questions 16	Question 17
A=3 points	A=9
B=4 points	B=7
C=5 points	C=3

Now total your scores up and see where you stand on sexuality.

90 points or more

The Cool Cat

Wow! You can consider yourself a chick magnet. You're sending out the right signals to women and you know how to highlight your assets to attract them. But beware of not making your appearance too perfect, because women may assume it's contrived or that you're too self-obsessed, which is a big turn-off for most women. They don't want a man who is egotistical. No woman wants to compete for the mirror with her partner.

47 to 89 points

The Pussy Cat

Most men will be within this rating. You're an average performer in using what you have to attract women. If you're closer to the 89 points you don't have that far to go to improve. Just look at the questions where you didn't rate so highly, and read the next chapter for hints on how to improve. If you're closer to the 47 points, you have a base that you need to work harder to improve. The next chapter will show you how.

Up to 46 points

The Alley Cat

You're happy roaming the backstreets, and probably think that any man who prefers women to beer is gay. Your mates are more important to you than women. But if you do want to be attractive to women, you need help! Women like men who have a great personality, who can make them laugh, who are sensitive to their needs, and who have ambition and brains to get ahead in life. Fortunately, you can learn most of these things. Just think of all the fun you will have when all of the women in your life start to look at you differently!

Chapter 11

MALE SEX APPEAL

What turns women on

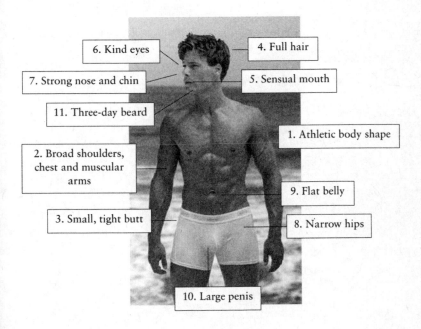

6. Kind eyes

4. Full hair

7. Strong nose and chin

5. Sensual mouth

11. Three-day beard

1. Athletic body shape

2. Broad shoulders, chest and muscular arms

9. Flat belly

3. Small, tight butt

8. Narrow hips

10. Large penis

In priority order, the parts of a man's body that appeal to women.

The first thing you'll notice about this chapter on what attracts women sexually to men is that it's half the size of the chapter on what turns on men about women. This is because, as we've said before, a woman's body has evolved almost as a sexual signalling device to radiate messages to men about her potential as a healthy, successful carrier of his genes. Female sex appeal is a sophisticated, complex process, but male physical sex appeal is much more basic and straightforward.

From the beginning of time, women have been primarily attracted to healthy, strong men who could obtain food and protect her and her children. That hasn't changed much. But twenty-first-century woman wants something more than her female ancestors: she wants a man who'll also fulfil her emotional needs. Thus her brain has evolved to look for two opposite requirements – hardness and softness.Hardness means her chosen mate will display virtues that will provide the best possible genetic inheritance for her offspring and give them a greater chance of survival. For that, she'll be seeking a John Wayne, Russell Crowe, or Bruce Willis kind of tough guy. One way this trait can be identified is by a man's body symmetry; by the way the left side of his body mirrors the right with even-length limbs. This is quite different to the way men view women. They look for symmetrical faces rather than bodies. Yet both sexes see these symmetries as indicative of youthfulness and health, in exactly the same way as symmetrical

flowers prove more attractive to bees because they have more nectar, and symmetrical animals tend to survive longer than non-symmetrical ones.

....

A man's body symmetry is more important to a woman than his facial symmetry – which is why champion boxers can still often attract beautiful women.

....

Many animals and insects are exactly the same. In the case of scorpion flies, the female only wants to mate with males who have symmetrical wings, as these males have greater resilience to overcome life's problems and setbacks. This resilience is in his genes and can, in part, be passed on to her offspring. Consequently, for scorpion flies, symmetry is seen as a health certificate, and therefore a logical reason for females to select these males as mates. Yet in humans, the female attraction to symmetrical, or tough, men can waver according to the woman's menstrual cycle.

....

A study in Scotland found that the kind of male face a woman finds attractive can differ depending on where she is in her cycle. If she is ovulating, she's attracted to men with rugged, masculine features. If she's menstruating, she is more likely to be attracted to a man with scissors shoved in his head.

....

When the possibility of conception is at its highest (about halfway through a woman's menstrual cycle) a woman is more likely to select the hardness of a more symmetrical male for a short-term relationship. In other words, she could be a candidate for a one-night stand with Russell Crowe once a month.

For long-term partners, however, women tend to choose men who will invest in the relationship and the raising of children, whether the men are symmetrical or not. But in judging attractiveness from appearance only (which is what we are doing here) symmetry plays a significant part in a woman's overall choices. In Britain, DNA evidence reveals that 10% of children born in marriage are not the offspring of the husband. It seems the wife chose him for his nurturing abilities, but sought good genes elsewhere.

What Science Shows

Research in the USA has found that attractive men are paid 12-14% more than their less attractive workmates (Hammermesh and Biddle). The worrying part of all this is that attractive individuals receive more favourable treatment in court, get shorter sentences and lower fines (Castelloe, Wuensch and Moore, 1991 and Downs and Lyons, 1990). In Pennsylvania, a study was made of the attractiveness of 74 male defendants before their criminal trials began and it showed that attractive defendants not only received lighter sentences, they were twice as likely to avoid a jail sentence than the unattractive defendants. This explains why the best con men are almost always attractive people.

A study of damages awarded in a staged negligence trial found when the defendant was better-looking than the victim, the victim received an average compensation of US$5,623, but if the victim was more attractive, he or she received an average compensation of US$10,051 (Kulka and Kessler, 1978). If everyone in a courtroom was blindfolded and couldn't see the defendants, the evidence shows the outcomes would be significantly different.

That may sound disheartening but, on the plus side, at least everyone has the chance to improve their appearance, and can make a conscious decision to increase their attractiveness to other people. For men, women's sexual responses are triggered visually by certain aspects of the male body. Here they are, in order of priority.

Women's Top Turn-Ons
1. Athletic body shape
2. Broad Shoulders, Chest and Muscular Arms
3. Small, Tight Bum
4. Full Hair
5. Sensual Mouth
6. Kind Eyes
7. Strong Nose and Chin
8. Narrow Hips and Muscular Legs
9. Flat Belly
10. Large Penis
11. Three-day Beard

Turn-on 1: Athletic Body Shape

Top of the attraction list for women is a man with an athletic-looking, V-shaped body. A strong, athletic body is a sign of good health and signals a man's potential to successfully catch food and fight off enemies. Even in our times of supposed gender equality, where bulging biceps and a broad chest are of little practical use, these signals still stimulate a woman's brain when she is assessing suitable partners. The V-shape also appeals to a woman because it's the opposite of what she is; she has an inverted V-shape. Wherever she has curves and softness, a man's body usually has angles and firmness and it's that difference which can prove so attractive.

Turn-on 2: Broad Shoulders, Chest and Muscular Arms

The upper body of the hunting male is wide and tapers to narrow hips, whereas a woman's body is narrower at the shoulders and widens at the hips. Men evolved these features to allow them to lug heavy weapons over long distances and carry home their kills.

Broad shoulders are a masculine feature, which is often copied by women who want to assert themselves. To do so, they place their hands on their hips to appear broader in the shoulders and to take up more space. Women who wear shoulder pads in business are seen as more assertive – just like the status that epaulettes confer upon men. The male chest developed to house large lungs to enable more effective distribution of oxygen and for him to breathe more efficiently when running and chasing. The bigger his chest, the more respect and power he commanded. When modern men achieve, their chests will still 'swell with pride' and teenage boys still equate a well-built upper torso with masculinity.

Men have longer forearms than women to allow them to be better aimers and throwers, and therefore better providers. Men's hairy armpits have always been a strong masculine characteristic. The armpit hair is to trap scent from the sweat glands that carry a musky-smelling pheromone to sexually stimulate women's brains. The same also happens with chest and crotch hair.

Women are certainly attracted to a well-defined male upper body but most dislike the 'muscle man' body-builder look because they feel such a man is likely to be far more interested in his own beauty than in hers. A fit, healthy appearance turns her on; the Arnold Schwarzenegger type turns her off.

The male chest also carries female feeding equipment – nipples and mammary glands. This is because the basic template for a human being is female in its structure and the nipples and mammary glands still remain even when the baby will be male. Male nipples are a low ranking feature in the attraction stakes but play a part in sex play. There are thousands of recorded incidents of men being able to produce breast milk for feeding in circumstances of extreme deprivation, such as the starvation that occurred in the concentration camps during World War II. Because men still carry this female equipment, one in 50 people diagnosed with breast cancer are men, and they die much more quickly than women.

You'll rarely hear about this because men diagnosed with breast cancer tend to be acutely embarrassed about having such a traditionally female sickness, and won't discuss it.

Turn-on 3: Small, Tight Bum

Male apes don't have protruding, hemispherical bottoms – only humans do. When we learned to walk on two legs, the gluteal muscles in the leg expanded dramatically to allow us to stand upright. The bum has always been the butt of many jokes and is the body part looked upon with both hilarity and disdain. Twenty-three per cent of all photocopier faults world-wide are caused by people sitting on them to photocopy their buttocks. So, why are many women so interested in men's bums, itch to pat them as their owners walk by and like to admire pictures of men with neat behinds? A small, compact bum is a favourite of women everywhere but few understand its magnetic attraction.

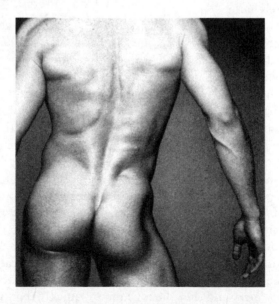

The secret is that a tight, muscular rear is necessary to make the strong forward thrusting motion during sex. A man with a fat or flabby derriere has difficulty with this forward movement and has a tendency to throw his entire body weight into the thrust. For women, this isn't ideal, as the man's weight can be uncomfortable on her and make it difficult to breathe. By contrast, the man with the small tight rear promises a far greater chance of doing a more effective job.

> *A small tight bum promises a*
> *greater chance of conception.*

Spanking the bare buttocks has long been a favourite of sadists and masochists and many men and women find it a sexual turn-on. The reddening of the buttocks resembles a woman's state of sexual arousal and the heightened stimulation of the many nerve endings in the buttocks is passed on to stimulating the genitals. In other words, when a woman pats a man's rear, she's actually encouraging him to have an erection.

Turn-on 4: Full Hair

Throughout history, hair on the head has been considered a badge of raw masculine power. In the Middle Ages hair was considered to have magical powers and locks would be cut off and stored in a sweetheart's locket or used in religious ceremonies. In the case of monks, removing the hair by shaving the head was seen as a sign of humility before God. When Samson had his hair cut off he lost all his strength. A full head of hair has always represented male strength and power and therein lies its attraction.

Around 50% of women place a high priority on a man having a full head of hair. It is a lower priority for the other 50%, many of whom also find balding and shaved heads attractive.

Male baldness is hereditary and caused by an over production of male hormones. These hormones flood the system and switch off certain hair papillae, usually on top of the head. Because of higher hormone levels, bald-headed men are usually more aggressive and hornier than their hairy-headed brothers, so baldness becomes a super-male signal. This masculine signal transmitted by a bald head highlights male and female sex difference and stimulates many women.

To some, it's a bald head. To others, it's a solar panel for a sex machine.

We conducted an experiment using images of male heads that had been computer-altered to display various degrees of baldness. We showed them to respondents who were asked to give their first impressions of each in a business environment. We found that the balder the man, the more power and success he was perceived to have, and the less resistance people would put up when he enforced his authority. The hairy-headed men, on the other hand, were thought to be the least powerful and less well paid. Thus, a bald head is a powerful display of testosterone. Many men are anxious about their actual, or impending, baldness and feel frustrated that there's little they can do about it – the only sure way of avoiding baldness being castration before puberty, which we don't recommend. But they should realise the clear trade-off for baldness is an enhanced aura of power and sexuality.

During the research for our best-selling book *Rude and Politically Incorrect Jokes* (HarperCollins), we found that only men tell bald jokes; you'll rarely hear a woman tell one. While this is partly because women may be sympathetic to men's discomfort about their baldness, it's also because a bald head is a masculine badge. So many women don't actually see it as a weakness to be made fun of, quite the opposite. They'll be turned on by it and will often kiss, or stroke, a man's hairless dome.

Turn-ons 5 & 6: Sensual Mouth and Kind Eyes

When men describe a woman's lips or eyes, they use words like moist, sexy, delicious, inviting, luscious and erotic. When women describe a man as having a sensual mouth or kind eyes however, they use words like caring, sensitive, responsive, protective and loving. These words aren't used literally, however, to describe the physical feature. Women use them to describe how they perceive a man's *attitude*. This is further evidence of the difference between the sexes: men see the actual feature itself, while women look beyond to seek the emotion.

As for eyes, a woman displays more of the white than a man because the female brain is set up as a close range communication tool. The white of an eye is an aid to face-to-face communication as it lets someone monitor the direction of another person's gaze, which gives clues to their attitude. Most other animals show little to no whites because they watch, instead, the body signals of other animals over greater distances. Also, a woman will show a preference for men with darker eyes because light eyes are more infantile in appearance.

Turn-on 7: Strong Nose and Chin

The strong male nose, chin and brow evolved to give a man protection from blows to the face during fighting or hunting and have remained powerful badges of masculinity. Males with high levels of testosterone have stronger, more protruding jaws than low-testosterone males, and the gesture of thrusting the jaw forward is seen as a gesture of defiance. The goatee chin beard enhances the perceived size of the chin so a man looks like he can 'take it on the chin'. Unfortunately, the goatee beard can be seen as having its origins with Satan, which can make it difficult for a man to gain acceptance and trust in business. Drawing the chin back is associated with fear and is a gesture used by 'chinless wonders' and so isn't popular with women.

Since the Roman times, the size of a man's nose has also been equated to the size of his penis but, much to Pinocchio's disappointment, there is no research to substantiate this myth. The only thing the nose has in common with the penis is the way it protrudes from the front of the body. What has been found, however, is that a man's nose expands with blood during sexual arousal and increases in temperature by up to six degrees, just like his penis.

Turn-on 8: Narrow Hips and Muscular Legs

The powerful, angular male legs are the longest of all primates and his narrow hips allow a man to run swiftly over long distances to chase and hunt. Women's wide hips cause many women to have difficulty running as their lower legs and feet often flay out to the side to balance body weight. Leading US neuropsychology professor Dr Devendra Singh discovered that women find male hips with a 90% hips-to-waist ratio the most appealing – the same ratio that 'feminine' lesbians prefer in 'masculine' lesbians. Men's legs are only attractive to women, however, in that they are symbols of masculine power and endurance.

Turn-on 9: Flat Belly

In ancient times when food was scarce, a large potbelly was a sign of high status showing its owner had the resources to afford to eat as much as he wanted. In modern society where food is plentiful, a protruding potbelly is seen as a sign of over-indulgence and low regard for personal health. Well-defined abdominal muscles have never been a prominent feature of the admired male anatomy. Such a look is a creation of health clubs and gym equipment-makers who are desperate to convince us that we can't live without a well-developed 'six pack'. Hercules and He-Man are about the only heroes who ever had them – Superman and Batman didn't. They certainly had flat bellies but never sported a washboard look. In fact, many past heroes looked much more like ads for Dunkin' Donuts.

Turn-on 10: Large Penis

The human male has the largest penis of all the primates. For thousands of years the length of a man's penis has been associated with his perceived power and prowess as a lover, but the power is more in the mind than in the actual organ. Despite the digitally-enhanced wedding tackle you can readily see on the Internet, the longest officially recorded penis is 14 inches, and there is no relationship between body size, nose size and shoe size and his penis size. The average male erection is 5.5 inches and most women's vaginal passage is 3.5 inches long, with most of the sensitivity within the first two inches, ending around the G-spot. The reality is that a man with a three-inch erection can deliver a more accurate service than a man with a seven-incher, as the shorter one can accurately hit the right spots. Women who appear excited about a long penis are reacting more to the perceived masculine power of the organ than to what its length will physically achieve. Women in a happy relationship rarely ever think about penis size but, in a bitter break-up, may talk about their former partner being small as a form of revenge.

The young man was terrified about the first time he'd have sex with his girlfriend as he was sure his penis was too small. Eventually, he realised he couldn't put it off forever, and nervously asked her back to his place. Tentatively, he began to take off his clothes, then turned the lights down low. Carefully, he started to peel off her clothes and caress her. Nervously, he finally put his erection in her hand and hoped that she might not notice its size. "No thanks", she said, "I don't smoke."

Evolution has not programmed women to be sexually aroused by the sight of male genitals, which is the opposite of what happens to men. Men's porn magazines show women with legs fully spread, either standing or lying, with views from the front and the rear, while all attempts to market pornographic images of men to women have failed. Their only success is in attracting a gay male audience.

When a man sees a naked woman, he becomes dumbstruck. When a woman sees a naked man she usually bursts into laughter.

It seems that a man's penis size rates at number 10 on a woman's attraction list because of its historical association with male power – the bigger the organ, the more respect he supposedly commands among other men. In New Guinea, men make a public display of their penises by covering them with one-metre-long sheaths, which they tie around the neck for support and to parade them around in public. The closest most western males have come to this statement is Speedo swimming trunks.

New Guinea natives wearing ceremonial penis sheaths and, below, Speedo swimmers. Different approach, same message.

....

*No fashion faux pas a woman
can make will ever compete
with men's Speedos.*

....

Turn-on 11: Three-day Beard

Male humans are the only primates that can grow significantly longer hair on the face than on the rest of the body.
Monkeys and chimps have the same length pelt over their
entire bodies. You'll never see an ape with a beard and
Cheetah the Chimp never had a handlebar moustache. Male
hormones cause long facial-hair growth. The higher a man's
testosterone on a given day, the faster it grows. Consequently,
the three-day beard serves as a strong visual badge of
masculinity, used particularly to effect by men who might be
seen by women as looking too boyish otherwise. Most women
would agree, for instance, that Tom Cruise looks far sexier
with growth on his chin than he does clean shaven. Stress and
illness suppress testosterone, which is why a sick or stressed
man doesn't need to shave very often. The man who sports a
5-o'clock shadow by midday, however, gives the impression
he's raring to perform.

What's wrong with this picture?

Tom Cruise sporting the macho three-day beard look.

What Women Want Long Term

Here are the results from surveys showing what women look for in a man –

What women look for in a man
1. Personality
2. Humour
3. Sensitivity
4. Brains
5. Good body

Men have two lists: their first impression list, and what they'd seek in a long-term partner, but women only ever have one list. Women want a man to be caring, intelligent, humorous, loyal and understanding, in contrast with the kind of visual assessments men make. If a man has a good body, she sees it as a bonus but – except for one or two days of the month when Russell Crowe tops her list – it usually ranks the lowest of her priorities. Unlike a man, she doesn't use a man's appearance and grooming as a measure of how he feels about her. Instead, she measures his love by how he treats her. If a man has lousy dress sense or starts developing a potbelly, while women may not like it, it's seldom a major issue. This fundamental difference between men and women causes much frustration and misunderstanding on both sides. Women need to understand that their appearance is important to a man and that it can seriously affect their relationship. Men need to learn that a woman measures the depth of their relationship by how he behaves towards her.

A woman wants a man who is soft, caring, understanding and will communicate, but is also strong, rugged and masculine. But she can't have him. He's already got a boyfriend.

Polls and surveys consistently show how important a woman's physical attractiveness is to men, particularly in the first meeting where he evaluates her attractiveness rating in less than ten seconds. For long-term and permanent partner selection, however, men use a different set of values. Women like their men to be attractive, but a man's physical shape and appearance is not critical to his business or social standing, it's just an added extra. How else could you explain Gérard Depardieu's success? Women start and finish with the same value list in partner selection. If a man can make a woman laugh, is sensitive to her needs, can converse on a range of subjects, has goals to continually improve his life, and is heterosexual to boot, he'll never be short of a date.

Solution

To become a more attractive man, you need to first work on your communication and relationship skills. Colleges and business courses everywhere can teach you how to be a good communicator, how to make friends and influence people and how to develop your sense of humour. As you can see from the list, women love men who can make them laugh. Buy books that show you how women think and feel. We recommend our book *Why Men Don't Listen and Women Can't Read Maps* (Orion) and *What Women Want Men to Know* by Barbara De Angelis (Thorsens) as excellent resources. Then step outside your comfort zone and apply for a better job. Women are attracted to men who demonstrate they are moving forward and are keen to improve their position in life. Even the women who are self-sufficient and financially independent are attracted to the man who stacks up as a good protector and provider. Even though she may not be so interested in his resources, her brain is still wired to be impressed by the man who is going places. He doesn't need to be Donald Trump, he just needs to have plans and goals and be seen to be acting on them. Take a college course to expand your overall knowledge. This lets you converse with women on a range of subjects. Men have been providing food for women for thousands of years, so learn how to cook – it stimulates the primal part of a woman's brain. Dancing has always been a woman's form of foreplay, so take lessons as soon as possible. A man who can cook and dance (not necessarily at the same time) is one of the most popular guys in town.

You can always tell the best year of a man's life – his haircut is still there.

Finally, join a health club and get yourself into shape. Change your hairstyle at least every three years. A man's hairstyle, moustache or beard is often stuck in the year that was the best year of his life, often when he was around age 20.

No longer are there reasons for a man not to have or do the things he wants in life – only excuses. Don't complain – just do it!

Chapter 12

"DOES THIS OUTFIT MAKE ME LOOK BIG?"

Why men lie

A man taking the ultimate lie-detector test.

The new man in your life swears he's over his ex, but you know he has a picture of her in his office desk drawer. Your female instincts tell you something is not quite right, but you can't put your finger on it.

Your girlfriend didn't see you last night as promised because she says she or her dog or her mother wasn't feeling well. But you know she's never ill, her mother is dead and she doesn't have a dog. You're suspicious. Are you being lied to?

Lie: *noun*, an action in which one person deliberately sets out to mislead another

Who Lies?

Everyone lies. Most lying occurs at first meetings where everyone wants to present themselves in the best light. Most lies we tell are White Lies. These are told as a way of allowing us to live together without violence and aggression because often we'd prefer to hear subtle distortions of the truth than the cold hard facts. If you have an extremely large nose, you don't want to hear the truth about it – you'd prefer to hear that it looks fine, that no one notices it or that it's the right size for your face.

Always tell the truth – and then run.
PROVERB

If you had told the absolute truth to every person you interacted with over the last week, where would you be right now? In hospital? Perhaps jail. If you'd spoken the exact words going through your mind as you were thinking them, how would they respond? One thing's for sure: you'd have no friends and you'd probably end up unemployed. Imagine this conversation:

"Hi, Maria. You look awful. Why don't you wear a bra to support those saggy breasts?"

"Hi, Adam. Why don't you see a dermatologist about all those ugly pimples on your face? You're a lousy dresser. And why don't you trim your nose hair?"

"That's a beautiful new car you've bought, Michelle. Your two hyper kids should wreck it in no time. As a parent, you're absolutely clueless."

These examples are truths. A lie would have been, "Hi, Maria, you look great." "Hi, Adam, you handsome hunk." "You're such a good mother, Michelle."

When was the last time you lied? Well, maybe you didn't actually lie, but just let someone make a wrong assumption based on what you did or didn't tell them, or just fibbed a little to avoid hurting their feelings. Maybe it was just a little white lie – you said you liked their haircut, decorating style or new partner when you didn't – or you didn't want them to hear bad news from you. Maybe you exaggerated a few little things on a loan or job application to present yourself in a better light.

When you were selling your car, possibly you forget to mention that constant oil leak from the motor when you said what great condition the car was in. When you advertised your house for sale you omitted to mention it was directly under an airline flight path. Maybe you dyed your hair to make yourself look seven years younger or combed your few remaining strands across your bald patch, thinking you could fool others into thinking you still have a fine head of hair. Have you ever worn high heels to pretend your legs are longer than they are, shoulder pads to feign authority, fake nails or make-up, or perhaps lied outright about your weight or age? We all constantly lie to each other. Parents lie to their children about sex and teenagers lie to their parents about having sex. Call them what you like – they're all lies.

Only enemies speak the truth. Friends and lovers
lie endlessly, caught in the web of duty.
STEPHEN KING

We lie for two reasons – to make a gain or avoid a pain. Fortunately, most people feel a sense of guilt, remorse or unease when they lie, and most find it impossible to hide. It then becomes possible for the other person to work out whether they're being told the truth – or lied to. With a little practice, it's easy to recognize the behavioural signals, and learn how to decode them.

Case Study: Sheelagh and Dennis's Story

Sheelagh was invited by Dennis to dinner at his home and so she dressed to impress. She went to the hairdresser that day to have her hair streaked with blonde, she made her face up carefully, she slipped into a sexy dress that was slightly revealing, she stepped into high heels, clipped on a pair of drop earrings and dabbed some expensive French perfume behind her ears. When she arrived, she was impressed with the way Dennis had set the scene for their evening. He'd turned the lights down low, had soft music playing in the background and had lit an open fire. As she entered the dining room, he presented her with a beautiful bouquet of flowers and led her gently to the candlelit table where he slowly poured her a glass of Champagne. As she sat there basking in all this glory, she noticed he was wearing the aftershave she'd mentioned she loved – Opium. All her senses – sight, sound, smell and touch – were aroused and turned up high. They casually talked for a while about her work and the events in her day. Dennis listened attentively, smiling and gazing into her eyes and encouraging her to talk. Sheelagh was completely overwhelmed by how caring and sensitive this man was – so unlike the other men she had dated. And she assumed he felt exactly the same way about her.

In polite terms, this scenario is called a romantic candlelit dinner. The reality, however, is that it's a complete fabrication of lies on both sides to try to gain personal advantage. Dennis's performance was entirely for Sheelagh's benefit. Champagne, dim lights and soft music were not normally part of Dennis's lifestyle and his usual topic of conversation was sport. The whole set-up was an elaborate ruse. Dennis wanted sex. Wild, uninhibited sex. He was experienced enough to know that if he set the scene the way he did, there was a much greater chance Sheelagh would give him what he wanted.

Sheelagh, on the other hand, was as much a liar as Dennis. She had adorned and decorated herself purely to stimulate the sexual part of his brain, thus increasing his testosterone level. She intentionally displayed most of the sex signals we discussed in Chapter 9 so that he would pay her plenty of attention. Everything they said and did that evening was to gain personal benefit. The whole evening, in short, was based on lies and deceit. Yet if confronted with this basic truth, both would, naturally, strenuously deny it.

Types of Lies

There are four basic types of lies – the White Lie, the Beneficial Lie, the Malicious Lie and the Deceptive Lie. As discussed, the White Lie is part of our social fabric and stops us from emotionally hurting or insulting each other with the cold, hard, painful truth. The Beneficial Lie is used by a person who intends to help others. For example, a farmer hiding Jews from Nazis who is asked if he's keeping any Jews in his house is seen as acting heroically when he lies. The rescue worker who pulls a child from the remains of a burning car and lies to the child that his mother and father are OK is saving the child, in the short term, from more trauma. Doctors who lie to a patient on their deathbed to lift their spirits or prescribe fake medication, placebos, to patients are also technically lying.

Research shows 30–40%
of patients gain relief from placebos.

It's the Deceptive Lie that is the dangerous one because the liar intends to harm or disadvantage the victim for their own benefit. For example, a friend of ours, Gerri, was once warned by one of her woman friends against a man who was paying her a great deal of attention. Gerri was a single parent who didn't get out much socially so, when she met a single father at her son's playgroup who seemed sweet, sensitive, intelligent, funny and, most importantly, interested in her, she was delighted. Margie, however, was quick to head off the burgeoning romance. She told Gerri that the man was a well-known womaniser, who specialised in breaking female hearts. Gerri, always careful around men because of the danger of her child becoming emotionally attached to a boyfriend, avoided him from that moment on. A month later, she happened to bump into him at the local shopping centre – with a beaming Margie on his arm.

There are two main ways of deceitful lying – concealment and falsification. In concealment, the liar doesn't actually tell a lie, they withhold information. Let's say, for example, Gerri had later happened to discover from another friend that this man had, in a past life, tricked an old girlfriend into signing over all her money to him and then fled with the cash, leaving her facing bankruptcy. You could hardly blame Gerri for not telling Margie. Margie might not believe her, anyway. But if

Gerri made the decision not to tell Margie, then she too would have been guilty of lying, this time by an act of concealment.

In falsifying, false information is presented as if it was true. Margie had presented Gerri with false information about an eligible man's nature in order to win him from her rival. This kind of lying is an intentional act, never an accident. Malicious lies are told either for revenge or gain. High-profile people such as actors, the wealthy and politicians are obvious targets for malicious lies for gain. Journalists who then submit those stories to trashy tabloids and magazines, knowing them to be untrue, can also benefit, just as much as their business, political and showbiz rivals.

Malicious lies, or rumour-mongering, are often used as weapons in competitive situations. Malicious liars set out to destroy the character and reputations of their victims, usually with devastating and lasting results.

A company might, for example, spread false information that its main competitor is in financial difficulties. Similarly, it is not uncommon for political parties to start rumours of inappropriate sexual behaviour by an opponent.

Imagine the effect if one of two men vying for the affections of the same woman were to spread a lie that the other had an STD or was a paedophile. Malicious lies work on the basis that no matter how outrageous or improbable the lie, if you throw enough mud, some will stick.

Types of Liars

A 'natural liar' is someone who does have a conscience but is confident of their ability to deceive, and has been doing so since childhood. Often they learned to lie to their parents to avoid terrible punishments that would be handed out if they told the truth. Many natural liars capitalise on this ability as adults by becoming trial lawyers, salespeople, negotiators, actors, politicians and spies.

An 'unnatural liar' is a person who, as a child, was convinced by his parents it was impossible for him to lie and that the parent and others would always detect it. These poor saps go through life telling everyone the truth about everything, insisting 'I can never tell a lie' and causing anger and trouble among everyone they meet.

One of the most dangerous liars a woman can encounter is the Romantic Liar. When a Romantic Liar is operating, most women have little idea of what's going on. Some Romantic Liars specialize in concealing the fact that they're married while others are expert at posing as lawyers, doctors and successful business people in order to win respect and sex appeal. These liars are limited only by their imagination. As a result, they can cause women enormous harm, emotionally, psychologically and, often, financially. The usual goal of the Romantic Liar is to extract money, accommodation, sex and other benefits from an unsuspecting woman. In return, he pretends to offer her excitement and love.

Therapists' rooms are filled with intelligent, resourceful women who have fallen victim to a Romantic Liar, with some otherwise smart women turning out to be serial victims who continually attract the same type of men. The emotional damage and lack of self-esteem resulting from these encounters usually far outweighs the loss of possessions and can leave a woman emotionally scarred, never trusting men again.

....

**The Romantic Liar secretly
believes he's James Bond.**

....

Romantic Liars can appear from anywhere and they thrive in Internet chat rooms where most people lie and anything goes. Many people believe that women who are sucked in by a Romantic Liar must be gullible or even stupid, but this is not the case. The Romantic Liar's main talent is his ability to act out a plausible lie long enough for his victim to become infatuated.

She becomes blinded to the lie or denies it, even when it is apparent to her friends and family.

It's always helpful for women to make an agreement with a close friend that, in the event of either falling madly in love with 'the one', the other is authorized to secretly conduct a police and bankruptcy check on him. If he applied for a position of trust anywhere in the world this would be standard practice, so why shouldn't it be the case when your own finances and emotions are up for grabs? The women who resist this idea with the catchphrase "Love will conquer all" are usually the ones who are repeatedly vanquished by the Romantic Liar.

People say they love the truth
but in reality they want to believe
that which they love is true.
ROBERT RINGER

If someone has lost weight, become sober, quit drugs or got a job in order to make themselves more appealing, you might want to question their motives. If you make a commitment to them, will they really stay thin, employed, sober and drug-free? Leopards rarely change their spots. Relationships based on honesty are the only ones that will last in the long term.

The lasting changes we make for ourselves
are the only permanent ones.

If you were the personnel manager of any corporation and someone applied for a responsible position of trust, you'd want to know as much as possible about them and their past, right? When considering a long-term partner, the same should apply. The best source of information is a person's past partner. If you or a friend can 'accidentally' bump into them, they are usually more than forthcoming with relevant information. While this may seem like snooping to some, it is standard practice for many romances in Japan. One family will present a *curriculum vitae* on their son or daughter to the family of the prospective son or daughter-in-law, and interviews and negotiation take place even before a first date is arranged. This avoids any skeletons appearing from a closet in the potential couple's future. The answer here is to always check the track record of any product you intend to keep for a long time. Don't become a victim of either romantic clichés or raging hormones.

Who Lies the Most?

Most women will enthusiastically claim that, without doubt, men lie far more often than women. Scientific studies and experiments show, however, that men and women tell about the same number of lies. It's the content of their lies that differs. Women tend to lie to make others feel better and men lie to make themselves look good. Women lie to keep the relationship safe. Women find it most difficult to lie about their feelings. Men lie to avoid an argument and love to lie about how wild they were when they were young.

....

A woman will lie to make you feel good.
A man lies to make himself look good.

....

This is the main difference between male and female lies. A woman will lie that someone looks wonderful in their new outfit, even though she thinks the person looks like a sack full of potatoes. In the same circumstances, a man will keep away from the person to avoid lying and will only lie if he is forced to give his opinion. He'll say the outfit is "interesting" or "lovely", he'll tell an indirect lie like "What can I say?" or "Words fail me" or he'll simply lie that he loves it. And when a man does tell a lie, most women are good at spotting it. A man will tell you he is second-in-charge of food distribution for an international company when he actually has a delivery run with Pizza Hut.

The number one question men ask that makes women lie: "How was I?"

In 2002, Robert Feldman at the University of Massachusetts in Amherst studied 121 couples as they had a conversation with a third person. One third of the participants were told to appear likeable while another third were instructed to seem competent, and the rest were asked just to be themselves. All participants were then asked to watch the video of themselves and identify any lies they had told during the conversation, no matter how big or small. Some lies were white lies, such as saying they liked someone when they really did not. Others lies were more extreme, such as falsely claiming to be the star of a rock band.

Overall, 62% of participants told an average of two to three lies every ten minutes.

**The truth will set you free,
but first it will piss you off.**
MAL PANCOAST

The most common form of lying is self-deception, which allows a person to smoke two packs of cigarettes a day while claiming to not be addicted, or convince himself that a calorie-laden dessert will not interfere with a diet.

The evidence is clear – women lie just as much as men, they simply lie differently. Because of women's super-awareness of body language and voice signals, men get caught far more often, which makes it seem like men lie more. They don't. They just keep getting caught.

Common Lies Men Tell Women

"I'm not drunk." This is an easy lie to pick, especially as it usually sounds like, "I'ym narg drmgthph." There is no reason for someone to say they're not drunk – unless they're drunk.

"I definitely didn't have sex with that woman." A man who has cheated will lie about it well past the point of all rationality because, in his mind, he has nothing to gain by telling the truth.

"Sex with my ex was lousy." Sex for men is one of life's constants – it's always good, no matter where or when. If a man says sex with his ex was lousy, he's definitely lying. When he tells you sex with his ex was better than with you, he's lying again, probably to make you angry. It's always the same for him – it's good.

"We're just friends." He says they're simply lifelong buddies and he has absolutely no other interest in her. But he keeps her away from you and won't let you meet her. Other variations of this one include: she's a lesbian; she just needs a friend; she just needs someone to talk to; she's going through a tough time and I just want to help her; she's sick and wants me to go and see her; she doesn't have feelings for me – she is just embarrassed. That's why she doesn't want you to be here when she's here.

Why Lies Fail

Most lies can be detected because they usually involve emotions that leak out as visual and verbal red lights. The bigger the lie and the more emotions involved, the more clues will be leaked by the liar. Trying to conceal these leaks creates an emotional struggle for most of us. The closer you are to a person, the harder it is to lie to them because of the emotions involved. For example, a husband will have difficulty lying to his wife if he truly loves her but would have no difficulty lying to an enemy if captured in warfare. Herein lies the key to the pathological liar – they have no emotional attachment to anyone, so all lying is easy.

Whether or not you see these clues is a different matter.

Why Women Are So Good at Spotting Lies

Most men know how difficult it is to tell even the smallest lie to a woman, face-to-face, without getting caught. If a man must lie to her, he'd do much better over the telephone. Most women have less difficulty lying straight to a man's face – and they can usually get away with it.

MRI brain scans reveal the average woman has between 14 and 16 key locations in both brain hemispheres when she is communicating face-to-face. These locations are used to decode words, tone of voice changes and body signals, and largely account for what is known as 'a woman's intuition'. A male typically has only 4 to 7 of these locations because male brains have evolved for spatial tasks rather than communication.

This female 'super-awareness' has a purpose – to defend her territory against strangers and to communicate with her children. A woman needs the ability to look at her offspring and quickly read the difference between pain, fear, hunger, injury, sadness and happiness. She needs to be able to rapidly assess the attitude of people who approach her nest – are they friendly or aggressive? Not having these survival skills would leave her exposed and in danger. A woman can even read the emotions of animals for the same reasons. She can tell you if a dog is happy, sad, angry or embarrassed. Most men can't even imagine how an embarrassed dog would look. The goal of a hunting male has always been to accurately hit his target, not talk to it, counsel it or try to understand it.

> *A man needs to accurately hit his target, not have a deep, meaningful conversation with it.*

As we discussed earlier, women's brains are organised for multi-tracking, allowing them to deal with a number of pieces of information at one time. This gives women the additional advantage of being able to read body signals and listen to what is being said while, at the same time, talking. Males, with their mono-tracking brains, focus on one piece of information at a time and consequently miss many of the body signals.

FBI agents are taught how to analyse 'micro expressions' – small, fleeting, split-second expressions that liars will make when lying. This is done using slow motion cameras. For example, Bill Clinton was shown to use a split-second frowning gesture just before he answered questions about Monica Lewinsky. A woman's brain is organised to read these signals when they occur and this explains not only why women are much harder to fool but also why they often make more perceptive negotiators than men.

Why Women Always Remember

Erik Everhart, assistant professor of psychology at East Carolina University, and his colleagues at the State University of New York in Buffalo found that boys and girls, aged 8 through 11, use different parts of their brains to recognize faces and expressions. Boys used more of their right brain while girls used more of their left. They found these differences help girls detect fine changes in facial expression, making them better at sensing people's moods. Reading someone's mouth or eyes requires finer discrimination than judging emotions in the entire face.

Women are very good at remembering what lie they told and who they told it to while men usually forget their lies. The

271

hippocampus – the part of the brain used in memory storage, retrieval, and language – is filled with oestrogen receptors, and grows more quickly in girls than in boys, giving women superior memory recall on emotionally charged issues.

Advice to Men

Don't waste your time telling a lie to a woman face-to-face. It's much too difficult. Call her on the phone or send her an email. Not only do women have a superior ability to uncover lies, they have the ability to remember them as ammunition for future arguments.

Young People Are More Likely To Lie, Cheat, Steal

The younger a person is, the more likely they are to deceive. In the USA, a 2002 survey involving nearly 9,000 teenagers and adults nationwide showed a significant number of 15 to 30-year-olds are willing to lie, cheat, and steal.

The survey covered 3,243 high school students, 3,630 college students, and 2,092 adults.

In the survey, 33% of the high school students and 16% of the college students admitted they had stolen merchandise from a store within the past year.

About one third of the students in each group said they were willing to lie on a resume, a job application, or during a job interview to get the job they wanted, and 16% of the high school students said they had already done it at least once.

61% of the high school students and 32% of college students admitted having cheated in an examination once in the past year.

> *"Can I get into trouble for something*
> *I haven't done?" asked the student.*
> *"No," replied the Headmaster.*
> *"Good – I haven't done my homework."*

The survey found 83% of the high school students and 61% of the college students said they had lied to their parents over the past year.

The researchers found that dishonesty and other unethical behaviours were less rampant among those over the age of 30 and that both sexes lied about the same amount.

Disturbingly, 73% of the 15- to 30-year-olds sampled said they believed that "most people will cheat or lie when it is necessary to get what they want."

From this study it would be easy to say that Americans are all a bunch of liars and cheats but similar studies throughout the Western world show the same trend – and these are the countries that consistently score higher than the rest when it comes to the honesty stakes.

Unfortunately, it is all a symptom of a larger moral crisis that pervades societies everywhere and reflects a real change in society's values. Parents teach their children that honesty is the best policy, but also tell them it's polite to pretend they like a birthday gift they've been given. They also teach children to lie with phrases like, "Don't give me that look!" "Look pleased when your grandmother kisses you" "Don't look so miserable. Put on a happy face."

Children get a mixed message about lying, and this has an impact on how they behave as adults. Most truths are told by children who are usually chastised for doing so. For example, when a fat person passes a child on the street, the child might be clearly heard asking his mother, "How come that man's so fat?"

Most parents don't realize that the severity of their punishments is one of the main reasons many children grow up to be such prolific liars. Much of these lying behavioural patterns are set when you're young and then triggered again in adulthood by figures of authority.

When Everyone You Know Lies to You

There are some people who believe that no one should be trusted and the world is full of liars. They usually feel this way for one of two reasons: first, they themselves are habitual liars and they assume that everyone else is just like them. The second, and more likely, reason is that their behaviour compels others to lie to them. In other words, they make it difficult for others to tell them the truth because others can see how aggressively or emotionally they react to the truth. If others see how angry, hurt or vengeful you become when they tell you the truth, they'll avoid telling it at all costs. If you are known as someone who is easily offended, you'll never know what others are really thinking or feeling as they'll distort to truth to pander to your negative reaction. If you demand that children tell you the truth and then punish them for it because the truth is not very palatable, you teach them to lie to you to protect themselves.

If you feel everyone around you is lying to you, you need to examine your own behaviour and attitudes first – the other person is only half of the equation.

Why the Lies of Friends and Family Hurt Most

The more intimate a relationship is, the more pain someone's deception will cause because you will be less likely to want to remove that person from your life. For example, a deceptive lie told by a parent or sibling will cut deep because the closer the person is, the more we trust them and open ourselves to them. A lie told by a brother, sister or child will hurt more than that of an acquaintance, but is likely to be forgiven because that person will always be our brother, sister or child. A lie by a close friend will also hurt but we can remove that person from our life, at least temporarily, by not contacting them. At the other end of the scale, we expect a used car salesman to lie to us, are not surprised if he does and we can choose never to see him again.

Clues to Unmasking the Liar

Because most people feel uncomfortable when they're lying they instinctively try to distance themselves from their lie. In the United States, the FBI recently discovered this valuable clue during the analysis of the words of suspects who were giving false alibis. The liars would leave references to themselves out of their lies and avoided using the words "I" or "me". Take the case of someone arranging to meet you but not showing up. If they call you later and say, "The car broke down and the mobile had a flat battery," you would instinctively be more suspicious than if they'd said, "My car broke down and I couldn't call you because the battery on my mobile was flat." Liars will also try to avoid using the name of the person they're lying about. They'd prefer to say, "I did not have sexual relations with that woman," instead of, "I did not have sexual relations with Monica."

Liars and Elephants

Like an elephant, an habitual liar never forgets. He has practised his lie in his head several times and can usually give a flawless performance. Ask someone to tell you what they did last weekend and they'll probably say something like, "Ah... I went to my brother's place after breakfast and then... ah... no, I saw him after lunch because I had to take my car in for a repair first... "

....

Beware the flawless performance.

CHINESE PROVERB

....

When people recall a day's events they will usually chop and change direction to try to get things in the right order. Not so with the liar. He has a perfectly rehearsed script and rarely gets it wrong.

Going Once, Going Twice

If you believe a person is lying to you, act as if you believe every word and eventually they'll betray themselves as they become overconfident in their performance. Then ask the liar to repeat the lie a second time. Good liars have practised their answers and can come back with an identical response. Next, leave a pause to allow the suspect to think they've got away with it, then ask them to repeat it a third time. Because they're not expecting a third encore and are in a relaxed state, they usually won't give a third identical response and their story will sound a little different.

Because of the stress associated with lying, a liar's voice becomes more high pitched. If he gets a text message on his phone from Charlotte and, as he's explaining it's a wrong number or he's never heard of her, you notice he's chirping like a canary, add a tick to your suspicions chart.

How to Read Between the Lines of What's Said

Have you ever had a conversation in which the speaker sounded convincing but the more he spoke, the less convincing you found him?

Let's examine some of the most commonly used words and phrases that can signal that a person may be attempting to disguise the truth or to mislead by trying to convince you of an emotion they don't really feel. The words 'honestly', 'sincerely' and 'frankly' indicate that the speaker is about to be considerably less frank, less honest or less sincere than he claims. Perceptive people unconsciously decode these words and get a 'gut feeling' that the speaker is trying to deceive them. For example, 'Frankly, this is the best offer I can give you,' translates to, 'It's not the best offer but maybe you'll believe it.' 'I love you' is more believable than 'I honestly love you'. 'Undoubtedly' gives reason to doubt and 'without a doubt' is a definite warning signal.

'Believe me, when I say,' often means: 'If I can get you to believe me, you'll do what I want.' The degree to which a person saying 'Believe me' tries to convince another person is proportionate to the extent of the deceit. The speaker feels that you won't believe him or that what he is saying sounds unbelievable, so he prefaces his remarks with, 'Believe me'. 'I'm not kidding' and 'Would I lie to you?' are other versions.

If you're going to be honest, frank, believable or truthful, you don't need to convince someone that's what you're doing.

....

What's the difference between lying to
the taxman and lying to your wife?
If you get caught, the taxman
still wants to screw you.

....

Some people simply develop the repetitive habit of using these types of words. They unconsciously use them to preface an honest statement, making it sound untrue. Ask your friends, relations and co-workers if they've noticed any of these words in your speech, and if they have (which is likely), you will begin to understand why some people never seem to be able to develop a trusting relationship with you.

The expressions, 'OK' and 'Right!' force the listener to agree with the speaker's point of view. 'You'd agree with that, right?'

The listener is forced to respond with his own 'Right' even if he doesn't necessarily agree with the speaker's point of view. 'Right' also shows doubt about the listener's ability to receive and understand what is being discussed.

'Only' and 'Just'

The words 'just' and 'only' are used to minimise the significance of the words that follow, to relieve a person's guilt or to put the blame for unpleasant consequences elsewhere. "I'll only take five minutes of your time" is used by time-wasters and others who want to take up to an hour of your time, whereas, 'I'll take five minutes of your time' is specific and more believable. The phrase 'ten minutes' usually means an unspecified amount of time between twenty and sixty minutes. 'Only £9.95' and 'just £40 deposit' are used to convince that the price charged is insignificant. 'I'm only human' is the catchphrase of someone who doesn't want to take responsibility for his or her blunders; 'I just wanted to tell you I love you' masks the timid lover's need to say, 'I love you' and no woman believes a man when he says, 'She's only a friend.'

When you hear someone use 'only' or 'just', you need to consider why that person is attempting to minimise the importance of what he or she is saying. Is it because they lack the confidence to say what they really feel? Are they intentionally trying to deceive? Are they trying to avoid their responsibilities? Close examination of 'only' and 'just', related to the context in which they occur, can reveal the answer.

When They Say, 'I'll Try'

'Try' is frequently used by people who are habitual under-achievers and failures to announce in advance that they probably won't succeed at a task or even that they expect to fail. When a person is asked to be faithful in a relationship, they may say, 'I'll try' or its equivalent, 'I'll do my best', both signalling impending failure. Translated, these expressions mean, 'I have doubts about my ability to do it.'

When the person ultimately fails he says, 'Well, I tried,' confirming that he had little intention or confidence in his ability to remain true. When you hear these phrases, ask the person to commit himself to a 'will' or 'will not' attitude. It is better that a person will not do what you want than 'try' and fail. 'Try' is as reassuring as a 'definite maybe'.

'With respect', and 'with all due respect' means the speaker has little or no respect for the listener and even contempt for him. 'I appreciate your comments, but may I say, with respect, I disagree.' This is a long-winded way of saying, 'What a load of bull' and is intended to deliver a blow to the listener, while cushioning his fall.

Here is a list of some of the more common expressions that are used to try to convince you the speaker is telling the truth when in fact they may be attempting to force you to believe what they are saying. Remember, however, that each phrase is not a guarantee of dishonesty and should be read in context.

'Trust me'
'I'd have no reason to lie'
'Truthfully speaking'
'I'm telling you the truth'
'Why would I lie?'
'To be totally frank/honest/truthful with you'
'Would I do something like that?'

Another common ploy to try to avoid being caught is the use of any phrase that puts the liar in a class of people who should be beyond reproach because they answer to a higher authority. Here are some examples:

'Honest to God'
'I swear on my mother's grave'
'As God is my witness'

'I swear to God'
'May God strike me dead'

We're not talking here about people of true faith or religious conviction. These people don't feel the need to use their faith or belief to try to convince you they are being honest because they are living their beliefs. You'll never hear the Pope say, 'I swear on my father's grave and may God strike me dead if I'm lying.'

Similarly, others can use an organisation to which they belong, an award they've received, or their family upbringing to convince you of their honesty. Here are a few you might recognize:

'My parents taught me better than that'
'I'm a loyal employee'
'I'm a member of (group/club)'
'I'm not that sort of person'
'I'd never stoop to such a thing'
'I have received the (award)'

The point here is that people of moral character don't need to continually try to prove it to you, they live their values and you can see it. The above responses are used to avoid directly answering the question.

Catching Liars With the Computer

Advances in computer science have produced three interesting ways of detecting liars using technology. The polygraph is the most well-known lie detector and measures a person's respiration, relative blood volume, and pulse rate. The lie is detected by physiological changes that take place when someone is being deceptive. These include an increase or decrease of heart rate and blood volume, changes in breathing and perspiration. If a person is being truthful, there should be no changes in these areas. How accurate the polygraph can be is still a question that's hotly debated. According to the American Polygraph Association, over 250 studies have been conducted on the accuracy of polygraph testing during the past 25 years, proving its accuracy. Recent research reveals that the accuracy of the new computerized polygraph system is close to 100%. These machines are now seen on American TV talk shows where the guests try to prove the guilt, innocence or faithfulness of their partners.

The polygraph is still not acceptable as evidence in court, however, unless directed by a judge. Skilled liars show less anxiety than novices and can sometimes pass polygraph tests, while truthful people can be intimidated into showing anxiety and be branded as liars. There are also physiological differences between people that can lead to polygraph unreliability.

What the Vocal Chords Say

Voice Stress Analysis is used to determine the truthfulness and level of stress indicative of deception by electronic means. These measure accepted physiological signposts, such as the automatic 'fight or flight' response. This technology is claimed to be effective on telephone speech or tape recordings and the manufacturers claim it can snag eight out of ten fibs. Priced at about US$50 for a portable machine, the technology mathematically calculates the stress levels in a human voice that change due to reduced blood flow to the vocal chords when someone is lying. During the presidential debates, one of these machines was used by *Time* magazine reporters to analyze Al Gore and George W. Bush. It registered 57 lies for Bush and 23 for Gore during their three debates.

Photographing the Lying Brain

Professors of Psychiatry, Ruben Gur and Daniel Langleben of the University of Pennsylvania School of Medicine, conducted a study using MRI (functional Magnetic Resonance Imaging machines) and found that the brain operates differently in cases of deception and honesty. They gave 18 volunteers a playing card – like the Ace of Hearts – and $20. Each person was placed in an MRI machine to measure their brain activity. As scans were taken, a computer presented the volunteers with different playing cards. When the computer presented the right card – in this case the Ace of Hearts – volunteers were told to lie about it being the wrong card.

Participants were told they would get paid more if they could fool the computer into believing them. The computer, however, knew beforehand which card they had and when they would be lying.

Scans of the participants' brains when they were lying revealed significant increased activity in the anterior cingulate cortex that sits about three inches behind the middle of the forehead and in the left pre-motor cortex, which is a few inches inside the skull near the left ear.

Gur and Langleben believe this discovery may signal the end of the polygraph test because MRI can distinguish between different types of thoughts. For example, brain signals may look the same on a polygraph when someone is lying as when they are thinking about the excitement of an upcoming vacation, but the two thoughts are dramatically different. MRI scans offer spatial resolution so this problem is eliminated.

Dr Jia-Hong Gao, associate professor at the Research Imaging Center at San Antonio, conducted similar experiments and his results showed the left and right cerebral hemispheres were engaged when someone pretended they had lost their memory. The imaging data revealed four principle areas of brain activation – in the prefrontal and frontal, parietal, temporal and sub-cortical regions. The parietal region is the brain's calculation centre.

Listening for Vocal Clues

There are three elements of the voice that can give away a liar – pitch, speed and volume. When a person is experiencing stress, the associated tension causes a tightening of the vocal chords that gives them a squeakier voice, and may increase their speed and volume. Studies show around 70% of people increase their pitch when lying. Conversely, if the liar is carefully thinking through the lie to be sure they deliver it effectively, they may begin to speak more slowly, decrease the volume and slow down their speed. When someone has been unexpectedly caught bending the truth their speech is likely to be peppered with ums, ahs, ers, stutters and pauses because they haven't had enough time to rehearse their lie. This is more noticeable in males than females as males have fewer facilities in the brain for language control. A man who slurs his words is likely to be lying as it reveals the person has a number of issues happening at the same time, and his brain is trying to deal with them all at once.

When someone slurs their
answer to your direct
question, be suspicious.

Keep in mind that the signals we are discussing here show a person is experiencing some kind of stress and are not guarantees they are lying. There are a small percentage of people who are comfortable about lying and don't show many stress-related signals and others, such as political or religious fanatics, can actually believe their own lies and therefore not display any signs of deceit. But most liars display many signs, most of the time.

Reading Body Language

In our book *Body Language* we explained how body signals account for over 60% of the messages sent between people and we recommend you read this book, as we will not be covering it here in detail. We will, however, discuss some of the signals you may see when someone lies. We have observed and recorded that both men and women significantly increase hand-to-face gestures when they are doubtful, uncertain, exaggerating or lying. Men's gestures are easier to spot because they are bigger than women's and men use more of them. These include eye and nose rubbing, ear pulling and collar tugging. For example, Bill Clinton was recorded touching his nose and face 26 times in front of the Grand Jury when answering questions about Monica Lewinsky.

Always Read Clusters

Never interpret a solitary gesture in isolation from other gestures or circumstances. If someone rubs his eye, it may genuinely be itchy, sore or tired. We've found lies come in groups called clusters and you need to see at least three signals before you can assume a lie is being told. If a person touches their mouth or nose, rubs their eye, pulls their ear, scratches their neck, puts their fingers to their mouth or rubs their nose there is no guarantee they are lying, but you should know that something is going on in their brain which they are not telling you. They may not necessarily be lying but they are probably hiding something. If they continually touch their face while saying, 'Trust me, believe me, to be perfectly honest and with all due respect,' it's reasonable to assume you've just been told a lie.

Smiling

Men and women smile just as much when they lie as when they tell the truth. A real smile however, comes fast and is symmetrical – the left side of the face mirrors the right side. A false smile comes slowly and is not symmetrical. When people are trying to show an emotion they don't feel, their facial expressions are not symmetrical. In other words they have a crooked smile.

It's in the Eyes

Traditionally, you've probably been taught to believe that a liar will never look you in the eye. This is true of children raised in Western and European cultures whose mothers told them, "I know you're lying because you won't look me in the eye." In many Asian, Japanese and South American countries, however, it's considered impolite or aggressive to hold extended eye contact so that rule does not apply. Besides, practised liars are competent at maintaining eye contact when lying, so reduced eye contact only becomes an implicating factor in uncovering deceit. Increased blinking is an important signal to note, as it's a sign of increased tension and the liar's eyeballs drying out from too much forced eye contact. The direction someone's eyes move when you ask them a question can help you spot a liar too, as it shows which part of their brain they are using and is a signal that's almost impossible to fake. When most right-handed people are recalling an event that actually happened they engage their left brain and look to their right. When they are inventing a story they engage their right brain and look to their left. In simple terms, right-handed liars look toward their left, left-handed liars look to their right. This observation is not foolproof but is a strong signal of deceit.

The Pinocchio Effect

Special imaging cameras that show blood flow in the body reveal that when a person is lying, his nose grows. Increased blood pressure inflates the nose and causes the nerve endings in the nose to tingle, resulting in a brisk rubbing action to the nose with the hand to satisfy the 'itch'. The same phenomenon occurs when a person is upset or angry. Scientists at the Smell and Taste Treatment and Research Foundation in Chicago found that when you lie, chemicals called catecholamines are released, causing tissue inside the nose to swell. You can't see the swelling with the naked eye but it's interesting to note that a man's penis also swells during a lie. So if you're not sure whether a man is lying or not, pull his pants down.

Here's a brief list of other giveaways indicating a man may be bending the truth:

1. Facial muscular twitching. The brain tries to prevent the face from showing any feedback.
2. No eye contact. His eyes will look away. If the room has a door, that's where he'll look.
3. Crossing of arms and/or legs. This is a defensive instinct.
4. Tight-lipped smile. This is a forced smile used by both sexes to feign sincerity.
5. The pupils of the eyes narrow.
6. Fast talking. A liar wants to get it over with.
7. The head will shake 'no' when giving a 'yes' answer or vice versa.
8. Hiding his hands. Men find it easier to lie with their hands in their pockets.
9. Mispronouncing words or mumbling. A liar thinks he is not lying when he does this.
10. Overstated friendliness/laughing. He wants you to like him so you will believe him.

How Not To Be Lied To

1. Sit in the higher chair. This is a subtle form of intimidation.
2. Uncross your legs, open your arms and lean back. Make yourself 'open' to the truth.
3. Don't ever tell them what you DO know – don't point out you know what they are saying is a lie.
4. Invade their personal space. When you get close, they'll get uncomfortable.
5. Mirror their posture and movement. This establishes a rapport and they'll find it harder to lie to you.
6. Speak in their style by listening to how they think. If the person says things like 'I HEAR you!' or 'That SOUNDS good,' you'll know he thinks auditorially or with his ears. If he says, 'I should have SEEN it coming' or 'I SEE what you mean,' you'll know he is visually oriented. If he says things like 'It HIT me like a ton of bricks' or 'I just FROZE in my tracks,' you'll know he thinks by feelings. Speak to him the same way. A good test is to ask someone to recite the alphabet. Some people will stare as if they are looking at the alphabet above the blackboard in grade school (visual), some people will sing the alphabet (auditory) and some people will tap out the letters (feeling). If you match their thinking method, you'll develop instant rapport.
7. Give them an 'out'. You need to make it easy for them to tell the truth. Pretend you didn't hear them correctly or tell them you didn't understand what they said. Always leave a way out so they can recant their words and tell the truth.
8. Stay calm. Never show surprise or shock. Treat everything they say with the same importance. The first time you react negatively you will lose any chance of being told the truth.
9. Don't accuse. Aggressive questions like, 'Why didn't you call me?' or 'Are you seeing someone else?' can make a liar reinforce the position. Use soft questions like, 'Where did

you say you were again?' and 'What time did you say you
arrived at the restaurant?'
10. Give them one last chance. Ignore the lie and say, 'What
can we do to avoid this happening again?' If they think
you've let them off the hook they're more likely to come
clean and at worst, they'll come up with their own
solution for not using that lie again.

Finally, we asked our female readers to send us the phrases
they hear from men that mask what they really mean:

A Dictionary of Male Speech Patterns

What he says – the lie	What he means – the truth
1. "I can't find it."	*"I can't see it, it didn't fall into my hands, so it must not exist."*
2. "It's a guy thing."	*"There's no rational thought pattern connected with it. It also explains my unjustifiable behaviour."*
3. "Can I help with dinner?"	*"Why isn't it already on the table?"*
4. "I'm getting more exercise lately."	*"The batteries in the remote are dead."*
5. "We're going to be late."	*"I have a legitimate reason for driving like a maniac."*
6. "Take a break, honey, you're working too hard."	*"I can't hear the television over the vacuum cleaner."*

7. "That's interesting darling." *"Are you still talking?"*

8. "We don't need material things to prove our love." *"I forgot our anniversary again."*

9. "It's really a good movie." *"It's got guns, knives, fast cars, and naked women."*

10. "You know how bad my memory is." *"I remember the words to the theme song of* Gilligan's Island, *the address of the first girl I kissed, and the registration number of every car I've ever owned, but I forgot your birthday."*

11. "I was just thinking about you, and got you these roses." *"The girl selling them on the corner was a real babe with great curves; I wanted to look at close up."*

12. "Call an ambulance! I think I'm dying." *"I cut my finger."*

13. "I heard you." *"I haven't the faintest idea what you just said, but you can stop talking now."*

14. "You really look terrific in that outfit." *"Please don't try on one more outfit, I'm starving."*

15. "I missed you." *"I can't find my socks, the kids are hungry, and we're out of toilet paper."*

16. "I'm not lost, I know exactly where we are." *"No one will ever see us alive again."*

17. "Nice dress."   *"Nice breasts."*

18. "I love you."   *"Let's have sex now."*

19. "May I have this dance? / Can I call you sometime? / Do you want to go to a movie/dinner?"   *"I'd eventually like to have sex with you."*

20. "Will you marry me?"   *"I want to make it illegal for you to have sex with other guys and I need a replacement for my mother."*

21. "You look tense – let me give you a massage"   *"I want to have sex with you within the next ten minutes."*

22. "Let's talk."   *"I am trying to impress you by showing that I am a deep, sincere man so maybe then you'd like to have sex with me."*

23. "I do help around the house."   *"I once threw a dirty towel near the laundry basket."*

24. "She's one of those militant, feminist lesbians."   *"She refused to have sex with me."*

Men will never understand women and women will never understand men. And that's the one thing that men and women will never understand.

Chapter 13

WHEN A HUNTER HANGS UP HIS BOW – RETIREMENT

In developed countries, the number of people approaching retirement is growing at an astonishing rate. Because of advances in medical science, not only do a larger proportion of the population now live to retire but they also live much longer after retirement. The number of those living for at least 10 years after retirement has doubled in the last 60 years.

Prior to 1940, only a small percentage of the population lived beyond age 65. Those who had not achieved financial independence either lived in poverty, kept working until they died or were supported by their children.

From the 1940s through to the 2020s, the worldwide average human life span will have risen by more than 50%, from age 46 to age 72. By the year 2020, more than 1 billion people will be 60 years old.

The 'Baby Boomer' Problem

When World War II ended in 1945, the world's birth rate exploded with a new generation known as the 'Baby Boomers'. They are the people born between 1946 and 1964 and there are 76 million of them who are now beginning to retire.

Inside every older person is a younger person — wondering what the hell happened.

Developed countries are now forced to devote a large and increasing part of their budgets to help support and care for this ageing population.

In many countries, compulsory contributions to a national retirement scheme have been introduced, but the problem is in the number of employed people making the contributions to these funds compared to the number retiring. In the USA, for example, the ratio has fallen since 1952 from 9:1 to 4:1. By 2010, Japan will have fewer than two people at work for every retiree and this is compounded by the fact that the Japanese now live longer than anyone else. Japanese women born in 1993 are expected to live 82.51 years and men are expected to live 76.25 years.

Governments everywhere are working on this problem continuously. Financial institutions are heavily marketing personal retirement funds. Bookshop shelves are stacked with books on financial independence and retirement planning. Retirement counselling has become big business. But there are two emerging problems not being given so much attention; first, the psychological effects retirement has on men and, second, how women cope with their partners and the effect retirement has on their relationship.

Graham's story

Graham thought retiring to the coast would be like having one long holiday. He'd spend his days in idyllic bliss – sunbathing, swimming, eating out, sleeping late and relaxing. And for the first few months, that's exactly what he did. But then the retirement blues set in, and with a vengeance.

He and his wife Ruth had bought a beautiful house near the beach with plenty of space, a garden and pool, and moved in two weeks after he'd finished working out his notice. They were looking forward to the kind of revelry they always loved on holidays, but Graham hadn't yet made the distinction between enjoying snatched holidays shoehorned into a busy working schedule, and the rest of his life.

Like most men of retirement age, work had been the focus of Graham's life. For over 40 years he had risen every day knowing exactly what he had to do. Now, for the first time in his life, he had nothing to do. He began to worry about how he was going to fill all that free time. He was well known in business and well respected. He had held an important position, attended meetings, trained new people and solved everyone's problems. At the beach however, no one knew him or wanted his opinion about anything. His status had gone. He missed the involvement with people at work and the daily mental stimulation it gave him. His problem-solving days were over.

It suddenly hit him that he had jumped off an express train at work and onto a mule train on the beach. Instead of juggling two or three things at once to save time, he was spinning things out to try to fill in time. The call he expected from businesses keen to snap up his services never came. For a while he kept in touch with friends at work but their calls became fewer and fewer. Yesterday he was Mr Important – today he was The Invisible Man.

Graham, suffering acutely from what was his abrupt loss of identity, was soon seeking more and more attention from Ruth, getting under her feet, and cramping her style. His most popular and regular refrain was, "What's for lunch?" Before he had retired, she had been free to do just as she pleased. Now she had him to deal with every minute of the day. Their relationship soon started showing the strain.

Over time, things finally began settling down, and Graham and Ruth made new friends. In fact, lunches and dinners became so numerous that Graham soon became a candidate for Weight Watchers. He became bored with sunbathing, did little swimming and rarely did anything in the garden. Sadly, he had become the type of person he had never had time for in his previous life. He would think about work every day and, at night, he'd often dream about it. He suspected his health was suffering but never talked to anyone about it, not even his doctor.

Suddenly, 18 months into his dream retirement, Graham suffered a major heart attack.

....

*An extremely famous businessman was at a cocktail party, the
first function he'd attended since his retirement. He looked around
the room, spied a very attractive woman and made a beeline
for her. "Hello," he said, holding out his hand. "You'll know who
I am, of course." She looked blankly back at him. "No," she
replied. "But if you go' and see the host, he'll remind you."*

....

Sex and Retirement

The way men and women handle approaching older age and
retirement highlights the difference in brain organization.

Since women make up 40–50% of the modern workforce,
you'd expect the psychological problems associated with
retirement would be the same for women as they are for men.
But because of the different brain structure and different
priorities men and women have, it becomes a remarkably
different experience. For many men it is an unmitigated disas-
ter and can even contribute to premature death. The same
applies to men who win the lottery or inherit large sums of
money and the younger it happens, the worse their experience.

....

*Most men who inherit large sums or
win big amounts of money go broke,
suffer worse health and die earlier.*

....

There have been numerous books written and studies carried
out on the problems facing retiring men, but there has been
little research done on retiring and non-working women in
retirement because their main problem is coping with a newly-
retired man.

When a Hunter Quits Hunting

For at least a hundred thousand years men have risen in the morning and gone out to find food for their families. A man's contribution to human survival was clear and simple – find an edible target and hit it. Consequently, the male brain evolved with specific areas to allow him successfully to do just that. That part is called the visual-spatial area. It is used to measure speeds, angles, distances and spatial co-ordinates and is also the area used by modern males for such tasks as reverse parallel-parking, map-reading, merging on a motorway, programming a video player, playing ball sports and hitting a moving target. In simple terms, it's the hunting part of the brain. The illustrations below are created from the brain scans of 50 men and 50 women, showing (in black) the active spatial areas of the brain.

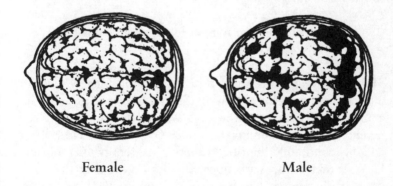

Female   Male

The areas of the brain used for hunting –
Institute of Psychiatry, London, 2000.

For tens of thousands of years, the male job description was specifically to hunt, so it makes sense that modern men's brains would be organised exactly as these scans show. Women evolved as nest-defenders – their role was to ensure the survival of the next generation. Their brains evolved with different areas of strength to deal with that task – hitting a moving zebra at 30 metres was never part of that responsibility. This helps to explain why female brain scans show minimal activity in the spatial areas.

How The Ancient Hunter Became Redundant

By the end of the eighteenth century, advanced farming techniques meant that hunting for food was no longer a priority. To deal with the frustration of no longer being required to chase and hit a target, men used two substitutes – work and sport. Both involve all the elements of hunting – stalking, chasing, aiming and hitting the target.

Consequently, 90% of all modern ball sports originated between AD 1800 and 1900 as a replacement for hunting. Again, this is why most men are obsessed with their work and sport, while most women are not.

Modern sport is a form of replacement hunting.

Then the twentieth century brought an even bigger blow for men: retirement. Not only were they no longer required to hit a moving target, they were not wanted for anything. And herein lies the problem for the modern retired man. He still has a highly configured hunting brain that is literally unemployed. He's all dressed up with nowhere to go. Not only that, he's sitting on a remote beach where no one knows him or even cares about him.

You know you're retired when you know all the answers but nobody ever asks you the questions.

How Women Deal with Retirement

Compared to men, most women tend to move smoothly into retirement without problems and just 'get on with life'. Men have always defined themselves by their work and *accomplishments*; women usually judge their own self-worth by the quality of their *relationships*. Studies on male and female values continually show that 70–80% of men everywhere say that the most important part of their lives is their work, and 70–80% of women say the most important priority is their family. As a result, retired women maintain the social networks they have built or slip easily into new ones. They spend the extra time they have available doing the things they have always done or take up new challenges that they never had time for during their working life.

Men value accomplishments,
women value relationships.

On retirement, many women join groups to improve their hobbies or interests. They may go back to school, spend more time caring for others or join sporting clubs. Their choice of activities almost always involves interaction with other people. A woman's identity is multi-faceted. She can be income-earner, carer, mother, grandmother, homemaker, socialiser, companion, wife and lover, at any given time, and often all at once. When a woman's income-earning life ends, she continues on with all the other facets of her life. In other words, a woman retains her identity. There is no drama. She simply gets on with things. She never retires.

Peter and Jennifer's Story

Jennifer had been looking forward very much to retiring with her husband Peter by her side. This would be a chance for them to do all the things they'd always dreamed about but had never had time for. Their children were grown up and married, so she didn't have to worry about them any more. Jennifer and Peter's lives were finally their own and, even though they'd been married 20 years, Jennifer often felt she didn't know her husband. He was always working, and often spent evenings and weekends in meetings or socially networking with business contacts. She sometimes felt he was a stranger. Now, she felt, they'd both have time to get to know each other all over again. It would be almost a second honeymoon.

She welcomed retirement with real excitement. She'd worked as a nurse most of her life and had found the work stressful and poorly paid, with little opportunity for promotion. In addition, she'd had to combine work with bringing up a family, which left her little time for herself. Finally, with retirement, she felt free.

When Peter finally retired, however, he seemed to be constantly in a bad mood from the time he woke up from the time he went to bed. He never wanted to do anything, just sit around at home and mope about how smoothly his company had moved on without him, and how infrequently his old colleagues called for the benefit of his advice and experience. Jennifer knew he was depressed, but she just couldn't persuade him to talk about his feelings. She felt he had finally shut her out of his life completely.

At first, she sat at home with him, hoping he might one day turn to her for help. But after a few months, she began to feel resentful that he was making her retirement as miserable as his own. She started going out more with her own friends. She'd go swimming with a group three times a week, play tennis two days, and took up art classes. Later, she began to learn Italian at her local college. She spent less and less time at home.

"You know," she told a close friend, "I'm loving being retired. The freedom... I adore it. The only thing I hate is having to go home again at the end of the day. I'm beginning to wonder what I ever saw in Peter. Spending time together for the first time in our lives, I realise we have nothing in common, and I wonder if we ever did. I don't even know these days whether I still love him, or even want to be with him any more."

Coping with a retired man in her life is often one of the biggest problems a woman faces. It can cause arguments, tears and even separation. He always seems to be 'under her feet', and may even start trying to take charge of her life, treating her as he may have once treated his employees, offering her solutions and advice when she really doesn't want them. And, frequently, he blames her for his own misery.

A 70-year-old couple have always been in great health because of the woman's insistence on healthy food and exercise. One day, they both die in a car crash. At the pearly gates, St Peter introduces them to their new life in Heaven.

He shows them to a fabulous mansion. "But how much will this cost?" asks the man. "It's nothing," replies St Peter. "It's free. This is Heaven."

Then he shows them the wonderful golf course to the back of the mansion. "But how much does it cost to join?" asks the man. "It's nothing," replies St Peter. "It's free. This is Heaven."

Finally, he takes them through to the restaurant attached and shows them the menu, full of the richest, most delicious dishes, all with heavy cream sauces. "But we only eat low-fat, low-salt, non-dairy, low-cholesterol meals," says the man. "Don't worry," says St Peter. "This is

Heaven. There are no calories in Heaven. You can eat as much as you like and still stay trim and healthy."
At that, the man screams and turns to his wife. "You absolute bitch!" he shrieks at her. "If you hadn't insisted on us eating all that health food and taking exercise, we could have been here ten years earlier!"

Why Men Can't Handle Retirement

Retirement is a big deal for most men and can turn out to be one of the most stressful periods in a man's life. It's not the loss of his job that causes so much stress; it's the loss of something far greater – the loss of his identity

When approaching retirement, a man will often want to deny that his working life is about to suddenly end. He feels he has so much knowledge and experience, obtained over a lifetime, that his employers and associates won't be able to lose all of his talent, and still continue. The fact that they feel they can, and probably will, usually feels like a solid kick in the guts.

Unable to face this, many men reassure themselves with the belief that they'll become consultants instead. It feels like a worthwhile step. On one hand, there won't be the need for long hours of work. On the other, they will still be important cogs in the wheel. They will be 'on call' to return to work to solve the problems that only they have the knowledge and experience to fix. Even if they never much liked their work, they still want the 'hunting pack' to need them to continue the chase.

....

A man always wants to think the
hunting pack still needs him.

....

For most men, however, this rarely happens. The newer generation have their own ideas and solutions, and now feel free to implement them and trial new ways of doing things without consultation.

On the last day of work, men will often make jokes about how they thought the end was near when they noticed their colleagues measuring their office, when their old computer was replaced with a brand new top-of-the-range model and their assistant started responding to orders with "Yeah, whatever". But still they rarely realise that, at the farewell bash, "Goodbye" really does mean goodbye.

Why So Many Men Go Downhill So Fast

Some men approach retirement casually, thinking it will be easy. They take it slowly, doing what they want when they want. But unless they have carefully prepared for their retirement, this honeymoon period is rarely the way things continue. The sudden loss of friends and associates, of their status and their feelings of importance, will soon give way to depression.

A man's loss of identity is, in many ways, similar to the death of a loved one. They begin with *denial*, followed by *depression, anger* and hopefully, eventually, *acceptance*.

The onset of depression can take place without being recognized. Firstly, the retired man will become disappointed with his new life. He may become withdrawn, lose his vitality and begin to become inactive. He may feel rejection, worthlessness and loss of libido. He may overindulge in food, alcohol or drugs. He regularly gets colds, flu and minor illnesses. He may reminisce, with abject disappointment, about the things he didn't achieve. It is critical to recognize this stage because if he doesn't pass through it, or fails to seek professional help, depression may become permanent, resulting in an unhappy, apathetic, and shortened life.

....

Retired men who failed to plan are constantly ill.

....

Signs of anger are usually the first indication that the depression stage is passing. Others are blamed for his dilemma; his partner or family are often targeted because, "They don't understand how I feel." His former employer will be blamed for not preparing him for retirement. He can't understand his employer's resistance to his returning to work part-time or in a consulting role, and he feels he has been shown an appalling lack of loyalty. This anger is often vented in a desire to take over the running of the household, particularly the finances and scheduling of social and family activities. He wants to be the CEO of the family now.

These intrusions can become very frustrating for his partner and arguments may start to occur regularly.

Yvonne's Story

Barry qualified as a plumber at age 20 and was working for himself by age 25. He had always been something of a research addict; he loved facts and figures and was very successful with his time management. By the time had decided to retire at age 50, he had built a highly successful plumbing business, was the boss and felt he was the best in the business.

He had always been motivated by the thought of the day he would retire and he and Yvonne could spend all their time together travelling and spending time with their children and grandchildren. One day, retirement arrived and within 4 weeks it was turning into Yvonne's worst nightmare.

Barry was now trying to be the CEO of the household. Not only that, he wanted to control Yvonne and everything she did! He volunteered to take over the family finances and gave her a budget for food; he wanted to know why she spent so much on items that he deemed unnecessary. They had no money problems but he wanted to know where every cent was going and why. It was driving Yvonne insane.

She loved to shop but now Barry had decided that they would do it together and he would make up a timetable, draw a map of where they would go and what they would be purchasing. If Yvonne went into a shop that was not on the timetable, Barry would want to know why she wanted to do this – didn't she have enough clothes or shoes already? On one trip, Yvonne needed a new bra and Barry sat outside the dressing room in the 'bored-husband-chair'. She quickly tried on as many bras as she could – she didn't want him to get annoyed with how long it took.

Meanwhile, outside the dressing room, Barry was collecting data from the shop staff and other shoppers about bras – how many they owned, why women thought they needed so many, why they were so expensive, the life expectancy of a bra and a range of other statistical questions. He would then give them his thoughts on the situation. Through consideration and analysis, Barry deduced that Yvonne only needed two bras and that more than that was a waste of money. For Yvonne, this was all too much. She didn't buy any bras that day – she decided to come back another time, alone.

Barry felt that Yvonne's days would be much more successful if she practised effective time management so he asked her to keep a daily diary on the hour, starting at 8am. Yvonne felt like she was an inmate in a concentration camp.

"What are you doing tomorrow?" he'd ask. "I'm going to the doctor" she'd respond. "The doctor won't take all day – so what will you do first thing in the morning?"

"I might do some vacuuming, wash clothes and anything else that needs doing."

To Barry's disciplined, organized mind this was too hard to understand. How could she function without a plan?

One day, to humour him she said, " I'll clean the shower first."

When it hadn't been done by 10am – she had decided to do some urgent washing instead – he became anxious. If she didn't do what was on Barry's diary it was too much for him to handle. His life had been an hour-by-hour schedule and just doing things when it suited her didn't suit him. He did notice, however, that at the end of each day Yvonne had achieved her tasks and more without an hourly diary to follow.

Yvonne began to sneak out of the house to get away from Barry and his diary system. "He needs to get a life!" she told her friends, "and I want mine back!"

> A retired couple were sitting at the dinner table having a conversation about old age. "The worst thing," said the woman, "is the forgetfulness."
>
> "What do you mean?" asked her husband.
>
> "Well, I keep getting to the middle of something, and forgetting what I was doing," she replied. "One day last week, I was standing at the top of the stairs, wondering if I'd just finished getting to the top, or was just starting to walk down to the bottom."
>
> "Huh!" said the man. "I never have that kind of problem."
>
> The woman smiled ruefully. "Then yesterday I was sitting in the car wondering if I'd just got in to drive somewhere, or had arrived back home and was just getting out."
>
> The man hurrumphed. "No, never suffered from that at all," he insisted. "My memory is perfect, touch wood." He rapped on the table twice, then looked startled. "Who's there?" he called.

The Downsides of Retirement

When arguments start about the different capabilities of a couple, and the different roles they're playing, this can be a dangerous time because couples begin to feel incompatible. Female partners can resent what they feel is an intrusion into what they see as a happy, orderly life. They may see their husband, for the first time in their lives, for breakfast, lunch and dinner. They can see he has so much free time – but he still never offers to help with the housework. Steadily, resentment, and anger, can grow. As this rises to the surface, the man begins to feel rejected, misunderstood and worthless. When things get really bad, separation, divorce, and even suicide are possibilities.

The men who survive the first three stages of retirement will usually accept their new phase of life and take up the challenge of planning a happy and useful new life.

Recognition of these stages is crucial and the man who has not thoroughly planned for retirement may take many years to go through them. If he does not pass through quickly, professional counselling should be sought to avoid negative attitudes becoming permanent, resulting in loneliness and unhappiness.

Men in high-stress occupations who retire to do nothing, die early.

In Western and European societies, the life expectancy of a man who retires to do nothing is five years. For high-stress occupations such as highly placed executives and doctors, it's as little as two years, five months. These men go from a highly disciplined and organised environment to nothing.

A man spends 30 to 40 years of his working life in a tightly structured, goal-oriented environment, so his retirement needs to be exactly the same. With the growing trend towards early retirement, rising life expectancy and better health, the period of retirement is likely to be longer too, so even more care needs to be taken. The critical difference between the two periods of life is that he is the one in complete control now. He can make all the decisions that will affect the rest of his life.

A Plan of Action

The time to start planning is years before you retire. This may not always be possible because of early redundancy. You may already be retired and going through the post-retirement stages. But generally the sooner you begin to plan, the better.

> *Studies show the earlier you plan for retirement, the better your health will be and the longer you will live.*

You need to approach your retirement as you would any big project. Start off by writing a business plan, preferably by hand. Begin with an overview of how you think you will live in your retirement, then take each item and break it down into detail. Discuss your plan with your partner, because that person is the one most likely to share it with you. Planning ahead will help you to be ready for what lies ahead – and anything that may go wrong.

An elderly woman saved a fairy's life. In return, the fairy gave the woman three wishes.

For the first wish, the woman said she'd like to become young and beautiful – and suddenly she was. For the second wish, she said she'd like to be rich – and suddenly she was. For the third wish, she pointed to her beloved cat and asked that he be turned into a handsome prince – and suddenly he was.

The fairy vanished into thin air, and the handsome prince walked up to the woman, and smiled. "Now," he said, taking her hand in his, "aren't you sorry you had me neutered?"

Social Activity

This should include activities that the man and the woman do alone, ones they do with their own friends, and those they do together. For instance, the man may choose to sign up for an investment course by himself at the local college, and decide to join a golf club with a group of his male friends. The woman may like to take an art class and go to the movies each week with a bunch of girlfriends. It's important that each have their own sets of activities and friends so, when they come together again, they'll always have plenty to talk about. They'll also then be able to retain their own distinct identities, rather than ending up merged into one.

An additional bonus is that they might each individually end up making good friends – who are then also invited back to meet the partners.

As a joint activity, a couple may sign up for a dance class together, or join a walking club that hikes around the outlying areas for a few hours each weekend.

Health

Start with a thorough medical check, and then set a good diet by reading books on the best eating habits for retirees. If you are overweight, seek advice on losing the excess. Today, there's a wide range of exercise programmes available for everyone. Walking is excellent, but you might also consider dancing, swimming or bike riding. Exercise takes time, but that's the one thing you'll have plenty of! The more often you exercise, the longer you will live and the better will be the quality of your life.

Sporting Activity

Retirement presents many men with the opportunity to participate in hunting, chasing and other spatial skills which, until now, they may not have had time to explore – such as golf, fishing or bowls. For the less active, archery, ten-pin bowling or target-shooting give spatial enjoyment.

*Why do they call it golf? Because all
the other four-letter words were taken.
And then they spelt it backwards.*

Community or Charity Work

For most retirees, these activities give a tremendous feeling of satisfaction and self-worth. This is the key to maintaining a man's sense of self-esteem because the greatest urge for men is to feel important. When a man finishes his working life, part of his identity and role in the big picture is taken away and he doesn't feel important any more. It is essential that his identity is replaced quickly.

Whatever a man's career has been, it would have included skills that others will want to use or learn. These could be knowledge of a certain trade, computer skills or financial expertise. Anything about which he has knowledge or experience – gardening, household maintenance, painting, collecting – can be passed on to others. In addition, there are many church-related charities crying out for help, and a myriad of social organizations dedicated to fund-raising and assisting those in need.

Spiritual

Spiritual activities may already involve a system of belief. If not, investigate belief systems that fit in with your philosophy of life, or take up hobbies like meditation or yoga.

Sex

A happy, healthy life should also include a fulfilling sex life. For those men and women with partners, time should be put aside for sex, particularly if there are special circumstances that mean extra care needs to be taken. Prescription drugs such as Viagra mean many more men – and women – can enjoy sex well into their later years. If a man or woman is alone, there is even more reason to seek out friends of the opposite sex, and not to shy away from the opportunity for close relationships.

> *Albert, 75, stood up in the dining room of the old folks' home one night and looked around at the women having dinner. "Hey ladies!" he shouted. "Anyone who can guess what's in my hand can sleep with me tonight!"*
>
> *There was a stunned silence. Finally, one elderly woman called back, "A house!" He looked at her. "Yes!" he roared back. "That's close enough!"*

Financial Planning

There are two choices here – to accept the limitations of your retirement income and plan carefully to live within them, or to plan to earn additional income. Many men have started successful businesses after their retirement, while others have taken up casual employment where their knowledge, experience or skills can be used.

Getting Organised

A planned retirement should become a diligently organised habit. Before you retire, about 90% of your day is made up of repetitive, organised activity. When you are working, you don't have to consciously decide to get out of bed at 6.30am, drive to work and start at 8am; you just do it every day. Your job may involve different problems but, most of the time, your approach to them will be the same as it has always been. Overall, your life is a routine, and you feel confident and in control.

In retirement, old habits don't apply. Unless you have planned otherwise, you have to decide whether or not to get out of bed every morning when you wake. When you do rise, you have to decide what to do next, even if it's as simple as deciding whether to walk to the shop and buy a newspaper, return home, make coffee and sit and read. Then, before you know it, it's lunch-time. After lunch, you may have to decide whether to read a book or have a nap, if there's nothing else more pressing on the agenda.

Do these things for the first 30 days of retirement and these will become your new habits, and will be very difficult to break. This is the point at which an overwhelming feeling of worthlessness sets in.

If, however, you plan to rise at a certain time, walk for 30 minutes then become involved in organized activities every day, all day, and you do this for 30 days, this will become your new habit. You won't need to keep deciding what to do next. Your life will be structured and, if your activities are properly chosen, you will find a new identity and have goals and feel that your life is worthwhile. It's never too late to start learning new things. You may want to write a book, become a teacher or take up a new sport. You may want to become a leader or participant in a favourite charitable organization, or start a new organization or club and gain recognition as its founder. You may even want to let it all hang out and become a nude model. Anything is possible when it's planned.

The concept of sitting under a palm tree doing nothing for the rest of your retired life is a myth promoted by retirement funds and lotteries. It just makes you fat, dull and boring. And sunburnt. Most men can do it for just a few weeks before they go crazy – or their wives murder them.

Paul and Dana's Story

Paul was an accounts manager whose working life had always been full of goals, deadlines and targets. He thought he'd probably retire at 65. When he was 57, however, his company was taken over by a competitor and, after years of loyal service, he became redundant overnight. When he heard that the new owners of his company were outsourcing the accounts department and had very different ideas to his, he realised it was definitely the end of that era.

His partner Dana had retired three years earlier and was looking forward to Paul's retirement. She was enjoying her own retirement a great deal. She now had the time to do so many of the things she had always wanted to do and she wanted so much to share her newfound happiness with Paul.

Dana was alarmed when Paul became gloomy about his redundancy. He sat around drinking too much and was becoming depressed. The drinking and depression were feeding on each other and Paul was going downhill fast.

Dana decided that professional help was needed. She convinced Paul to see a retirement counsellor who she heard had a good reputation for dealing with newly retired men. The counsellor helped Paul understand why he felt the way he did and showed him how to tackle the next phase of his life. Paul decided to accept the challenges the counsellor put to him.

The first step was to have a thorough medical exam and then to see a financial planner. They would then take a holiday to relax and plan the rest of their lives.

The medical results showed Paul was fine apart from being nine kilos overweight and having slightly heightened blood pressure and cholesterol. He visited a naturopath who showed him healthy eating habits and gave him an exercise programme.

You know you're getting old when your back goes out more than you do and when you sink your teeth into a steak, they stay there.

The financial counsellor really put Paul's mind at rest. First, he helped them complete a detailed budget. Next, he explained how Paul's redundancy payment, combined with some savings and investments and his and Dana's retirement funds would be sufficient to cover their budgetary needs. In 10 to 15 years, proceeds from the sale of their home would be more than enough to finance their later years in a retirement village if that was what they chose to do.

After all this advice, Paul felt a huge burden had been lifted from his shoulders. They set off on their holiday in a positive frame of mind. They had started to plan their journey – one that would take 25 years or more to complete.

Their next challenge was a big one, to decide what they would do with the rest of their lives. They needed a plan that took into account their individual and joint goals.

They decided to modify their eating habits, throw out the old cookbooks and replace them with healthy recipes that concentrated on their dietary requirements. Next, they agreed they'd walk vigorously every day for at least 45 minutes and join a walking club for an extended walk several times a month. This would have the added advantage of introducing them to new people. They signed up to learn T'ai Chi, as friends who did it always seemed relaxed and calm, and the exercise would be beneficial. Dana already played tennis once a week and was on the club committee. She was also in a patchwork group and was trying her hand at writing a book.

Paul had played golf a few times but, although he enjoyed it, he never found time to play regularly. He had a set of clubs and decided to give it a go.

Their finances gave them enough to meet living expenses, but no room for any extravagances. Paul, therefore, decided he would investigate the possibilities of studying a bookkeeping course through Adult Education, and set their monthly outgoings at a firm level they could afford.

This left one more area to plan – community or charity work. "What have we done in our lives that we could share with others less fortunate?" they asked themselves. "Who are we most concerned about?"

They concluded that their greatest achievement was bringing up four happy, successful and well-adjusted children. Paul had always been concerned about the welfare of teenagers, and they understood the problems they faced without family support. He decided to enquire about a youth counselling course and become a youth counsellor.

The pair committed their plan to writing and put it into a time-frame. When they sat back and looked at it, they felt excited, and as though they couldn't wait to get started.

Today, Paul and Dana are healthy and happy, enjoying life and helping others. They are so busy they need to run a detailed diary. Retirement is proving to be the most wonderful time of their lives. At a time when a man and a woman are thrown together more than at any other period in their lives, it becomes vital that they have learned all the lessons of *Why Men Lie and Women Cry*. For only then will they be able to live happily, peacefully and lovingly, understanding each other's strengths – and weaknesses – and be able to get out as much from their relationship as they put in.

We firmly believe that using the tools offered in *Why Men Lie and Women Cry* can help all men and women have closer, more fulfilling and sexier lives. Use them wisely and use them well. Good luck!

References

Alder, Harry, *NLP in 21 Days*, Piatkus (1999)

Allen, L.S., Richey, M.F., Chai, Y.M. and Gorki, R.A., 'Sex Differences in the Corpus Callosum of the Living Human Being', *Journal of Neuroscience*, 11, pp. 933–942 (1991)

Amen, Daniel G., *Change Your Brain, Change Your Life*, Times Books (2000)

Andrews, Simon, *Anatomy of Desire: The Science and Psychology of Sex, Love and Marriage*, Little, Brown (2000)

Aquinas, Thomas, *Summa Theologica*, translated by the Fathers of the English Dominican Province, London: Burnes Oates & Washburn. (1922) [Distinguishes between the degrees of turpitude of various kind of lie.]

Arons, Harry, *Hypnosis in Criminal Investigation*, Illinois: Charles C. Thomas (1967)

Augustine, 'Lying' and 'Against Lying', in *Treatises on Various Subjects*, R.J. Deferrari (ed), New York: Catholic University of America Press. (1952) [Early and highly influential prohibition against all forms of lying.]

Bailey, F. Lee, and Aronson, H., *The Defense Never Rests*, New York: Signet (1972)

Bailey, F. Lee, *For the Defense*, New York: The New American Library, Inc. (1976)

Bandler, Richard and Grinder, John, *Frogs into Princes: Neuro-Linguistic Programming*, Moab, UT: Real People Press, (1979)

Barry, Dave, *Dave Barry's Complete Guide to Guys*, New York: Ballatine Publishing Group (2000)

Bart, Dr Benjamin, *The History of Farting*, Heron (1993)

Beatty, W.W. and Truster, A.I., 'Gender Differences in Geographical Knowledge', *Sex Roles* 16, pp. 565–590 (1987)

Beatty, W.W., 'The Fargo Map Test: A Standardised Method for Assessing Remote Memory for Visuospatial Information', *Journal of Clinical Psychology*, 44, pp. 61–67 (1988)

Belli, Melvin, *My Life on Trial*, New York: Popular Library (1977)

Benbow, C.P. and Stanley, J.C., 'Sex differences in Mathematical Reasoning Ability: More facts', *Science* 222, pp. 1029–1031 (1983)

Berenbaum, S.A., 'Psychological Outcome in Congenital Adrenal Hyperplasia', in *Therapeutic Outcome of Endocrine Disorders: Efficacy, Innovation, and Quality of Life*, B. Stabler and B.B. Bercy (eds), pp. 186–99, New York: Springer (2000)

Berne, Eric, M.D., *Games People Play*, Grove Press, Inc. (1964)

Black, H., 'Amygdala's Inner Workings', *The Scientist*, 15[19]:20, Oct. 1 (2001)

Block, Eugene B., *Voice Printing – How the Law Can Read The Voice Of Crime*, Veronica School District 47J, Petitioner v. Wayne Action, et ux, Guardians ad Litem for JAMES ACTON 515 US –, 132L Ed 2d 564, 115 S Ct — |No 94-590| US Supreme Court Reports, 132 L Ed (Drug Abuse Screening by Urinalysis Decision.) Argued March 28 (1995). Decided June 26 (1995)

Bok, S., *Lying: Moral Choice in Public and Private Life*, New York: Pantheon (1978)

Botting, Kate and Douglas, *Sex Appeal*, London: Boxtree Ltd. (1995)

Brasch, R., *How Did Sex Begin?*, New York: David McKay (1997)

Budesheim, T.L. and Depaola, S.J., 'Beauty or the Beast? The Effects of Appearance, Personality, and Issue Information on Evaluations of Political Candidates', *Personality and Social Psychology Bulletin*, 20, pp. 339–348 (1994)

Buss, David M., *The Evolution of Desire*, Basic Books (1994)

Buss, D.M. and Kenrich, D.T., 'Evolutionary Social Psychology', in *The Handbook of Social Psychology* (4th ed.) D.T. Gilberts, S.T. Fiske and G. Lindzey (eds) (Vol. 2, pp. 982–1026). Boston: McGraw-Hill (1998)

Carper, Jean, *Your Miracle Brain*, New York: HarperCollins (2000)

Castellow, W.A., Wuensch, K.L. and Moore, C.H., 'Effects of Physical Attractiveness of the Plaintiff and Defendant in Sexual Harassment Judgements', *Journal of Social Behavior and Personality 5*, pp. 547–562 (1990)

Chang, K.T. and Antes, J.R., 'Sex and Cultural Differences in Map Reading', *The American Cartographer* 14, pp. 29–42 (1987)

Cole, Julia, *After the Affair*, Vermilion, G.B. (2000)

Cox, Tracey, *Hot Relationships*, Bantam, Australia (1999)

Crick, Francis, *The Astonishing Hypothesis*, New York: Macmillan (1994)

Dawkins, Richard, *The Blind Watchmaker*, New York: Norton (1987)

Dawkins, Richard, *The Selfish Gene*, (2nd ed), New York: Oxford University Press (1990)

De Angelis, Barbara, *Secrets about MEN Every Woman should Know*, Thorsons, UK (1990)

Dedopulos, Tim, *The Ultimate Jokes Book*, Parragon Book Service Ltd, UK (1998)

Downs, A.C. and Lyons, P.M., 'Natural observations of the Links Between Attractiveness and Initial Legal Judgements', *Personality and Social Psychology Bulletin*, 17, pp. 541–547 (1990)

Eagly, A.H., Ashmore, R.D., Makhijani, M.G. and Longo L.C., 'What is Beautiful is Good But …: A Meta-Analytic Review of Research on the Physical Attractiveness Stereo-Type', *Psychological Bulletin*, 110, pp. 109–128 (1991)

Eibl-Eibesfeldt, I., *Ethology: The Biology of Behavior*, (2nd ed), New York: Holt, Rinehart & Winston (1975)

Ekman, Paul, *Telling Lies*, W.W. Norton (2002)

Ekman, Paul, and Friesen, W.V., *Unmasking the Face*, Lexington, MA: Lexington Books (1975)

Everhart, D.E., et al., 'Sex-Related Differences in Event-Related Potentials, Face Recognition, and Facial Affect Processing in Prepubertal Children', *Neuropsychology*, 15, pp. 329-41, July (2001)

Farrell, Warren, *Women Can't Hear What Men Don't Say*, Australia: Finch Publishing (2001)

Fast, J. M., *Body Language*, New York: Evans and Company (1970)

Ferris, Stewart, *How to Chat-Up Women*, UK: Summersdale Publishers (1994)

Fisher, Helen, *Anatomy of Love*, New York: Norton (1992)

Fisher, Helen, *The First Sex*, London: Random House (1999)

French, Scott and Van Houten, Paul, PhD., *Never Say Lie - How to Beat the Machines, the Interviews, the Chemical Tests*, Boulder, Colorado: Palladin Press (1987)

Fromm, Erich, *The Forgotten Language*, New York: Grove Press, Inc. (1951)

Garner, Alan, *Conversationally Speaking*, (2nd ed), Los Angeles: Lowell House (1997)

Glass, Lillian, *He Says, She Says*, New York: Putnam (1992)

Gray, John, *Mars and Venus in the Bedroom*, Australia: Hodder & Stoughton (1955)

Gray, John, *Men, Women & Relationship*, Australia: Hodder & Stoughton (1995)

Greenfield, Susan, *Journey to the Centers of the Mind*, New York: Basic Books (1998)

Grice, Julia, *What Makes a Woman Sexy*, New York: Dodd, Mead, (1998)

Gron, G., et al., 'Brain Activation During Human Navigation: Gender-Different Neural Networks as Substrate of Performance', *Nature Neuroscience*, 3, pp. 404–8 (2000)

Grotius, Hugo, *On the Law of War and Peace*, translated by F. Kelsey, Indianapolis: Bobbs-Merrill. (1925) [Defines lying in terms of the rights of those to whom the lie is addressed.]

Gur, R.C. et al., 'An FMRI Study of Sex Differences in Regional Activation to a Verbal and a Spatial Task', *Brain and Language*, 74, pp. 157–70 (2000)

Gur, R.C. et al., 'Sex Differences in Brain Gray and White Matter in Healthy Young Adults: Correlations with Cognitive Performance', *Journal of Neuroscience*, 19, pp. 4065–72 (1999)

Hammersmith, D. and Biddle, J.E., 'Beauty and the Labor Market', *American Economic Review*, 84, pp. 1174–1194 (1994)

Harrelson, Leonard, *Lie Test: Deception, Truth and the Polygraph*, Partners Publishing Group (1998)

Heisse, John W. Jr., *Simplified Chart Reading*, self-published, Burlington, Vermont (1974)

Heisse, John W. Jr., 'The 14 Question Modified Zone of Comparison Test', *Stressing Comments*, International Society of Stress Analysts, Vol 3, No 7, June, pp. 1–4 (1975)

Heisse, John W. Jr., M.D., *Audio Stress Analysis: A Validation and Reliability Study of The Psychological Stress Evaluator (PSE)*, self-published, Burlington, Vermont (1976)

Heisse, John W. Jr., M.D., *The Verimetrics Computer System: A Reliability Study*, self-published, Burlington, Vermont (1992)

Hodgson, D.H., *Consequences of Utilitarianism*, Oxford (1967)

Holden, Robert, *Shift Happens*, Hodder & Stoughton (1998)

Holden, Robert, *Laughter the Best Medicine*, Thorsons (1993)

Horvath, Frank, PhD., 'Detecting Deception: The Promise and the Reality of Voice Stress Analysis', *Journal of Forensic Sciences*, JFSCA, Vol 27, No. 2, pp. 340–351 (1982)

Hoyenga K.B. and Hoyenga, K.T., *Gender-Related Differences*, Allyn & Bacon, p. 343–345 (1993)

Inbau, Fred E. and Reid, John E., *Truth and Deception: The Polygraph ("Lie Detector") Technique*, Baltimore: The Williams & Wilking Company (1969)

Johnson, Gary, *Monkey Business*, Gower Publishing (1995)

Juan, Dr. Stephen, *The Odd Body and Brain*, Australia: HarperCollins (2001)

Kant, Immanuel, 'On a Supposed Right to Lie from Benevolent Motives', in *The Critique of Practical Reason and Other Writings in Moral Philosophy*, Chicago: University of Chicago Press (1949)

Kenton, Leslie, *Ten Steps to a Young YOU*, Vermilion UK (1996)

Kinsey A.C., Pomeroy W.B. and Martin C.E., *Sexual Behaviour in the Human Male*, Philadelphia: Saunders (1948)

Knapp, Mark L., *Nonverbal Communication in Human Interaction*, New York: Hold, Rinehart, Winston (1978)

Kreeger, K.Y., 'Yes, Biologically Speaking, Sex Does Matter', *The Scientist*, 16[1], pp. 35–6, Jan 7 (2002)

Kriete, R. and Stanley, R., *A Comparison of the Psychological Stress Evaluator and the Polygraph*, presented at the First Annual Seminar of the International Society of Stress Analysts, Chicago (1974)

Kulka, R.A. and Kessler, J.R., 'Is Justice Really Blind? The Effect of Litigant Physical Attractiveness on Judicial Judgement', *Journal of Applied Social Pyschology*, 4, pp. 336-381 (1978)

LeVay, S., *The Sexual Brain*, Cambridge, Massachusetts: MIT Press (1993)

Lewis, D., *Convention: A Philosophical Study*, Cambridge, MA: Harvard U.P. (1969)

Lieberman, David J., *Never be Lied to Again*, St. Martin's Press (2000)

Lippold, O., 'Physiological Tremor', *Scientific American*, Vol. 224, No. 3, pp. 65–73 (1971)

Lorenz, Konrad, *King Solomon's Ring*, New York: Crowell (1952)

Lorenz, Konrad, *On Aggression*, New York: Harcourt (1974)

Maccoby, Eleanor and Jacklin, Carol N., *The Psychology of Sex Differences*, Stanford University Press (1974)

Marshall, Hillie, *The Good Dating Guide*, UK: Summersdale Publishers (1998)

Maynard, Smith J., *The Theory of Evolution*, New York: Cambridge University (1993)

McKinlay, Deborah, *Love Lies*, London: HarperCollins (1994)

Miller, Gerald R. and Stiff, James B., *Deception Communication*, Newbury Park: Sage Publications (1993)

Moir, Anne and Jessel, David, *BrainSex*, New York: Dell (1992)

Moir, Anne and Bill, *Why Men Don't Iron*, HarperCollins Publishers (1998)

Morris, Desmond, *Bodywatching*, New York: Crown (1985)

Morris, Desmond, *The Naked Ape*, New York: Dell (1980)

Morris, Desmond, *People Watching*, UK: Vintage (2002)

Nierenberg, Gerald, I. and Calero, *How to Read a Person Like a Book*, New York: Cornerstone Library (1971)

O'Neill, W.C., *Report of the Special Hearing Officer of the Secretary of State of Florida, Regarding Public Hearings of the Department of State of Florida: Psychological Stress Evaluation*, Florida Secretary of State, Tallahassee, Florida (1974)

O'Toole, George, *The Assassination Tapes – An Electronic Probe into the Murder of John F. Kennedy and the Dallas Cover up*, New York: Penthouse Press Ltd. (1975)

Pease, Allan and Barbara, *Why Men Don't Listen & Women Can't Read Maps*, UK: Orion (2001)

Pease, Allan, *Rude and Politically Incorrect Jokes*, UK: Robson Books (1999)

Pease, Allan, *Signals: How to Use Body Language for Power, Success and Love*, New York: Bantam Books (1984)

Pease, Allan, with Garner, Alan, *Talk Language*, UK: Simon & Schuster (1998)

Pease, Raymond, and Dr. Ruth, *My Secret life as a Gigolo*, Sydney: Pease International (2002)

Penny, Alexandra, *How to Keep your Man Monogamous*, UK: Bantam Books (1990)

Platt, Vanessa Lloyd, *Secrets of Relationship Success*, UK: Vermilion (2000)

Pittman, Frank, *Private Lies*, Norton (1990)

Quilliam, Susan, *Body Language Secrets*, HarperCollins (1997)

Quilliam, Susan, *Sexual Body Talk*, New York: Carroll & Graff (1992)

Reid, John E., Inbau, Fred E., and Buckley, Joseph B., *Criminal Interrogation & Confessions*, Baltimore: Williams & Wilkins Co. (1986)

Reinisch, J.M., et al., (eds.) *Masculinity and Femininity, The Kinsey Institute Series*, Oxford University Press (1987)

Ringer, R.J., *Winning Through Intimidation*, Los Angeles: Fawcett Crest (1973)

Roffman, Howard, *Presumed Guilty*, New York: A.S. Barnes and Company, Inc. (1976)

Roger, L.J., *The Development of Brain and Behaviour in the Chicken*, Wallingford: CAB International (1995)

Rogers, Lesley, *Sexing the Brain*, GB: Weidenfeld & Nicolson (1999)

Samenow, Stanton E., *Inside the Criminal Mind*, New York: Times Books (1984)

Schipp, Thomas, PhD and Kryzysztof, Izdebski, 'Current Evidence for the Existence of Laryngeal Macrotremor and Microtremor', *Journal of Forensic Sciences*, (1980)

Shaywitz, Sally and Bennett, 'How is the Brain Formed?', *Nature*, 373, pp. 607–609 (1995)

Shaywitz, B.A., et al., 'Sex Differences in the Functional Organization of the Brain for Language', *Nature*, 373, pp. 607–9 (1995)

Staheli, Lana, *Affair-Proof Your Marriage*, Staheli Inc. (1995)

Stein, D.G., 'Brain Damage, Sex Hormones and Recovery: A New Role for Progesterone and Estrogen?', *Trends in Neuroscience*, 24, pp. 386–91, July (2001)

Stewart, J.E. II, 'Defendant's Attractiveness as a Factor in the Outcome of Trials', *Journal of Applied Social Psychology*, 10, pp. 348–361 (1980)

Tannen, Deborah, *Talking From 9 to 5*, New York: Morrow (1994)

Tannen, Deborah, *That's Not What I Meant*, New York: Ballantine (1986)

Tannen, Deborah, *You Just Don't Understand: Women and Men in Conversation*, New York: Morrow (1990)

Tucker, Nita, *How NOT to Stay Single*, USA: Crown Publishers (1996)

Whiteside, Robert, *Face Language II*, Hollywood FL: Frederick Fell (1988)

Wilson, Glenn D. and Nias, David, *The Mystery of Love*, London: Open Books (1976)

Wolf, Naomi, *The Beauty Myth*, New York: Anchor (1992)

Picture Credits

Advertising Archives p203
Bridgeman Art Library p206; 209; 212cl; 223b
Empics: 251br
Getty Images: p202; 211tr; 213bl; 218; 223t; 244; 252
Hulton/Getty: p212b
Kobal Collection: p193; 207t; 217
Panos Pictures: p210; 215cl; 251bl
Peter Newark's Pictures: p 11
Picture Bank: p 207b
Popperfoto: p201
Rex Features: p211tl; 215cr; 239; 246; 247; 249; 253
Robert Harding Photo Library: p214; 216
Ronald Grant Archives: p212cr; 213br
Ripswear Inc: p237

Why not use Allan Pease as guest speaker for your next conference or seminar?

Pease International (Australia) Pty. Ltd.
Pease International (UK) Ltd.
P.O. Box 1260
Buderim 4556
Queensland 4556
AUSTRALIA
Tel: ++61 (7) 5445 5600
Fax: ++61 (7) 5445 5688
e-mail: (Aust) info@peaseinternational.com
(UK) ukoffice@peaseinternational.com
website: www.peaseinternational.com

Also by Allan Pease:
Video programs
Body Language Series
Silent Signals
How to make Appointments by Telephone
The Interview
Why Men Don't Listen and Women Can't Read Maps

Audio Cassette Programs
The Four Personality Styles
How to Make Appointments by Telephone
How to Remember Names, Faces & Lists
Questions Are the Answers
It's Not What You Say

Books
Body Language
Talk Language
Write Language
Questions are the Answers
Why Men Don't Listen and Women Can't Read Maps
Why Men Lie and Women Cry
The Ulitmate Book of Rude and Politically Incorrect Jokes
Why Men Can Only Do One Thing At A Time and Women Never Stop Talking

**Please send for a catalogue of sales and management
programs and other material by Allan Pease**
183 High Street
Henley in Arden
West Midlands B95 5BA
UNITED KINGDOM
Tel: ++44 (0) 1564 795000
Fax: ++44 (0) 1564 79053